The Opera Singer's Career Guide

Understanding the European *Fach* System

Pearl Yeadon McGinnis

Edited by Marith McGinnis Willis

THE SCARECROW PRESS, INC.
Lanham • Toronto • Plymouth, UK
2010

Published by Scarecrow Press, Inc.
A wholly owned subsidary of The Rowman & Littlefield Publishing Group, Inc.
4501 Forbes Boulevard, Suite 200, Lanham, Maryland 20706
http://www.scarecrowpress.com

Estover Road, Plymouth PL6 7PY, United Kingdom

British Library Cataloguing in Publication Information Available

Library of Congress Cataloging-in-Publication Data

McGinnis, Pearl Yeadon.
  The opera singer's career guide : understanding the European Fach system /
Pearl Yeadon McGinnis ; edited by Marith McGinnis Willis.
        p. cm.
  Includes bibliographical references and index.
  ISBN 978-0-8108-6915-8 (pbk. : alk. paper) — ISBN 978-0-8108-6916-5 (ebook)
  1. Opera—Vocational guidance. 2. Singing—Vocational guidance. 3. Vocal
registers. I. Willis, Marith McGinnis. II. Title.
  ML3795.M354 2010
  782.1023'4—dc22   2010010096

∞™ The paper used in this publication meets the minimum requirements of
American National Standard for Information Sciences—Permanence of Paper
for Printed Library Materials, ANSI/NISO Z39.48-1992.

Printed in the United States of America

This book is dedicated to all my students, who showed me the joys that teaching can bring, and to all future students and prospective opera "stars" who want to follow their *dream trail* to a career in opera.

—Pearl Yeadon McGinnis

As an art form, opera is a rare and remarkable creation. For me, it expresses aspects of the human drama that cannot be expressed in any other way, or certainly not as beautifully.

—Luciano Pavarotti, *Pavarotti: My World*

Contents

Foreword

The Opera Singer's Career Guide: Understanding the European Fach *System* will be a vital part in guiding an opera singer through a career in the European system. Dr. Pearl Yeadon McGinnis, Ph.D., most recently professor and director of Opera Workshop and the Collectors Series at Missouri State University, Springfield, Missouri, had a distinguished career as an international opera singer.

My own operatic career began in the Young Artists Development Program of the Metropolitan Opera in New York City under the guidance of maestro James Levine. My genuine love of performing opera led me to the European theater, with my first engagement at the Hannover Staatsoper. I learned the *"Fach"* system on the job over twelve years in Europe and worldwide before continuing my operatic career and teaching in the United States.

Now, in retrospect, I realize that this book would have been a great technical resource and immense help in the accomplishment of my career. This book will therefore serve well as a learning tool for all who truly desire to teach, coach, or perform opera.

At Pearl's request, I feel it both an honor and a privilege to critique this indispensable guide for my dear friend and colleague! With my highest admiration,

Karen Bureau
dramatic soprano

Foreword

The first time I saw and heard Pearl Yeadon was in the summer of 1976 at the voice studio of Lee and Sally Sweetland in Los Angeles. It was a wonderful experience; as Pearl sang Elsa from Richard Wagner's *Lohengrin* she actually was Elsa. Thus began our many long years of a warm-hearted friendship. Pearl loved singing and people and enjoyed sharing her passion for singing with everyone, regardless of where they were from or their position. She understood how to kindle inspiration in the next generation with her experience and knowledge.

It is my great honor to contribute information to this successful book. I hope all readers of this book find it a companion for the satisfying journey into the wonderful world of opera, a world Pearl so loved and lived.

Alexander Senger
tenor, concert and opera soloist, and artistic director,
Operamobile/Kleines Musiktheater, Niedersachsen, Germany

Editor's Preface

*T*he *Opera Singer's Career Guide: Understanding the European* Fach *System* is based on the firsthand experiences of my sister, Dr. Pearl Yeadon McGinnis, as an opera singer in Germany during the 1980s and 1990s. Sprinkled with conversations with opera colleagues, conductors, and directors, this delightful book will take you on a journey through a wealth of information about the European *Fach* system, *Fach* categories, life as an opera singer, and what is needed to succeed in this career field.

Although my singing career led me into the Broadway musical genre, I also shared my sister's love of opera and was fortunate to be able to costar with her in a series of benefit concerts, "Great Moments from Broadway and Opera," during the 1990s and early 2000s. Inevitably we always sang several opera duets. When she began this book in 2005, I was her initial sounding board and editor.

Following her unexpected death in January 2007, I gladly took responsibility for ensuring that her book would be published. Working on it has kept me close to her and given me an increased depth of knowledge about the world of an opera singer, as well as an appreciation of how much she loved her craft and the joy she felt about singing and life in general.

My sister often referred to her journey through the world of opera as "the dream trail," and that was the working title of this book. It is fitting that the culmination of her dream of being an opera singer is this book, designed to impart her love of opera and the joy it brought into her life and to others. I feel she has accomplished this.

Author's Acknowledgments

No book of this size and scope would be possible without the help of many colleagues and friends. Special thanks and recognition go to my sister Marith McGinnis Willis for her wise and insightful contributions to chapter 3, as well as the patient editing and polishing of this manuscript.

To those who helped make my European experience such a pleasure I extend my thanks and appreciation: to *Intendant* Giancarlo del Monaco, who launched my opera career; director Andreas Prohaska; collegues Jimmy McCrae, soprano Kathleen McCalla, baritone Mauro Augustini, coach Rita Loving, Professor Herbert von Nöe, and the late maestro Alexander Sander.

To Sarah Tannehill-Cutler, Jody Kienzler, Jerry Daniels, Chrissellene Petropoulos, and Judith Blegen, opera singers all, many thanks for contributing ideas and experiences.

I wish to thank my student readers, Beth Driver and Geovonday Jones, for the many hours devoted to this book in its early stages. And to my accompanists at Missouri State University, Dr. Peter Collins and Jeannie Raney—your moral support and friendship meant the world to me.

Many thanks to tenor Alexander Senger, founder and artistic director of Operamobile / Kleines Musiktheater in Niedersachsen, Germany, for his friendship and information on fees, audition requirements, and contracts.

An overwhelming thank you to Bianca Mergell of Bäerenreiter-Verlag, Kassel, Germany, for the kind permission to use information from the 2006 Kloiber *Handbuch der Oper* in the body of this text, and as the basis for several of the appendixes.

Editor's Acknowledgments

There are many people I wish to thank for their assistance to me in completing my sister's book. First, I wish to extend my thanks to Pearl's good friend Dr. Karen Bureau, dramatic soprano, and her late mother, Mrs. Jule T. W. Bureau, for their early suggestions toward editing the original manuscript, and to Karen for assisting me in compiling audition arias for the female *Fach* categories. I also wish to thank Dr. Andrew Childs, lyric tenor, for his valuable suggestions and his research in compiling all the audition arias for the male *Fach* categories. A superb job!

To Suzane Lutz and Deborah Scheierl of the Munich Opera (Bayerische Staatsoper) *Pressebürro*, thank you for being so most gracious in offering your assistance in providing a copy of a 2007–2008 *Spielplan* (season plan), and Mr. Wilfried Hösl, the Munich Opera photographer, who gave his kind permission to use his photos from the Munich Opera.

I extend my thanks also to Ms. Juliane Cobes, *Pressereferentin* of the Staatstheater Kassel, for providing examples of *Wochenplans* and *Probeplans*, and to Kassel photographer Dominik Ketz for the use of his photos. Gratitude is extended to Herbert Raith for the use of his photos from Theater Ulm's 1984 production of Puccini's *Manon Lescaut*.

Viel und Dank to good friends Werner and Carole Gaubinger, who assisted with translation of German words in the appendixes and with contacting sources in Germany.

Thank you niece Pamela and husband, Glenn Glasell, for submitting the cover photo showing opera at its dramatic best. And a thank you to editors Renée Camus and Kellie Hagan of Scarecrow Press, and copy-editor Glenn Novak, for their help through the whole editorial journey.

Finally, my love and gratitude to my husband, Colonel Richard Willis, who continually encouraged me to "finish the book" and helped with research, photos, computer problems, and the preparation of many meals.

Introduction

Amerian singers are some of the most expressive, energetic, and effective performers in the opera world today. Vocal training in America efficiently produces many exciting singers with beautiful, well-trained voices. However, an area seldom addressed during vocal study, whether privately or in an educational institution, is how to prepare for an opera career in Europe. Pivotal to this is an understanding of the European system of voice classification called *Fach*—a system used by European opera houses to hire singers and cast their operas, and by opera singers to ensure the longevity of their careers.

Also lacking was information about how to prepare the voice for auditions within this *Fach* system, as well as finding and maintaining a job in the European opera community.

During my twelve years as an opera singer in Europe, primarily Germany, I became increasingly aware of the importance and value of the *Fach* system, and when I began teaching, I included information about this important aspect of opera—thus the genesis of this book. My intent was to provide all the information necessary for an opera student or a professional opera singer contemplating a career in Europe. This book includes descriptions of the European *Fach* system, definitions for each *Fach* category, and suggestions on how to use the *Fach* system to train young voices, from lighter to heavier categories, and how to develop and maintain a career in the field of opera.

Also included is information on preparing for audition arias, the many different types of opera auditions, and descriptions and types of op era contracts. A state-level German opera house is analyzed, including descriptions of the various performance spaces, the makeup of an ensemble, the jobs and functions of all opera house personnel, contract negotiations, a typical schedule for rehearsals and performances, the duties and responsibilities of ensemble members, and opera house administration. Practical details about establishing and maintaining residency in Europe are also discussed.

Also included are a glossary of opera words and terms, and appendixes that list opera agencies; opera houses in Austria, Germany, and Switzerland; opera roles by *Fach*, including the newly researched and defined roles for children, young lyrics, and beginners; and suggested audition arias by *Fach*.

Scattered throughout the book are quotes from famous singers, conductors, and directors, as well as anecdotal stories about the interesting occurrences on and off the opera stage that make the opera profession so fascinating. Enjoy!

1

The *Fach* System

A merican opera singers are an integral part of today's international opera world. Attend any musical performance in Europe and you will see one or more Americans on stage. They are expressive and energetic actors and often have wonderful rapport with the audience. Beautiful voices come from all countries, but Americans often seem to have an energy and expression that speaks directly to the audience, an attribute developed by an American culture that encourages personalities that are outgoing, energetic, and free-spirited.

Americans have earned a reputation for being superbly trained, confident, and able to learn new music quickly. They are also acknowledged as effective interpreters of plot and character. For these reasons European opera houses are most willing to hire Americans, especially houses in German-speaking countries. For the purposes of this book, the term "German" will refer to the countries of Germany, Austria, and Switzerland, as their use of the *Fach* opera system is identical.

Many Americans have their first professional opera engagement in one of the more than 350 full-time opera houses in these countries, or as an apprentice singer in one of 26 opera studios. There are also more than 500 theaters that regularly present operas, including independent theaters, private theaters with permanent facilities, theaters without a regular ensemble, touring theaters, and summer festivals.[1]

What Americans often overlook, or simply don't know, is that to facilitate being hired in Europe, to keep that job, and maintain a career, they need to understand the European *Fach* system of operatic vocal categorization. Many American opera singers, even those who have performed in American regional opera and recognize the term *Fach*, still do not understand how integral the system is to the efficiency of European opera houses. In Europe the *Fach* system is used to hire and fire singers, organize the season, ensure that there are enough enscmble singers to cover all roles, and even to balance the budget. Almost every aspect of being a professional opera singer in Europe is enhanced or restricted by this system.

THE DEFINITION OF *FACH*

Fach in German means specialty or category. In the opera world, *Fach* has more than one meaning. First of all, it refers to the system used to cast operas. It also refers to a voice type or vocal category—not just soprano, alto, tenor, and bass, but what "kind" of soprano, alto, tenor, and bass (for example, soubrette soprano, or character tenor).

Twenty-five *Fach* categories are considered standard, and several others are not always listed but are preferred for some roles. An example is the *Hochdramatischer Sopran*, or "high" dramatic soprano, required for the role of Isolde in Wagner's *Tristan und Isolde*. All categories will be described in chapter 2, "*Fach* Categories."

This idea of putting each singer into a specific category is seen by Americans as restrictive but by European opera house directors as a sound organizational principle. Americans often resist being narrowly defined, even when it could help them find work. They feel that they should be able to sing their favorite arias or perform their favorite roles. They often resent being limited to a certain style of music or type of character based on their vocal or even physical characteristics—that is to say, their *Fach*. However, in Europe these *Fach* categories are the primary tool for creating opera organization.

THE *FACH* SYSTEM

European opera companies use the *Fach* system to form companies and cast operas. They do so to ensure they have enough members with the appropriate voice types or specialties needed to adequately cast productions.

This is similar to typecasting in movies, TV, and the theater, all of which also cast people based on vocal characteristics, physical characteristics, and age. In opera, as in the theater, a young person could be cast as an older person, but only if his or her vocal characteristics are suitable. Those characteristics determine that person's *Fach*. Makeup does wonders for covering up any disparity in age, and there is also the advantage of the audience being at some distance from the performers. In TV and movies this is more difficult, due to the proximity of the camera's eye; it is done, but with extraordinary makeup techniques. The movie *The Curious Case of Benjamin Button* is an example of a middle-aged actor, Brad Pitt, playing a man of all ages.

In the world of professional opera, a twenty-four-year-old soprano might love singing arias from *Carmen, Aida,* and *Tosca,* but it is highly unlikely she would initially be offered a *Fach* contract to sing any of these leading roles. They would go to the more mature and experienced singers with vocal qualities that match the character soprano or dramatic soprano *Fach* categories.

FACH AS A VOICE CATEGORY

When singers use the word *Fach*, it is in reference to the different vocal categories, or even a type of role they feel qualified to perform. In this respect, *Fach* defines the qualities that represent an individual singer's complete vocal package. Some of the various uses of this word are as follows:

Terms	Translations
Fach- (Fächer)	branch, specialty, department
das ist gerade sein Fach	that is his specialty
von Fach	by profession/by specialty
das ist nicht mein Fach	that is not in my category/my specialty
er versteht sein Fach volkommen	he is an expert in his subject

When one is just beginning to develop a career, it is best to concentrate on the *Fach* that best fits one's current vocal characteristics and then move into other *Fach* categories with age and experience. Therefore, knowing how the *Fach* system works, and how to develop one's voice within this system, will assist a singer in marketing himself or herself in the opera world.

THE ELEMENTS OF *FACH*

There are many factors that determine a singer's *Fach*. These include the singer's basic vocal equipment, combined with his or her physical appearance, age, and experience.

How a singer's voice sounds is the initial factor in determining that singer's *Fach*. This relies heavily on the characteristics of the vocal apparatus, which are directly related to the physiology of the individual. An extremely petite soprano seldom has a huge dramatic voice, nor does a tall, statuesque, large-boned soprano usually have a bright, high, flexible coloratura voice. (For a complete discussion of the vocal apparatus, see William Vennard's book *Singing: the Mechanism and the Technic*.)[2]

Certainly exceptions exist, such as Dame Joan Sutherland, an imposing woman close to six feet tall. She originally studied Wagner, until she discovered that she had a talent for lyric coloratura and dramatic coloratura repertoire, especially the Bellini and Donizetti operas. Beverly Sills was also a tall, statuesque singer. She was first recognized internationally as a Handel expert but quickly became famous as a bel canto specialist, that is to say, "the singing of cantabile (flowing) passages with purity, smoothness, and artistic finish, in the traditional Italian manner."[3] However, most opera singers can be initially categorized by their physical build, which will most often correspond to their vocal sound.

Opera roles were developed to correspond to this connection between physical build and vocal sound. Fairies, imps, and elves are sung by children or lyric, light voices. The young characters in an opera, a son or daughter, are sung by younger, lighter voices. Kings, fathers, counts, devils, and apparitions will have the darker voices. This same typing is found in the American musical world. The tenor is usually the good guy and has a higher, more melodious and soothing voice than the dangerous but sometimes still-attractive scoundrel, who is usually a baritone or bass with a vocal quality that can sound rough and threatening. A great example of this is the vocal comparison of the hero Curley versus the villain Jud in Rodgers and Hammerstein's *Oklahoma!*

Likewise, an opera's sweet young thing, such as Barbarina in Mozart's *Le nozze di Figaro*, will have a high, light voice, while the more mature woman, perhaps touched with madness, such as Elektra in Richard Strauss's *Elektra*, will sing with a richer, more dramatic sound.

Another example of this physical build/vocal sound connection is seen in tall, powerfully built, heroic-looking dramatic tenors such as Tristan in Wagner's *Tristan und Isolde*, whereas a stereotypical Tristan would look and sound out of place in light lyric tenor roles such as Don Ottavio in Mozart's *Don Giovanni*, Idamante in *Idomeneo*, or Ferrando in *Così fan tutte*.

Voice

"Voice" is the first element in determining a person's *Fach*. It is wise to regard the voice as an instrument and evaluate it as dispassionately as one would when considering any other instrument. Singers often refer to their voice as if it were a separate entity. "My voice is a little off today," they will say. Or, "I'm not in good voice today." In some respects, this is true.

The voice is made up of several factors. Everyone is born with a certain genetic makeup that determines the size of the vocal cords (*Stimmbänder*), technically called the "vocal folds." A person's basic physical characteristics also determine the width and length of the vocal folds, the musculature around the vocal folds, and other characteristics of the vocal apparatus. This includes the consistency of the mucus (*Schleim*), which provides lubrication; the shape and size of the resonating areas, which help give the voice size and color; and the use of breath (*Atem*), without which it is not possible to produce a tone.

Soprano Lilli Lehmann (1848–1929), a legendary German opera singer during the late nineteenth and early twentieth centuries, emphasized the use of the breath as follows: "The breath becomes voice through the operation of the will, and the instrumentality of the vocal organs. To regulate the breath, to prepare a passage of the proper form through which it shall flow, circulate, develop itself, and reach the necessary resonating chambers, must be our chief task."[4]

> *Fach* = voice (vocal folds, mucus membranes,
> muscles, resonators, breath)

Range

Range is the second element in determining *Fach*, and it has two meanings. The first is the actual number of notes that a voice is capable of singing, from the lowest note to the highest. This is determined partly by the physical makeup of the voice and also by training. A professional singer would not necessarily perform with the full range of the voice. An example would be Birgit Swenson, dramatic soprano, whose voice extended from the baritone F♯ to the f♯3 in the high coloratura range. Most of her roles required only middle c (c1) to an occasional high c (c3) or c♯3.

> NOTE: The system of range in this book is based on c1 as middle c on the piano keyboard; c2 is the second c to the right; c3 (the dreaded high c) is the third c to the right, and so on. The first c below middle c is written as a lowercase c; the next to the left on the keyboard is capital C, (the low C for a bass), the next C1, and so on. The range for a young dramatic soprano, for example, would be written c1–c3.

Range also refers to that part of the voice that can be consistently sung with the most ease and beauty—"the extent of pitch covered by a melody or lying within the capacity of a voice."[5] This will be the area of

the singer's range—high, low, or in-between—where the singer can perform most effectively. This is often called a singer's *tessitura* (Italian for
"texture") and also indicates the pitch region in which most of the notes
of a given role lie.

$$Fach = voice + range$$

Size

The size of the voice is also determined by the basic vocal apparatus but
can be developed further through training. Size can refer to many factors,
such as the sheer amount of sound a singer can produce, or the voice's
dramatic effect. A singer must often use a large voice in order to sing with
heavy orchestrations, or a light voice to sustain high, soft lines. Other elements add to the impression of size, such as breath control, the ability to
sustain the sound characteristic of the voice over extended periods, and
the timbre of the voice.

$$Fach = voice + range + size$$

Timbre

Timbre is the tone color (*Klangfarbe*) of the voice, often referred to as the
basic vocal quality. Timbre is determined partly by the construction of
the basic vocal apparatus and in a great part by training. Elements in
understanding the timbre of a voice are harmonics, partials, overtones,
and harmonic spectrum, all of which refer to the resonance of the voice,
which produces its characteristic color. The famed vocal teacher of the
late nineteenth century Giovanni Battista Lamperti stated that "the presence of resonance in head, mouth, and chest (overtones) is proof that your
voice is full-grown, full-fleshed."[6]

$$Fach = voice + range + size + timbre$$

Physical Build

A singer's physical appearance is a major determining factor in *Fach*.
Height, build, and innate personality all contribute to the basic appearance of the singer. Certain elements of physical build can be changed on
stage. Legendary Italian tenor Mario del Monaco always wore lifts in his
shoes and boots when he was in costume, which changed his five-foot
nine-inch frame to an imposing six feet. A tall soprano can magically
become shorter, when joining a not-so-tall tenor for a duet, by the simple

expedient of crouching down slightly at the knees. Physical characteristics other than build are often less of a challenge, as costumes, makeup, and wigs can disguise a multitude of flaws and inadequacies.

However, the impression a singer makes when auditioning—without a costume, makeup, or wig—is often used to judge if this person fits the *Fach* sought by the opera house. It is difficult to look short and delicate, if auditioning for the sweet young girl next door, when genetically gifted with a tall frame and powerful build. Since physical build usually goes along with the basic characteristics of the voice, outward appearance is an initial indicator of vocal sound.

Fach = voice + range + size + timbre + physical build

Age and Experience

When determining *Fach*, it is also important to consider age and experience. For example, two of the *Fach* category terms, lyric and dramatic, are quite opposite in their characteristics. Very young singers, those in their late teens or early twenties, could have the potential of being a dramatic soprano, mezzo, tenor, or baritone, but it would be unwise to perform those roles on stage at that age. It is best they stay with the lyric, younger-sounding roles. Even Lamperti emphasized this maturation process: "It is a pity that young singers, who are studying voice, immediately sing songs and arias, literally before they know how to open their mouths, instead of earnestly studying the real support of the voice (the mechanism of the breath) in order to develop the voice and make it smooth and flexible."[7]

A general rule would be that the more dramatic the role, the more age and experience one needs in order to be able to perform it effectively. Just as an athlete needs years of practice and experience to reach the Olympics, so too does an opera singer need age and experience to cope with the physical and emotional demands of many roles, especially the dramatic roles.

A wonderful exception to this rule was the phenomenal voice and artistry of soprano Astrid Varney (1918–2006). In 1941, at the age of twenty-three, she premiered at the Metropolitan Opera singing Sieglinde in Wagner's *Die Walküre*, a dramatic soprano role. Six days later she replaced the ailing Helen Traubel as Brünnhilde in the same opera, another heavy dramatic soprano role.[8] More than forty years later, during a performance of Pietro Mascagni's *Cavalleria rusticana* at the National Theater in Munich, when Varney sang her first solo line as Mamma Lucia, the critics wrote that it was as if the clouds had parted and the sun shone through and filled the entire hall with warmth and sound. Few opera singers have had her natural gift of a voice that was wide as well as brilliant, and as vibrant as it was dramatic, or the capacity at such a young age to perform the most dramatic and difficult of operatic roles.

As vocal characteristics and physical build usually match, a young singer will normally be cast in lyric roles that also demand a young-appearing singer. An older singer with years of experience and enhanced training will usually look the part of an older dramatic character, as well as have a more mature-sounding voice.

Susanna in Mozart's *Le nozze di Figaro* is considered a typical role for a young, lyric soprano. However, it is one of the longest soprano roles, at approximately one hour and twenty minutes of actual singing. One must be very careful that the length of the role does not put too much demand on a young singer. Although Susanna is a wonderful role for a young lyric to study and perform, in a European opera house the singer could be performing this physically demanding role two to three times a week, in rotation with other roles.

$$Fach = \text{voice} + \text{range} + \text{size} + \text{timbre}$$
$$+ \text{physical build} + \text{age and experience}$$

Desire

After all the physical and vocal qualities are analyzed, there is another important quality in each singer that must be considered when determining *Fach*. Quite simply, this is whether the singer truly enjoys singing in a certain tessitura, or feels drawn to performing a specific style, such as dramatic as opposed to lyric roles. Singers should ask themselves if coloratura (quick moving) passages are fun to sing as well as challenging, or is it more comfortable to sing music full of portamento (gliding from one note to another) and legato (flowing without breaks between notes) passages. If a singer is more confident as an actor, should that singer therefore seek the "buffo" or comic roles? Or if a singer is more comfortable letting the voice convey most if not all of the emotion required, should that singer therefore concentrate on the more classic roles, where there is less physical acting? For example, an extremely dramatic role such as Leonore in Beethoven's *Fidelio* could be performed without physical dramatics and still be effectively passionate just using the voice.

These considerations are a combination of the singer's personality mixed with age and experience and are not as easily defined. However, anyone who has performed for any length of time quickly learns that the voice/body is quite comfortable in a certain style of music or drama, and not as comfortable in something else. However, effective acting skills, combined with the correct vocal sound for the role, will add the physical and emotional excitement to make a role come alive.

$$Fach = \text{voice} + \text{range} + \text{size} + \text{timbre}$$
$$+ \text{physical build} + \text{age and experience} + \text{desire}$$

Frequency of Performance

A further consideration when choosing the proper *Fach* is to know which roles can be performed several times a week without vocal fatigue, especially if one has to rehearse new roles or perform others in rotation during the same period. There is an enormous difference in performing a role with only forty-five minutes of singing, such as Agathe in Carl Maria von Weber's *Der Freischütz*, three times a week, versus Susanna, with her one hour and twenty minutes of singing in *Le nozze di Figaro*. So keep in mind that the *Fach* must be carefully chosen not only because of all the elements discussed, but for what could easily be performed several times a week.

$$Fach = \text{voice} + \text{range} + \text{size} + \text{timbre} + \text{physical build}$$
$$+ \text{age and experience} + \text{desire} + \text{frequency of performance}$$

SERIOUS AND CHARACTER *FACH*

In Europe, *Fach* vocal descriptions are organized in two subcategories: serious and character. Serious (*Seriös*) refers to the roles most Americans think of as leading roles, or diva roles, if sung by a woman. Character (*Charakter*) roles usually require more acting but also can be leading roles.

Serious Category (*Seriöse Fächer*)

The serious category roles, often the leading roles, are the protagonists of the story and usually the most dramatic characters. Since dramatic music is usually accompanied by a large orchestra, a large, powerful voice is necessary to portray these roles effectively, as well as the physical build and personality to be imposing on stage.

The serious roles include many of the leading roles categorized as *erste Partien*—literally, first roles or lead roles. European opera houses consider the serious roles to be all those that demand voice and personality as well as significant experience and an artistic ripening to portray effectively. Leonora in Verdi's *Il trovatore* is an example of such a role, as are Escamillo and Don José in Bizet's *Carmen*, Leonore in Beethoven's *Fidelio*, King Philip in Verdi's *Don Carlos*, and Tristan and Wotan in the Wagnerian operas *Tristan und Isolde* and *Die Walküre*.

When casting a serious role, the primary consideration is not only the role's dimension or length but also its importance within the matrix of the opera. An example of a small role being filled by a *Seriöse Fächer* is that of the hermit (a holy man revered by the whole district in which the opera takes place) in Weber's *Der Freischütz*. It is usually cast with a serious bass. This is because his choral-like aria at the end of the third act is an important intercession that prevents the main character's banishment.[9] As in this case, the importance of a role to the plot dictates that leading singers perform even short roles.

In other cases, the difficulty of an aria will require it to be cast with a *Seriöse Fächer*. One such role is the Italian Singer in Richard Strauss's *Der Rosenkavalier*, which is cast with a leading young dramatic tenor (*Jugendlich-dramatischer Tenor*), also referred to as a spinto tenor, even though it is classified as a small role (*kleine Partie*). Luciano Pavarotti performed this role, which consists of one aria, "Di rigori armato il seno," early in his career and, needless to say, made quite an impression.

Below is a listing of the serious *Fach* categories (*Seriöse Fächer*) as listed in the Kloiber *Handbuch der Oper*, considered the standard reference in establishing *Fach* categories.[10] These same terms are used to define voice categories in casting operas in the United States, so their English equivalency is also listed.

Seriöse Fächer	**Serious Categories**
Lyrischer Sopran (c–c3)	lyric soprano
Jugendlich-dramatischer Sopran (*Spintosopran*) (c–c3)	young dramatic soprano/acting soprano
Dramatischer Koloratursopran (c–f3)	dramatic coloratura soprano
Dramatischer Sopran (g–c3)	dramatic soprano
Hochdramatischer Sopran (g–c3)	high dramatic soprano
Koloratur-Mezzosopran (g–b2)	coloratura mezzo-soprano
Dramatischer Mezzosopran (g–b2 or c3)	dramatic mezzo-soprano
Dramatischer Alt (g–b3)	dramatic alto
Tiefer Alt (Kontra-Alt) (f–a2)	low alto
Contratenor (c1–c3)	countertenor
Haute-Contre (*Altino*) (g–b2)	high countertenor (male alto)
Lyrischer Tenor (c–d2)	lyric tenor
Jugendlich-dramatischer Tenor (c–c2)	young dramatic tenor
Heldentenor (c–c2)	heavy dramatic tenor
Lyrischer Bariton (*Spielbariton*)* (B–a♯1)	lyric baritone (acting baritone)

Kavalierbariton (A–g1)	cavalier baritone
Heldenbariton (*Hoher Bass*) (G–f♯1)	dramatic baritone (high bass)
Seriöser Bass (*Tiefer Bass*) (C–f1)	serious bass (low bass)

*The Kloiber lists *Lyrischer Bariton* and *Spielbariton* as two separate *Fach* categories—the *Lyrischer Bariton* in the serious category and the *Spielbariton* in the character category. In chapter 2, "*Fach* Categories," they are described as one *Fach* and are listed as such here.

Acting/Character Roles (*Spiel und Charakter*)

The second subcategory, *Spiel und Charakter*, also referred to in Europe as acting roles, includes many roles Americans would categorize with the Italian term *comprimario*, or secondary roles. These acting/character *Fach* categories offer the singer the opportunity to play many interesting and challenging parts, which include the comedic or buffo characters. Many of these delightful roles are the most important ones in an opera and are differentiated from the serious category by the requirement to act and portray elaborate characterizations vocally as well as physically. These are actors who can sing.

Just as with the *Seriös* categories, singers specializing in the *Spiel und Charakter Fächer* have to possess an effective voice. Some young tenors with physically imposing and beautiful voices will specialize in these acting/character categories until they have the requisite years of experience to support more dramatic singing. For example, the gradual change to a Tristan in Wagner's *Tristan und Isolde,* later in a career, is a natural combination of vocal growth and acting experience combined with an innate desire to sing these roles—a desire that was probably present when the tenor was young. Lamperti said it well: "A tenor possesses the most delicate type of voice; it demands a very earnest and carefully prepared course of study." Similarly, "One of the most eminent dramatic sopranos 'found herself' only after singing light roles for twenty years."[11]

The character or acting categories should be considered by young singers for several reasons: first of all, it is easier to find that first job in the character *Fach* categories. This is because there are more of these roles in most operas, while there is usually only one hero, one heroine, and one villain. And these roles are usually shorter in musical length than the serious roles, and less desirable to the established singers. Also, starting in character roles provides the utmost training as an actor while allowing the time needed to gain experience and vocal maturity.

This does not imply that a singer who specializes in character roles is any less skilled musically than the *Seriös* category singers. On the contrary, specialists in these *Fach* categories are tremendous actors as well as singers, able to portray someone like Marie in Donizetti's *La fille du régiment*, who prances around the stage costumed as a military officer, or the dance master, *Tanzmeister*, in Strauss's *Ariadne auf Naxos*, who constantly makes acerbic comments to the audience and other performers during the opera.

Character roles are also often a lead part, *erste Partie*, but many character roles also would be classified as the buffo, or comic secondary roles. Other examples of *erste Partien* lead character roles include Carmen in Bizet's *Carmen*, Marthe in Charles Gounod's *Faust*, the Witch in Engelbert Humperdinck's *Hänsel und Gretel*, Loge in Richard Wagner's *Das Rheingold*, and Don Alfonso in Mozart's *Così fan tutte*. Following is a listing of the *Spiel und Charakterfächer*.[12]

Spiel und Charakterfächer	**Acting and Character Categories**
Lyrischer Koloratursopran (c1–f3)	lyric coloratura soprano
Spielsopran (*Soubrette*) (c1–c3)	acting soprano (soubrette)
Charaktersopran (b–c3)	character soprano
Lyrischer Mezzosopran (*Spielalt*) (g–b2)	lyric mezzo-soprano (acting alto)
Spieltenor (*Tenorbuffo*) c–b1	acting tenor (comic tenor)
Charaktertenor A–b1	character tenor
Charakterbariton A–g1	character baritone
Spielbass (*Bassbuffo*) E–f1	acting bass (comic bass)
Charakterbass (*Bassbariton*) E–f1	character bass (bass baritone)
Schwerer Spielbass (*Schwerer Bassbuffo*) D–f1	heavy acting bass (heavy comic bass)

PREPARING *FACH*-APPROPRIATE ROLES

Once the appropriate *Fach* has been determined, the singer then prepares as many roles as possible in this *Fach* category. Voice teachers, coaches, competition judges, and opera professionals can all assist with these choices. Singers should not be discouraged if their initial *Fach* is not yet in keeping with their ultimate goal. As they gain vocal maturity and performance experience, they can move into another *Fach* at any time.

When studying roles within a particular *Fach*, it is preferable to learn the entire role, not just the arias. Knowing the complete role makes an enormous difference in the presentation of an aria in an audition and to the general confidence of a singer. It is important to remember that whatever *Fach* is chosen to be the primary *Fach*, it should be music that can be sung every day—comfortably!

When preparing roles, singers should not only concentrate on learning the roles in their primary *Fach* but should also learn a few roles in a lighter *Fach*, as well as a few in a heavier *Fach*. (These lighter/heavier *Fach* categories would be those that immediately bracket the primary *Fach* category.) This is advised because there is always the possibility that, once one has an opera contract in the primary *Fach*, a vacancy might provide the opportunity to occasionally sing a role in a different *Fach*, one that is closely related to the primary *Fach*. For example, a *Jugendlich-dramatischer Sopran* (young dramatic soprano) who has learned roles such as Agathe in *Der Freischütz* should also learn a few lighter lyric soprano roles, such as Micäela in Bizet's *Carmen*, and a few heavier dramatic soprano roles, such as Tosca in Puccini's *Tosca*.

Age and experience will be the determining factors in deciding which roles in each category could be learned. A young dramatic soprano might have the stage presence and vocal power to perform a dramatic role such as Tosca. But she would not necessarily have the size of voice, nor probably the experience, to portray a Wagnerian role such as Isolde in *Tristan und Isolde*, even though both roles are listed in the dramatic soprano *Fach*.

On the other hand, there are dramatic sopranos who may not want to sing some of the *Jugendlich-dramatischer Sopran* roles, especially those demanding considerable coloratura, such as Elvira in Verdi's *Ernani*. Nor may they want to tackle the elegant lyric lines, or endless recitative, of the Countess in Mozart's *Le nozze di Figaro*, unless this type of singing fits comfortably within their tessitura. However, this same soprano probably could be comfortable singing other *Jugendlich* roles, such as Maddalena in Giordano's *Andrea Chénier* or Giorgetta in Puccini's *Il tabarro*, and would have no trouble singing these roles in rotation with Isolde.

FACH AND COMPETITION ARIAS

One of the problems young singers have is determining the correct arias to present in competition. The Metropolitan Opera National Council audition judges regularly see young competitors who have chosen arias from their favorite operas, or in emulation of their favorite singers, rather than from the most appropriate *Fach* for their abilities and current skill level.

For example, a young lyric soprano might choose to sing a heavy dramatic aria, followed by something from the coloratura *Fach* category. This can give the judges the impression that the singer does not have any realistic knowledge of her current vocal, acting, or experience-related capabilities. The judges are looking for a "complete package" in one area of expertise, in this case the lyric soprano *Fach*. Therefore, the arias chosen for competition must reflect an age-appropriate *Fach*, not what the singer thinks he or she might be capable of doing later. A competition is not the time to play jack-of-all-trades, master of none. Otherwise, the judging committee could be reluctant to advance the singer to the next level, even though that person may have demonstrated the most potential.

FACH ADVICE FROM THE EXPERTS

Following is some advice from three successful professionals on the subject of *Fach*, from *Great Singers on Great Singing* by bass Jerome Hines. First, Zinka Milanov (1906–1989), dramatic soprano, Metropolitan Opera:

> I never gave more than I had. . . . I always tried to put my piano, my *mezza voce* [medium fullness of tone], my legato in all my parts. . . . You're a soprano or you're a mezzo-soprano. You're a dramatic voice or you're a lyric. But to be a full lyric and go and sing dramatic parts is wrong. . . . The danger lies in singing roles outside your natural vocal category.[13]

Placido Domingo (1941–), tenor, Metropolitan Opera:

> I think there is one very important thing—especially when we sing in theaters as big as the Metropolitan—not that you have to sing loudly, because that's impossible. You sing with *your* voice in a small house and you sing with *your* voice in a big house. You don't change the technique.[14]

Magda Olivero (1910–), dramatic soprano, Metropolitan Opera:

> I feel that when one has reached a certain age and position in a career . . . and knows how . . . she permits herself this luxury [of singing dramatic roles] . . . but the young people beginning their careers—[and singing] *Aida, Trovatore*—it is not good. When they are just beginning, they must let their bones form themselves.[15]

Good advice for singers of any age!

NOTES

1. *Deutches Bühnen Jahrbuch* (Hamburg: Genossenschaft Deutscher Bühnen-Angehöriger im Verlag der Bühenschriften-Bertriebs-Gesellschaft mbH, 2006), 12.
2. William Vennard, *Singing: the Mechanism and the Technic* (Ann Arbor, Mich.: Edward Brothers, 1967).

3. C. O. Sylvester Mawson, *Dictionary of Foreign Terms,* 2nd ed. rev. and updated by Charles Berlitz (New York: Thomas Y. Crowell, 1975), 45.

4. Lilli Lehmann, *How to Sing,* trans. Richard Aldrich (New York: MacMillan, 1929), 13.

5. *Webster's New Collegiate Dictionary* (Springfield, Mass.: G. & C. Merriam, 1975), 1110.

6. Giovanni Battista Lamperti, *Vocal Wisdom.* Transcribed (1931) by William Earl Brown, trans. Lillian Strongin (New York: Taplinger Publishing, 1957), 23.

7. Ibid., 4.

8. Donald Arthur, *Fifty-Five Years in Five Acts: My Life in Opera* (Evanston, Ill.: Northwestern University Press, 1998).

9. Gustav Kobbé, *The Definitive Kobbé's Opera Book,* rev. and updated by George Henry Hubert Lascelles, Earl of Harewood (New York: G. P. Putnam's Sons, 1987), 135.

10. Rudolf Kloiber, Wulf Konold, and Robert Maschka, *Handbuch der Oper* (Kassel, Germany: Bärenreiter-Verlag, 2006), 897–898.

11. Lamperti, *Vocal Wisdom,* 22.

12. Kloiber et al., *Handbuch der Oper.*

13. Quoted in Jerome Hines, *Great Singers on Great Singing* (New York: Limelight Editions, 1988), 166–167.

14. Quoted in ibid., 104–105.

15. Quoted in ibid., 205.

2

Fach Categories

Twenty-five main *Fach* categories are unilaterally recognized in the opera world, and several additional, specialized categories have been delineated for certain opera roles.

The *Handbuch der Oper*, by Rudolf Kloiber, is considered the standard reference in all matters concerning *Fach* categories, especially in the European opera community. If there is a dispute of any kind between the opera house and a singer, either party can refer to this reference book as an authority on the *Fach* category designated for every role. Although "the Kloiber," as it is often referred to, also states that there is no absolute definition for each *Fach*, the categories listed in this reference have been agreed upon as guides for both singers and opera houses by the people who know the roles and their requirements best: the directors, conductors, and the singers themselves.

The *Handbuch der Oper* also describes operas alphabetically by composer, with a comprehensive analysis of important factors such as the personnel needed, length and organization of the opera, setting, the plot and history of the opera, origin of the libretto and story, the historical style, and the history of the composition. The *Handbuch der Oper* is highly recommended for all teachers and students of opera, as well as the professional opera singer.

Following are descriptions of *Fach* categories, including those for the child, young lyric, and beginner (*Anfängerin*), not listed as *Fach* in the Kloiber, along with examples of roles. Categories are listed from the lightest and highest voices to the lowest and most dramatic. (For a more comprehensive listing of roles, refer to appendix D, "Opera Roles for Children, Young Lyrics, and Beginners," and appendix E, "Opera Roles by *Fach.*")

CHILD CATEGORIES (c1–a2)

A child whose voice has not yet gone through puberty.

One of the most delightful aspects of opera is that it gives even young children a chance to perform on stage as soloists and in groups. Although not listed as a *Fach* category in the Kloiber (which is intended as a guide for established *Fach* assignments only), these roles help define the concept of *Fach* by illustrating the development of voices from the lightest and most elementary of vocal roles—those of a child—through the heaviest and most complicated of roles.

Opera fans are familiar with the "Chorus of Street Boys" in the first act of Bizet's *Carmen*, sung by children as they march enthusiastically around the stage. In Puccini's *Madama Butterfly*, Cio-Cio San's death scene is passionately sung to her very young son (a mute role), and operas such as Puccini's *La bohème*, Leoncavallo's *Pagliacci*, and Verdi's *Il trovatore* use children on stage to add realism to the crowd scenes.

Children play cupids, moths, spirits—all the most delicate of sounds and personalities. Although these roles are often cast with beginners or light lyric voices, they are most effective when performed by children. In Menotti's *Amahl and the Night Visitors*, the production notes specifically state that the role of Amahl must be sung by a boy.[1]

The fact that there are many more roles for boys than for girls is most likely a reflection of the long tradition in Europe of training young male voices in boys' choirs. In today's opera world, roles for "child" are often sung by boys or girls interchangeably, unless specifically requested by the composer.

Examples of Child Roles

- Yniold, *Pelléas et Mélisande*, Debussy
- Harry, *Albert Herring*, Britten
- Melia, *Apollo et Hyacinthus*, Mozart
- Boy, *Die Zauberflöte*, Mozart
- Street vendor, *Louise*, Charpentier
- Cobweb, *A Midsummer Night's Dream*, Britten
- Amahl, *Amahl and the Night Visitors*, Menotti

SOPRANO CATEGORIES

Beginner Soprano (c1–c3), *Anfängerin Sopran*

A light, high voice with a youthful quality.

Not described in Kloiber's *Handbuch der Oper*, this category encompasses roles that are usually listed following the opera's main cast of characters or within the body of the work and can be sung by beginners (*Angfängerin*). They are included in this chapter to show the progression of voice development from one *Fach* to another.

Most of these roles will be small roles (*kleine Partien*) or medium roles (*medium Partien*). However, *Anfängerin Sopran* could be considered a *Fach*, as this would be the designation written into a contract for a young soprano who is accepting her first contract in a European opera house and who does not yet have the experience or reputation to qualify for a more established *Fach* contract. These singers most often portray roles that include children, teenagers, and young adults.

Even though classified as a beginner, this soprano is still expected to effectively portray roles. However, the characters tend to be one-dimensional and described by their function, such as the "shepherd boy" in Puccini's *Tosca*, or the "priestess" in Verdi's *Aida*. Many of the selections for this voice will simply be labeled "soprano" or "voice," as in Richard Strauss's *Die Frau ohne Schatten*, or the "love pair" in Puccini's *Il tabarro*.

In the opera *Louise*, by Charpentier, there are over thirty small roles listed as a *kleine Partien* in the Kloiber that are suitable for beginners. In a delightful street scene in act 2, all types of characters could be sung by young voices, to include a rag picker, policemen, painter, sculptor, junk dealer, watercress vendor, carrot vendor, and students.

Almost every opera has at least one small role that could be suitable for the *Anfängerin*, a category that gives the singer ample experience and time to develop acting and vocal skills.

Examples of Anfängerin Sopran Roles

- Shepherd boy, *Tosca*, Puccini
- Temple singer, *Aida*, Verdi
- Priestess, *Aida*, Verdi
- Soprano voice, *Il tabarro*, Puccini
- Inez, *Il trovatore*, Verdi
- Love pair, *Il tabarro*, Puccini
- Stimme, *Die Frau ohne Schatten*, R. Strauss
- Ein Modistin, *Der Rosenkavalier*, R. Strauss

Soubrette (Acting) Soprano (c1–c3), *Soubrette (Spielsopran)*

A young soprano with a bright, flexible voice who appears energetic and youthful on stage.

A soubrette soprano usually plays supporting roles such as a sister, friend, or secondary character. The range of a soubrette soprano is relatively limited, but the music still demands a voice capable of singing with heavier voices and being heard over the orchestra. Sometimes the role requires more acting and thus would be listed as a *Spielsopran* (acting soprano).

Papagena, from Mozart's *Die Zauberflöte*, would be the most typical of these roles and is a delightful personality to portray. She first appears in the opera as an "old woman in disguise" in answer to the birdman Papageno's plea for a wife of his own. In spite of his negative reaction to her, she decides she really wants him and later appears as a cute "bird girl," the perfect match to the birdman.

Examples of Soubrette Soprano Roles

- Giannetta, *L'elisir d'amore*, Donizetti
- Grilletta, *Lo speziali*, Haydn
- Marie, *Der Waffenschmied*, Lortzing
- Gretchen, *Der Wildschütz*, Lortzing
- Serpetta, *La finta giardiniera*, Mozart
- Barbarina, *Le nozze di Figaro*, Mozart
- Papagena, *Die Zauberflöte*, Mozart
- Lucieta, *Le donne curiose*, Wolf-Ferrari

Lyric Coloratura Soprano (c1–f 3), *Lyrischer Koloratursopran*

A high, bright, flexible voice that shines in the upper register.

Lyric coloratura sopranos usually portray younger heroines, so must be capable of portraying a sweet, delicate image on stage. These roles are sometimes played by a young soubrette soprano and then would be referred to as a *Lyrischer Koloratursoubrette*. An effective and energetic actress, she usually sets up the action and manipulates the other characters with her brains and personality.

Examples range from Adina in Donizetti's *L'elisir d'amore*, who first scorns the attentions of a true-hearted peasant lad but later takes matters into her own hands when she realizes his devotion to her, to Blonde the English maid in Mozart's *Die Entführung aus dem Serail*, who matches her wits against Osmin, the overseer of the harem, who then complains about the English allowing their women so much liberty.[2]

Other examples include Despina, the maid of two spoiled young sisters in Mozart's *Così fan tutte*; Sophie in Richard Strauss's *Der Rosenkavalier*, an untouched innocent who falls in love with the young Octavian; and Madame "Silver-Voice" in Mozart's *Der Schauspieldirektor*, an opera diva dueling with her rival. The emotional and acting range of this category is enormous.

Examples of *Lyrischer Koloratursopran, Koloratursoubrette* Roles

- Adina, *L'elisir d'amore*, Donizetti
- Norina, *Don Pasquale*, Donizetti
- Marie, *La fille du régiment*, Donizetti
- Nedda, *Pagliacci*, Leoncavallo
- Manon, *Manon*, Massanet
- Sophie, *Der Rosenkavalier*, R. Strauss
- Despina, *Così fan tutte*, Mozart
- Zerbinetta, *Ariadne auf Naxos*, R. Strauss
- Silberklang, *Der Schauspieldirektor*, Mozart
- Blonde, *Die Entführung aus dem Serail*, Mozart

Dramatic Coloratura Soprano (c1–f3), *Dramatischer Koloratursopran*

A high, bright, flexible voice capable of considerable power in the upper range.

This *Fach* demands tremendous acting, energy, and characterization. Examples include Donna Anna in Mozart's *Don Giovanni*, who has been raped and spends the opera trying to get revenge, although secretly acknowledging that she loves the scoundrel who violated her; Leonora in Verdi's *Il trovatore*, who takes poison at the end of the opera rather than give in to the advances of the Count di Luna; Marguerite in Gounod's *Faust*, who has killed her own child and goes mad; Violetta in Verdi's *La traviata*, who dies of consumption; and Fiordiligi, one of two sisters in Mozart's *Così fan tutte* trying to remain faithful to their fiancés, who have disguised themselves as exotic Albanians to test the women's love.

Although the role of the Queen of the Night, in Mozart's *Die Zauberflöte*, is listed under this category, it is considered almost as a separate entity because of its vocal difficulty. Many lyric coloraturas are specialists as the Queen, and singers who can master the coloratura intricacies of her aria "O zittre nicht, mein lieber Sohn" can base a career on this role.

Examples of *Dramatischer Koloraturasopran* Roles

- Anna Bolena, *Anna Bolena*, Donizetti
- Marguerite, *Faust*, Gounod

- Cleopatra, *Giulio Cesare*, Handel
- Poppea, *L'incoronazione di Poppea*, Monteverdi
- Fiordiligi, *Così fan tutte*, Mozart
- Leonora, *Il trovatore*, Verdi
- Donna Anna, *Don Giovanni*, Mozart
- Rezia, *Oberon*, Weber
- Violetta, *La traviata*, Verdi
- Queen, *Die Zauberflöte*, Mozart
- Konstanze, *Die Entführung aus dem Serail*, Mozart

Lyric Soprano (c1–c3), *Lyrischer Sopran*

A voice with warm, beautiful color capable of long, seamless phrases and beautiful top notes.

A lyric soprano usually portrays young women, and this *Fach* includes small roles as well as lead characters. The characters are usually one-dimensional and relatively static, although some portray considerable elegance, passion, and deep emotion. Examples include Micaëla, the faithful fiancée of Don José in *Carmen*, and Marzelline in Beethoven's *Fidelio*, who is in love with Fidelio, not knowing Fidelio is a woman in disguise. Other examples are Gretel in Humperdinck's *Hänsel und Gretel*; Lauretta, the young daughter in Puccini's *Gianni Schicchi*; and the servant Liù, who loves Calaf in Puccini's *Turandot* and stabs herself to death rather than tell the princess Calaf's name.

Although these singers must be excellent actors, they are known almost as much for the exquisite music they sing as for their characterizations. A good Micaëla can steal the show from Carmen by a beautifully rendered "Je dis que rein ne m'epouvante," considered by many to be the most effective and beautiful aria in the whole opera. Lauretta's "O mio babbino caro" literally interrupts the fractured vocal phrases and frenetic comic action in *Gianni Schicchi* and allows the audience to luxuriate in long lines and beautiful sound. The heart-rending pathos of Pamina's "Ach, ich fühls" in *Die Zauberflöte* mirrors every young woman's dreams and doubts about love.

Examples of *Lyrischer Sopran* Roles

- Marzelline, *Fidelio*, Beethoven
- Micaëla, *Carmen*, Bizet
- Gretel, *Hänsel und Gretel*, Humperdinck
- Pamina, *Die Zauberflöte*, Mozart
- Susanna, *Le nozze di Figaro*, Mozart
- Lauretta, *Gianni Schicchi*, Puccini
- Liù, *Turandot*, Puccini

- Marie, *Prodaná Nevesta*, Smetana
- Zdenka, *Arabella*, R. Strauss
- Wellgunde, *Das Rheingold*, Wagner

Young Dramatic Soprano (c1–c3), *Jugendlich-dramatischer Sopran*

A young dramatic soprano voice with great power.

Also called a spinto soprano or a German dramatic soprano, *Jugendlich* has no adequate translation in English. It literally means "youthlike." The term refers to sopranos and tenors exclusively. *Jugendlich-dramatischer Sopran* refers to a young-looking dramatic soprano with a powerful and beautiful voice capable of long lyric phrases but of a greater volume capability than the lyric soprano. An example of a *Jugendlich* role would be Agathe in Weber's *Der Freischütz* in the German category, or Desdemona in Verdi's *Otello* in the Italian. German language mastery is an absolute necessity, as well as Italian, when specializing in this *Fach*. This singer must have extremely good diction because of roles that feature dialogue or recitative, such as those in *Der Freischütz* and *Die Zauberflöte*. This *Fach* is often used to cast the lead in operettas such as *Die Fledermaus* by Johann Strauss.

A *Jugendlich-dramatisher Sopran* must be capable of considerable vocal and dramatic interpretation, such as Magda in Menotti's *The Consul*, who, desperate to save her husband from the injustice of a bureaucratic system, throws papers all over the stage in a violent dramatic outburst; Giorgetta in Puccini's *Il tabarro*, who is forced to watch when her husband suddenly raises his cloak to reveal her murdered lover; and Agathe, in Weber's *Der Freischütz*, who is accidentally shot by her fiancé Max, who was aiming at a bird.

The *Jugendlich-dramatischer Sopran* usually dies at the end of the opera. Examples are Leonora in Verdi's *Il trovatore*, who agrees to marry the Count in exchange for the release of her lover and then drinks poison, and Desdemona in Verdi's *Otello*, who is unjustly smothered in her bed by her jealous husband, who, when learning the truth of her fidelity, stabs himself. These characters run a wide gamut of emotions, such as the Countess in Mozart's *Le nozze di Figaro*, willing to forgive an errant husband, and Donna Anna in Mozart's *Don Giovanni*, violently swearing vengeance on the lothario Don Giovanni who has violated her, among others. There is no end to the gorgeous music and wonderfully dramatic situations for this singing actress.

Examples of *Jugendlich-dramatischer Sopran* Roles

- Rusalka, *Rusalka*, Dvořák
- Maddalena, *Andrea Chénier*, Giordano
- Magda Sorel, *The Consul*, Menotti

- Countess, *Le nozze di Figaro*, Mozart
- Mimi, *La bohème*, Puccini
- Cio-Cio San, *Madama Butterfly*, Puccini
- Tatyana, *Eugene Onegin*, Tchaikovsky
- Desdemona, *Otello*, Verdi
- Elisabeth, *Tannhäuser*, Wagner
- Elsa, *Lohengrin*, Wagner
- Eva, *Die Meistersinger von Nürnberg*, Wagner
- Agathe, *Der Freischütz*, Weber
- Leonora, *Il trovatore*, Verdi
- Donna Anna, *Don Giovanni*, Mozart

Character Soprano (a–b2), *Charaktersopran/Zwischenfachstimme*

A bright, metallic voice with the power to portray dramatic characters.

Also called a between-category voice (*Zwischenfachstimme*), this *Fach* category does not require an easy top range, as is needed for Verdi roles, nor does it exemplify the warm beauty of sound preferred for Mozart roles. Instead, singers in this *Fach* must have the ability to clearly and effectively portray complicated personalities. This soprano is known as an actress first and a singer second, although the voice has to have the same brilliance on the top as a *Jugendlich*, the same flexibility as a coloratura soprano, and the same lasting power as a dramatic soprano. This voice must also be powerful enough to carry over the thick orchestration in Puccini operas, high enough to negotiate the extreme tessitura of a Salome in Richard Strauss's opera by the same name, and flexible enough to sing the beautiful lines of Bizet's *Carmen*.

Examples of *Charaktersopran/Zwischenfachstimme* Roles

- Carmen, *Carmen*, Bizet
- Mrs. Sedley, *Peter Grimes*, Britten
- Mélisande, *Pelléas et Mélisande*, Debussy
- Volpino, *Lo speziale*, Haydn
- Hexe, *Hänsel und Gretel*, Humperdinck
- La Follie, *Platée*, Rameau
- Ginevra, *Mona Lisa*, Schillings
- Margret, *Feuersnot*, R. Strauss

Dramatic Soprano (g–c3), *Dramatischer Sopran*

A powerful, brilliant voice, physically and vocally imposing on stage.

This soprano must have a voice that can cut through heavy orchestrations and the ability to sing effectively for long periods while always commanding the attention of the audience. A powerful and electric actress with the ability to portray changing moods and character, this *Fach* specialist revels in character studies. Examples include the young innocent maiden Manon in Puccini's *Manon Lescaut*, who is on the way to a French convent when she meets the attractive Des Grieux and ends up banished and abandoned in what is now Louisiana, and the Chinese "ice princess" Turandot in Puccini's *Turandot*, who decapitates any suitor who fails to answer three riddles.

When *Intendant* Giancarlo del Monaco staged *Turandot* at the Karlsruhe Opera in 1996, the decapitated heads of the spurned suitors were mounted along the front of the palace walls, with the blood flowing down in brilliant rivers. This was a magnificent effect and a not-so-subtle hint for the violent passion that underlies this opera. An interesting note: the dramatic soprano playing Turandot was fifty-five years old when she sang this role—a testament to the fact that this *Fach* can be sung by the more mature, experienced voice.[3]

Other examples include Ariadne in Strauss's *Ariadne auf Naxos*, who despairs of ever finding love again and then immediately falls for the first man she sees; Aida, who dies with Radames in the tomb scene; Lady Macbeth, who kills her king and then lies about it; and Tosca, who rather than accept the amorous attentions of the evil Scarpia throws herself off the top of a military fortress in Rome.

The range of emotions portrayed by the dramatic soprano is a challenge and probably one of the reasons many young singers dream of singing these roles.

Examples of *Dramatischer Sopran* Roles

- Leonore, *Fidelio*, Beethoven
- Ellen, *Peter Grimes*, Britten
- Alceste, *Alceste*, Gluck
- Santuzza, *Cavalleria rusticana*, Mascagni
- Minnie, *La fanciulla del West*, Puccini
- Tosca, *Tosca*, Puccini
- Turandot, *Turandot*, Puccini
- Marschallin, *Der Rosenkavalier*, R. Strauss
- Ariadne, *Ariadne auf Naxos*, R. Strauss
- Arabella, *Arabella*, R. Strauss
- Lady Macbeth, *Macbeth*, Verdi
- Leonora, *La forza del destino*, Verdi
- Aida, *Aida*, Verdi
- Sieglinde, *Die Walküre*, Wagner

High Dramatic Soprano (g–c3), *Hochdramatischer Sopran*

The most powerful and mature of soprano voices, with a smooth line, beautiful color, effortless volume, and endless staying power.

Although recent editions of Kloiber's *Handbuch der Oper* do not provide a separate list of these roles, the description of this *Fach* is based on the 1985 edition of the *Handbuch*.

Usually assigned to dramatic sopranos, these roles can be regarded as examples of the culmination of vocal development and experience in a soprano's career. It would be wise to avoid these roles as a young singer, as they are the most demanding of any of the dramatic roles, both for the voice and for the acting abilities, as well as the stamina of the singer.

The *Hochdramatischer Sopran* is almost exclusively a German category. This soprano has the same power in the voice as the dramatic soprano, but more of it and must be capable of singing for a longer time without becoming tired vocally or physically. This voice must be as powerful in the middle and low ranges as in the top. Although these roles tend to be more static on stage, this singer must be able to portray effective characters with her voice and physical stature.

Brünnhilde in Wagner's *Die Walküre* is an excellent example of this *Fach*. Where else does a soprano, with shield, spear, and helmet, make such an impression that she reappears in two more operas (*Siegfried* and *Götterdämmerung*)!

Examples of *Hochdramatischer Sopran* Roles

- Elektra, *Elektra*, R. Strauss
- Senta, *Der fliegende Holländer*, Wagner
- Venus, *Tannhäuser*, Wagner
- Ortrud, *Lohengrin*, Wagner
- Isolde, *Tristan und Isolde*, Wagner
- Brünnhilde, *Die Walküre*, Wagner

Beginner Mezzo-Soprano (g–b2), *Anfängerin-Mezzosopran*

A young mezzo with a flexible voice; appears energetic and youthful on stage.

Although not listed as a *Fach* category in Kloiber's *Handbuch*, young mezzo-sopranos have many possibilities for interesting small roles in opera. They are sometimes cast in child roles, if an appropriate child is not available. Examples would be one of the "six children's voices" in Strauss's *Die Frau ohne Schatten*, or the shepherd boy in Puccini's *Tosca*.

This singer could perform one of the three young maidens in Strauss's *Daphne*, or a short solo role such as Pinkerton's American wife, Kate, in *Madama Butterfly*, who has come to Japan with her husband to take away his son, Butterfly's child. The Musician in Puccini's *Manon Lescaut* has a beautiful short scene and a little aria that provides a sudden elegant line and mellow sound to an act that had been passionate and angular.

Although most *Anfängerin-Mezzosopran* roles are not long, this singer could be performing every evening in a startling array of roles and styles. An excellent way to start an operatic career.

Examples of *Anfängerin-Mezzosopran* Roles

- Ascanio, *Benvenuto Cellini*, Berlioz
- Kate, *Madama Butterfly*, Puccini
- Musician, *Manon Lescaut*, Puccini
- Shepherd boy, *Tosca*, Puccini
- Young maiden, *Daphne*, R. Strauss
- Annina, *La traviata*, Verdi
- Shepherd, *Tannhäuser*, Wagner
- Child's voice, *Die Frau ohne Schatten*, R. Strauss

Lyric Mezzo-Soprano/Acting Alto (g–b2), *Lyrischer Mezzosopran/Spielalt*

A strong mezzo or alto voice with effective coloratura ability.

This voice must have a pleasing timbre and be flexible enough to handle coloratura passages as well as have enough bite to give an effective dramatic impression when necessary. This *Fach* could be listed as two separate *Fach* categories, lyric mezzo-soprano and character (or acting) alto, and some operas specify a preference for one over the other in certain roles. (See appendix E for *Lyrischer Mezzosopran* and *Spielalt* roles.) The singer should ideally have a slender figure, since she performs a great variety of roles that are considered "pants roles" (*Hosenpartien*), that is, young male characters that are sung by women. Examples include Cherubino in Mozart's *Le nozze di Figaro* and Hänsel in Humperdinck's *Hänsel und Gretel*. She also portrays beautiful, seductive maidens such as the gypsy Mercédès in Bizet's *Carmen* or the tavern wench Maddalena in Verdi's *Rigoletto*.

Examples of *Lyrischer Mezzosopran/Spielalt* Roles

- Mercédès, *Carmen*, Bizet
- Hänsel, *Hänsel und Gretel*, Humperdinck
- Charlotte, *Werther*, Massenet
- Dorabella, *Così fan tutte*, Mozart
- Suzuki, *Madama Butterfly*, Puccini
- Dryade, *Ariadne auf Naxos*, R. Strauss
- Mignon, *Mignon*, Thomas
- Maddalena, *Rigoletto*, Verdi

- Flosshilde, *Das Rheingold*, Wagner
- Cherubino, *Le nozze de Figaro*, Mozart
- Magdalena, *Die Meistersinger von Nürnberg*, Wagner

Coloratura Mezzo-Soprano (g–b2), *Koloratur-Mezzosopran*

A mezzo voice with vocal weight, color, and agility, that is, the ability to sing florid coloratura passages over a wide range and with extreme rapidity.

A rich, dramatic mezzo sound, this *Fach* has almost the same voice as a lyric mezzo-soprano but with the extra ability of singing *con agilata*, with extreme speed and agility. A coloratura mezzo could also sing lyric mezzo roles, or those in the dramatic mezzo *Fach*, depending on the size of the voice and the singer's preference. Mezzos such as Marilyn Horne achieved worldwide prominence by specializing in these roles.

Examples of *Koloratur-Mezzosopran* Roles

- Johanna Seymour, *Anna Bolena*, Donizetti
- Rinaldo, *Rinaldo*, Handel
- Urban, *Les Huguenots*, Meyerbeer
- Isabella, *L'italiana in Algeri*, Rossini
- Rosina, *Il barbiere di Siviglia*, Rossini
- Angelina, *La Cenerentola*, Rossini

Dramatic Mezzo-Soprano (g–b2 or c3), *Dramatischer Mezzosopran*

A rich, powerful voice; physically and vocally imposing on stage.

Dramatic mezzo-sopranos often have the same range as a dramatic soprano, but the soprano can sing in a slightly higher tessitura for a longer time, while the mezzo has more bite and power in the lower register. The dramatic mezzo-soprano must have a powerful presence on stage and make her character noticeable even when surrounded by the most famous of dramatic tenors and sopranos. Amneris in *Aida* is equal in importance to Radames and Aida, and if you ask the mezzo, even more!

The emotional range portrayed by the characters in this *Fach* category also demands the extreme characterizations expected of dramatic sopranos. Amneris, the King of Egypt's daughter, must watch the man she loves die in a tomb with her rival, Aida. Herodias, wife of Herodes (King Herod), watches as her dissolute daughter Salome, who was spurned by Jochanaan (John the Baptist), demands his death; and when soldiers carry out the order and bring the bloody head back on a silver platter, Herodias witnesses her husband order Salome's own death. Whether a spurned other woman or a taunting temptress, this *Fach* is always vocally and dramatically challenging.

Examples of *Dramatischer Mezzosopran* Roles

- Adalgisa, *Norma*, Bellini
- Amneris, *Aida*, Verdi
- Second Dame, *Die Zauberflöte*, Mozart
- Dalila, *Samson et Dalila*, Saint-Saëns
- Herodias, *Salome*, R. Strauss
- Eboli, *Don Carlos*, Verdi
- Countess, *Pique Dame*, Tchaikovsky
- Preziosilla, *La forza del destino*, Verdi
- Kundry, *Parsifal*, Wagner
- Brangäne, *Tristan und Isolde*, Wagner

ALTO CATEGORIES

Dramatic Alto (g–b2), *Dramatischer Alt*

A large, flexible voice with a metallic tone, well-developed top range, and powerful low notes.

The emphasis in this *Fach* is on the power of the voice and ability to carry off dramatic situations as an actor. Many of the roles are also similar to those for a dramatic mezzo, but this voice tends not to have a usable high c (c3), which many of the dramatic mezzos can claim. The voice would be typically more metallic in timbre, with extremely effective middle and low registers and the ability to carry through thick orchestrations. The rich, full quality of this voice lends credence to the more mature characterizations that these roles demand.

Always challenging to portray, dramatic alto characters include witches, gypsies, and old mothers, as well as nobles and queens. This *Fach* has more than enough variety to satisfy the most demanding actor-singer.

Examples of *Dramatischer Alt* Roles

- Mama Lucia, *Cavalleria rusticana*, Mascagni
- Neris, *Medea*, Cherubini
- Genoveva, *Pelléas et Mélisande*, Debussy
- Witch, *Rusalka*, Dvořák
- Third Dame, *Die Zauberflöte*, Mozart
- Pythia, *Melusine*, Reimann

- The Mother, *The Counsul*, Menotti
- Azucena, *Il trovatore*, Verdi
- Ulrica, *Un ballo in maschera*, Verdi

Low Alto/Contralto (f–a2), *Tiefer Alt/Kontra-Alt*

A huge, warm, and even voice with an extreme low range.

If this voice had a soprano top, it would be the German *Hochdramatischer Sopran*. An extremely rare voice, it is also known as a contralto (*Kontra-Alt*). A character in this *Fach*, such as Gaea in Richard Strauss's *Daphne,* is required to have the f below middle c, and it must be sung easily and beautifully. Utilizing such a vocal range adds to the depth of character for these roles. Many of these roles could also be performed by the dramatic alto.

Examples of *Tiefer Alt (Kontra-Alt)* Roles

- Genoveva, *Pelléas et Mélisande*, Debussy
- Erda, *Siegfried*, Wagner
- Third Dame, *Die Zauberflöte*, Mozart
- Norn, *Götterdämmerung*, Wagner
- Gaea, *Daphne*, R. Strauss
- Princess, *Suor Angelica*, Puccini
- Zita, *Gianni Schicchi*, Puccini
- Ulrica, *Un ballo in maschera*, Verdi

TENOR CATEGORIES

Beginner Tenor (c–a1), *Anfänger-Lyrischertenor*

A light, high tenor voice with a youthful quality.

Young tenors have it made! Many grow up to be stars and on their way portray an endless array of charming, witty, engaging, energetic, and delightful small roles. Again, this *Fach* is not listed in Kloiber's *Handbuch der Oper*, but the term *Anfänger* would be part of the language of his contract.

A tenor with an *Anfänger* beginner contract will usually not portray any of the children's roles—the young lyric sopranos or lyric altos can do that. These tenors have their own world of adolescents, young heroes, and sidekicks of all sorts. Examples include Violetta's servant Joseph (Giuseppe) in *La traviata*; a prisoner in Beethoven's *Fidelio* who drags himself from the deepest pits of the dungeon out into the courtyard to enjoy a brief moment of fresh air while singing in the "Prisoners' Chorus," one of the significant passages of the score; and an animal handler in Strauss's *Der Rosenkavalier*.

Gershwin's *Porgy and Bess* has a wealth of parts suitable for a beginner tenor. A cook, a farmer, a soldier, a crab seller—all roles a beginner tenor can be performing almost every evening while he is developing the skills to move up into the more demanding and prestigious roles.

Examples of *Anfänger-Lyrischertenor* Roles

- Zwei Juden, *Die toten Augen*, d'Albert
- Soldier, *Frau Diavolo*, d'Albert
- Prisoner, *Fidelio*, Beethoven
- Nereus, *Mefistofele*, Boito
- Owlur, *Knas Igor*, Borodin
- Crab seller, *Porgy and Bess*, Gershwin
- Landowner, *La fille du régiment*, Donizetti
- Servant, *Alessandro Stradella*, Flotow
- Giuseppe, *La traviata*, Verdi
- Messenger, *Il trovatore*, Verdi

Countertenor (c1–c3), *Contratenor*

A male voice with the ability to sing in the falsetto, or soprano, registers, with beautiful tone, power, and agility.

This is a relatively new category, although historically this voice dates back to the early years of opera (the 1600s) when men, specifically *castrati*, portrayed women's roles. Men now choosing this *Fach* are responding to the new challenge in the opera world for voices that can perform the opera roles of Monteverdi, Handel, and Hayden with a sound and style appropriate to the original productions of these operas. This voice sings most of the time in the soprano or alto registers. While this voice sings primarily in falsetto, the character could also sing some of the lower notes in full voice as dramatic contrast.

This voice type is now in great demand. Alfred Deller, an English singer, was the first to popularize this sound in the 1950s and 1960s with his Deller Consort, which specialized in Renaissance and baroque music.[4] Tenors such as David Daniels and Andreas Scholl have attained great success in the opera world in a great variety of roles demanding vocal brilliance, beautiful color, and highly developed acting skills. Oberon, the King of the Fairies, in Benjamin Britten's *A Midsummer Night's Dream*, is a typical role for this *Fach*.

Examples of *Contratenor* Roles

- Oberon, *A Midsummer Night's Dream*, Britten
- Echnaton, *Akhnaten*, Glass
- Ottone/Narcisco, *Agrippina*, Handel
- Cesare/Tolomeo, *Giulio Cesare*, Handel
- Nerone/Ottone, *L'incoronazione di Poppea*, Monteverdi
- Edgar, *Lear*, Reimann
- Ernesto, *Il mondo della luna*, Haydn
- Mephistophiles, *Historia von D. Johann Fausten*, Schnittke

High Countertenor (g–b2), *Haute-Contre*

A rich tenor voice with a brilliant, well-developed falsetto and a seamless "passagio."

A high countertenor, specifically as used in French repertoire, is sometimes called a male alto (*altino*). This singer is able to mix the voice from the higher tenor range into the alto range with a seamless transition into the middle and higher female registers—the *passagio*. This results in the ability to sing slightly lower roles than the countertenor. It is interesting to note that one of these high countertenor roles is in Claudio Monteverdi's *L'Orfeo*, first produced in 1607.

Examples of *Haute-Contre* Roles

- Renaud/Danish knight, *Armide*, Gluck
- Orfeo, *L'Orfeo*, Monteverdi
- Amor/Castor, *Castor et Pollux*, Rameau

Lyric Tenor (c–d2), *Lyrischer Tenor*

A soft, warm, flexible voice with an extremely effective and easy top range.

This singer is sometimes called a Mozart tenor if he has particularly beautiful sound and good coloratura ability. He is usually the leading man, the young hero, or the best friend of a leading man, so must be attractive and personable on stage.

The variety of roles in this *Fach* is considerable, ranging from the higher-range Mozart roles such as Idamante in *Idomeneo* or Don Ottavio in *Don Giovanni* to the young dramatic tenor roles such as Tamino in *Die Zauberflöte*. This is the tenor *Fach* used most often in operetta, so it is advisable to have extremely good diction and proficiency in spoken dialogue. He is the handsome Alfredo in Verdi's *La traviata*, who furiously abandons Violetta when he lets himself be persuaded that she loved him only because of money; the somewhat befuddled Don Ottavio in Mozart's *Don Giovanni*, unable to protect Donna Anna's honor; and the Duke in Verdi's *Rigoletto*, who kidnaps Rigoletto's daughter, seduces her, and is unrepentant.

Examples of *Lyrischer Tenor* Roles

- Nemorino, *L'elisir d'amore*, Donizetti
- Ernesto, *Don Pasquale*, Donizetti
- Baron, *Der Wildschütz*, Lortzing
- Walter, *Tannhäuser*, Wagner
- Idamante, *Idomeneo*, Mozart
- Ferrando, *Così fan tutte*, Mozart
- Alfredo, *La traviata*, Verdi
- Fenton, *Falstaff*, Verdi
- Tamino, *Die Zauberflöte*, Mozart
- Duke, *Rigoletto*, Verdi
- Don Ottavio, *Don Giovanni*, Mozart
- Belmonte, *Die Entführung aus dem Serail*, Mozart

Acting (Comic) Tenor (c–b1), *Spieltenor/Tenorbuffo*

A slim, flexible voice with the capacity to take on various sounds and colors.

This tenor, often referred to as a "buffo" tenor, is expected to be a tremendous actor known for his characterizations. Singers in this *Fach* category have a fantastic time on stage portraying all sorts of wonderful characters. They often engage in physical antics—leaping, dancing, or wobbling—anything to help develop the stage personality. Disguises, quavering voices, wigs and spectacles that fall off are all part of the repertory of this imaginative singing actor.

There is no age specification for this category. Young tenors often begin in this *Fach*, gaining experience and building stamina while trying out varied characterizations. Older tenors, at the end of their careers, often choose to sing these roles and have great fun doing so, as well as extending their longevity in the opera world.

Examples of *Spieltenor/Tenorbuffo* Roles

- Jaquino, *Fidelio*, Beethoven
- Dancaïro/Remendado, *Carmen*, Bizet
- Beppo, *Pagliacci*, Leoncavallo
- Basilio/Don Curzio, *Le nozze di Figaro*, Mozart
- Spoletta, *Tosca*, Puccini

- Monostatos, *Die Zauberflöte*, Mozart
- Pedro, *Corregidor*, Wolf
- Goro, *Madama Butterfly*, Puccini
- David, *Die Meistersinger von Nürnberg*, Wagner
- Pedrillo, *Die Entführung aus dem Serail*, Mozart

Young Dramatic Tenor (c–c2), *Jugendlich-dramatischer Tenor*

A large, powerful, brilliant voice with a beautiful timbre and staying power.

Also known as a spinto tenor, this voice must be able to sing long dramatic phrases and appear imposing on stage. Although extremely powerful, and often with a baritone quality, this voice should still have a basically tenor sound.

These tenors definitely need to be good actors and effectively portray the leading man. Examples include Don José, who abandons his military post in pursuit of the beautiful but elusive Carmen; Des Grieux, in Puccini's *Manon Lescaut*, who falls instantly in love with the fifteen-year-old Manon, who is on the way to a convent. (She doesn't get there.)

Others include Canio, the clown in a small family traveling show, who murders his young wife, Nedda, in Leoncavallo's *Pagliacci*; Radames, in Verdi's *Aida*, who is condemned to a suffocating death in a tomb and discovers his lover Aida is waiting there for him; Apollo, a sun god; Lohengrin, a hero; and Cavaradossi, a dilettante painter—all epitomize the tragic, romantic hero.

Examples of *Jugendlich-dramatischer Tenor* Roles

- Florestan, *Fidelio*, Beethoven
- Don José, *Carmen*, Bizet
- Faust, *Faust*, Gonoud
- Canio, *Pagliacci*, Leoncavallo
- Des Grieux, *Manon Lescaut*, Puccini
- Rodolfo, *La bohème*, Puccini
- Cavaradossi, *Tosca*, Puccini
- Johnson, *La fanciulla del West*, Puccini
- Calaf, *Turandot*, Puccini
- Samson, *Samson et Dalila*, Saint-Saëns
- Manrico, *Il trovatore*, Verdi
- Radames, *Aida*, Verdi
- Lohengrin, *Lohengrin*, Wagner
- Max, *Der Freischütz*, Weber

Dramatic Tenor (c–c2), *Heldentenor*

A voice similar to the Jugendlich or spinto tenor but with a baritone sound and an extended top.

This *Fach* demands a voice of unusual power, with the capability to sing long phrases for endless amounts of time with no decrease in voice or energy. This singer needs to be dramatically effective on stage through the size of the voice as well as his physical presence. Typical roles would be Tristan in Wagner's *Tristan und Isolde*, or Siegfried in *Siegfried*. Of the Italian roles, Otello in Verdi's *Otello* is the most typical for this voice.

As with the *Jugendlich-dramatischer Tenor*, these roles are very rewarding if you are able to stand on stage and sing for large blocks of time. The first duet in *Tristan und Isolde* is forty-five minutes of singing. Just the duet! Not to mention that this tenor is often fighting battles right before important arias. No wonder this *Fach* is one of the last steps in a dramatic tenor's career.

Examples of *Heldentenor* Roles

- Peter, *Peter Grimes*, Britten
- Paul, *Die tote Stadt*, Korngold
- Canio, *Pagliacci*, Leoncavallo
- Baccus, *Ariadne auf Naxos*, R. Strauss
- Otello, *Otello*, Verdi
- Rienzi, *Rienzi, der lezte Tribunen*, Wagner
- Tannhäuser, *Tannhäuser*, Wagner
- Lohengrin, *Lohengrin*, Wagner
- Tristan, *Tristan und Isolde*, Wagner
- Schujskij, *Boris Godunov*, Mussorgsky
- Siegfried, *Siegfried*, Wagner
- Siegfried, *Götterdämmerung*, Wagner

Character Tenor (A–b1), *Charaktertenor*

A bright, powerful voice and extremely effective actor.

Also known as a *Zwischenfachstimme*, a between-category voice, the character tenor is similar in vocal and physical type to the *Spieltenor/Tenorbuffo* but with a slightly lower voice. This *Fach* is often sung by an older singer with the age and experience to portray a great variety of roles and extremely complex characters, whether dramatic or comic. This singer must be able to command the stage with his voice as well as his personality.

A young tenor can also easily make a career by specializing in this *Fach*, as well as the buffo roles. In Wagner's *Siegfried*, Loge and Mime are both integrally important to the plot development, and it is just plain fun to be a dwarf crawling around in holes under rivers looking for the ring of power. In Strauss's *Salome*, Herodes commands his stepdaughter Salome to dance for him (the famous "Dance of the Seven Veils") and later orders her killed by his guards (not because of her dance).

Examples of *Charaktertenor* Roles

- Lord Puff, *The English Cat*, Henze
- Herodes, *Salome*, R. Strauss
- Sturmwald, *Doktor und Apotheker*, Dittersdorf
- Guillot, *Manon*, Massanet
- Spalazani, *Les contes d'Hoffmann*, Offenbach
- Dr. Cajus, *Falstaff*, Verdi
- Altoum, *Turandot*, Puccini
- Loge/Mime, *Siegfried*, Wagner
- Rodolphe, *Guillaume Tell*, Rossini
- Riccardo, *I quattro rusteghi*, Wolf-Ferrari

BARITONE CATEGORIES

Beginner Baritone (B–g1), *Anfänger-Bariton*

A light, high baritone voice with a youthful quality; flexible actor.

The *Anfänger-Bariton*, like the *Anfänger-Lyrischertenor*, is not an established *Fach* listed in the Kloiber. However, a contract for this category will stipulate *Anfänger*, and this young baritone will be performing some sort of small solo almost every evening during a typical season. This could be as many as 120 performances over a ten-and-a-half-month season—a number of performances that would far exceed the norm, usually 60 to 80, assigned to older, more established singers.[5]

By being scheduled to sing so frequently, the beginner baritone has the chance to learn from the older and more accomplished singers. Unlike a major soloist, who is on stage for most of the opera, the young baritone makes one or two short entrances and then can stand in the wings and watch the action.

As with the other beginner categories, these roles are often listed just by function, such as "peasant," "Earth," "blacksmith," "notary," or "painter." This *Fach* is a great opportunity to develop acting skills in a variety of roles.

Examples of *Anfänger-Bariton* Roles

- Peasant, *Frau Diavolo*, Auber
- Pompeo, *Benvenuto Cellini*, Berlioz
- Neuling's friend, *Billy Budd*, Britten
- Painter, *Louise*, Charpentier
- Blacksmith, *Peer Gynt*, Egk
- Fiorello, *Il barbiere di Siviglia*, Rossini
- Jim, *Porgy and Bess*, Gershwin
- A Mandarin, *Turandot*, Puccini
- Notary, *Intermezzo*, R. Strauss
- Servant, *La traviata*, Verdi
- Earth, *Rappresentazione de anima e di corpo*, Cavalieri

Lyric Baritone (B–a#1) acting baritone, *Lyrischer Bariton (Spielbariton)*

A smooth, beautiful, flexible voice with a bel canto line and effective top notes.

Many a dramatic baritone started his career in this *Fach* category. The beautiful vocalism required of this voice, combined with interesting and demanding character studies, ensures ample time for a young artist to develop artistic sensitivity and vocal stamina. Examples include Papageno, the bird catcher for the Queen of the Night in *Die Zauberflöte*, who is chased by a dragon, threatened by three strange ladies, and then has to try to communicate with a lock on his mouth.

Figaro, in Rossini's *Il barbiere di Siviglia*, is in control of every situation as he manipulates the other characters in his opera; and Renato, in Verdi's *Un ballo in maschera*, plummets to the ultimate depths of despair when he learns that his faithful friend, the Governor, is in love with his wife and that she loves him as well. It is interesting to note that for years this opera was censored because the plot contained a successful conspiracy against an established official—not a popular notion in the mid-nineteenth century.[6]

Wolfgang Brendel is a modern example of this *Fach* and is also a leading interpreter of Verdi dramatic baritone roles. Awarded the German Order of Merit in 1995 and the honorary title of *Kammersänger* by the Munich State Opera, he is now one of the most sought-after baritones of his generation.[7]

Examples of *Lyrischer Bariton* Roles

- Claudio, *Béatrice et Bénédict*, Berlioz
- Zurga, *Les pêcheurs de perles*, Berlioz
- Billy Budd, *Billy Budd*, Britten

- Belcore, *L'elisir d'amore*, Donizetti
- Dr. Malatesta, *Don Pasquale*, Donizetti
- Albert, *Werther*, Massanet
- Guglielmo, *Così fan tutte*, Mozart
- Papageno, *Die Zauberflöte*, Mozart
- Ping, *Turandot*, Puccini
- Figaro, *Il barbiere di Siviglia*, Rossini
- Harlekin, *Ariadne auf Naxos*, R. Strauss
- Renato, *Un ballo in maschera*, Verdi

Cavalier Baritone (A–g1), *Kavalierbariton*

A brilliant voice with warm, beautiful color capable of singing coloratura passages, smooth lyric lines, and dramatic passages without effort.

This *Fach* could be considered the *divo*-baritone of the opera stage. Most of these roles are leading characters, and when this person is performing, no one looks at anyone else. He should be a personable figure and able to portray various characters sympathetically and easily. Although this voice often has an easy tenor top, it needs to have a recognizable baritone vocal color. Whereas the other baritones are not necessarily known for their general "good looks," this one is! A true cavalier baritone is one of the most difficult voices/actors/personalities to find. Therefore, making a match with this *Fach* is a guarantee of success for a young singer.

The *Kavalierbariton* is exactly that—a "cavalier" or gallant gentleman—irresistible to the ladies. The bullfighter Escamillo fatally fascinates Carmen. Don Giovanni has his way with every woman he sees and loves all of them equally. Lescaut in *Manon Lescaut* sells his young sister to an old geezer in Paris, and Onegin in Tchaikovsky's *Eugene Onegin* ignores the young and innocent Tatyana until she grows up and marries money and power. Scoundrels and good guys abound in this *Fach*.

Examples of *Kavalierbariton* Roles

- Don Fernando, *Fidelio*, Beethoven
- Escamillo, *Carmen*, Bizet
- Valentine, *Faust*, Gonoud
- Onegin, *Eugene Onegin*, Tchaikovsky
- Graf, *Der Wildschütz*, Lortzing
- Lescaut, *Manon*, Massenet
- Count, *Le nozze di Figaro*, Mozart
- Don Giovanni, *Don Giovanni*, Mozart
- Lescaut, *Manon Lescaut*, Puccini
- Marcello, *La bohème*, Puccini

- Posa, *Don Carlos*, Verdi
- Wolfram, *Tannhäuser*, Wagner

Character Baritone (A–g1), *Charakterbariton*

A focused, flexible voice capable of assuming many differing characterizations but also possessing a powerful vocal instrument.

Similar to other character voices, the *Charakterbariton* must be able to steal the attention away from the lead characters when he is on stage, and the voice should be able to cut through heavy orchestrations. Many singers happily spend their careers in this *Fach*, as the roles are fascinating, challenging, and satisfying.

Character baritones romp their way through rascals, dwarfs, evil police chiefs, and even play some really nice guys. Alberich, a treacherous gnome who dwells in the bowels of the earth in Wagner's *Siegfried*, is a wonderful role for a young baritone, and a secure career can be built on this one character alone. Beckmesser in Wagner's *Die Meistersinger von Nürnberg* is comedic, dishonest, and sympathetic at the same time; while Scarpia, the evil chief of police in Puccini's *Tosca*, is the ultimate in jealous possessiveness and evil intent as he exults in his power and exclaims that to possess Tosca "he would renounce his hopes of heaven."[8] There's enough variety and drama in this *Fach* to keep any singer-actor happy.

Examples of *Charakterbariton* Roles

- Sebastiano/Moruccio, *Tiefland*, d'Albert
- Wozzeck, *Wozzeck*, Berg
- Besenbinder, *Hänsel und Gretel*, Humperdinck
- Johannes, *Der Evangelimann*, Kienzl
- Schaunard, *La bohème*, Puccini
- Scarpia, *Tosca*, Puccini
- Paolo, *Simon Boccanegra*, Verdi
- Alberich, *Siegfried*, Wagner
- Alberich, *Das Rheingold*, Wagner
- Beckmesser, *Die Meistersinger von Nürnberg*, Wagner

Dramatic Baritone/High Bass (G–f♯1), *Heldenbariton/Hoher Bass*

An imposing, powerful voice with an extended range and a large, warm sound.

The dramatic baritone/high bass, sometimes called a *Helden* baritone, should be a commanding, regal figure on stage, with powerful stature and a voice capable of singing dramatically without sounding forced. This voice must also carry effortlessly through thick orchestrations. Examples of typical roles would be Wotan in Wagner's *Das Rheingold* and *Die Walküre*, Igor in Borodin's *Prince Igor*, and Macbeth in Verdi's *Macbeth*.

This singer needs a powerful, dramatic sound and when he is on stage should be the center of attention. A good example is the Dutchman in Wagner's *Der fliegende Holländer*, a mythical sea captain who is condemned by the devil to sail the sea until Judgment Day unless he can find a woman who would love him faithfully to the death. The Dutchman finally meets Senta . . . they fall in love . . . her former lover entreats her to remember their love . . . the Dutchman overhears and returns to his ship, thinking he is rebuffed . . . Senta rushes to a cliff overhanging the sea . . . proclaims her love and flings herself to her death . . . and the Dutchman's phantom ship sinks into a whirlpool. It's the usual opera plot: boy meets girl, boy loses girl, girl kills herself, boy follows suit.

This is perhaps the ultimate *Fach* for an acting baritone, and the characterizations are as difficult as they are varied. From kings to police chiefs to princes to prophets and phantom sea captains, this *Fach* is seasoned with every character type known to opera and offers both a challenge and career goal for the mature baritone. Note: Scarpia is also a role sung by this *Fach*, as well as by *Charakterbaritons*.

Examples of *Heldenbariton/Hoher Bass* Roles

- Igor, *Knas Igor*, Borodin
- Don Pizarro, *Fidelio*, Beethoven
- Tonio, *Pagliacci*, Leoncavallo
- Boris, *Boris Godunov*, Mussorgsky
- Scarpia, *Tosca*, Puccini
- Jack Rance, *La fanciulla del West*, Puccini
- Jochanaan, *Salome*, R. Strauss
- Macbeth, *Macbeth*, Verdi
- King Philip, *Don Carlos*, Verdi
- Amonasro, *Aida*, Verdi
- Wotan, *Das Rheingold*, Wagner
- Wotan, *Die Walküre*, Wagner
- Amfortas, *Parsifal*, Wagner
- Wanderer, *Siegfried*, Wagner
- Der Holländer, *Der fliegende Holländer*, Wagner

BASS CATEGORIES

Beginner Bass (E–f1), *Anfänger-Bass*

A young bass voice with the color and range to sing bass repertoire.

Not listed in the Kloiber, this young bass, like all *Anfänger* voices, would need to have the range to qualify as a bass but would not yet have the experience to perform the full bass repertoire. As there are many operas with small roles stipulated for "bass," this singer could perform many times a week and often in many different roles within the same opera. The Russian repertoire is an especially rich source of short, interesting, and effective roles for the development of both a voice and a career.

Examples of *Anfänger-Bass* Roles

- President, *Peer Gynt*, Egk
- Foquier-Tinville, *Andrea Chénier*, Giordano
- Pallante, *Agrippina*, Handel
- Hotel Direktor, *Neues vom Tage*, Hindemith
- Ruffiack, *Le Grand Macabre*, Ligeti
- Brühllmann, *Werther*, Massanet
- Kuzka, *Khovanschchina*, Mussorgsky
- Benoit, *La bohème*, Puccini
- Raimondo, *Rienzi, der lezte Tribunen*, Wagner
- Billy Jackrabbit, *La fanciulla del West*, Puccini

Character Bass/Bass-baritone (E–f1), *Charakterbass, Bassbariton*

A huge, rich voice, able to sing long dramatic phrases easily.

This singer must be an excellent actor capable of portraying many different character types. This *Fach* can be assigned to an acting bass if he has the required acting skills and a rich, full sound.

Many of these roles are for older men who have developed the mature, dark color of the low bass. The roles are challenging, demanding refined characterizations of difficult personalities. Figaro, in Mozart's *Le nozze di Figaro*, is one of the more famous of these roles. This character is constantly frustrated by the knowledge that his boss, the count, is illicitly interested in Figaro's soon to be wife, Susanna. Masetto in Mozart's *Don Giovanni* takes a beating meant for his master but still serves him faithfully. Don Alfonso, in Mozart's *Così fan tutte*, makes a bet with his two young friends that their lovers will not remain faithful, a bet he wins. And Angelotti in Puccini's *Tosca* gets to hide in a well. Enough variety for anyone!

Examples of *Charakterbass/Bassbariton* Roles

- Figaro, *Le nozze di Figaro*, Mozart
- Masetto, *Don Giovanni*, Mozart
- Don Alfonso, *Così fan tutte*, Mozart
- Sprecher, *Die Zauberflöte*, Mozart
- Crespel, *Les contes d'Hoffmann*, Offenbach
- Geronte, *Manon Lescaut*, Puccini

- Angelotti, *Tosca*, Puccini
- Graf Waldner, *Arabella*, R. Strauss
- Monterone/Sparafucile, *Rigoletto*, Verdi
- King, *Aida*, Verdi
- Daland, *Der fliegende Holländer*, Wagner
- Hunding, *Die Walküre*, Wagner

Acting Bass/Bass Buffo (E–f1), *Spielbass/Bassbuffo*

A rich, full sound, capable of flexibility and effective coloratura passages.

This *Fach* is used to portray many different characters. As the term "buffo" implies, this bass plays comic as well as dramatic characters. This actor must possess the ability to control others on stage through energy and presence, rather than through the sheer physical size or beauty of his voice.

The *Spielbass/Bassbuffo* category features many of the same roles listed in the next category, the heavy acting bass, although in the bass buffo/ acting bass *Fach* the singer's acting ability takes precedence over his vocal sound. The devil Méphistophélès in Gounod's *Faust* is a wonderful example, as he commands the stage with his intensity and creates a real fear factor enhanced by Gounod's brilliant orchestration. Osmin, in Mozart's *Die Entführung aus dem Serail*, guards the harem, although not very effectively. Baron Ochs in Richard Strauss's *Der Rosenkavalier* tries to seduce a young boy who is pretending to be a young girl, sung by a young mezzo-soprano, of course. Caspar, "a forester of dark visage and of morose and forbidding character" in Carl Maria von Weber's *Der Freischütz*, is in league with the devil.[9]

Many older male singers find this *Fach* a comfortable place for the latter part of their careers, and the acting and singing challenges are a fitting tribute to their many years of experience and success.

Examples of *Spielbass/Bassbuffo* Roles

- Plumkett, *Martha*, Flotow
- Caspar, *Der Freischütz*, Weber
- Méphistophélès, *Faust*, Gounod
- Colline, *La bohème*, Puccini
- Van Bett, *Zar und Zimmermann*, Lortzing
- Ochs, *Der Rosenkavalier*, R. Strauss
- Falstaff, *Die lustigen Weiber von Windsor*, Nicolai
- Lunardo, *I quattro rusteghi*, Wolf-Ferrari
- Abul Hassan, *Der Barbier von Baghdad*, Cornelius
- Osmin, *Die Entführung aus dem Serail*, Mozart
- Daland, *Der fliegende Holländer*, Wagner

Heavy Acting Bass/Heavy Bass Buffo (D–f1),
Schwerer Spielbass/Schwerer Bassbuffo

A huge, rich voice with an ability to fill spaces with effortless sound.

In this *Fach*, the physical size of the voice is not as important as for the next *Fach*, the *Seriöser Bass*. But this singer must be able to command the stage, and the audience's attention, with refined and energetic characterizations of many types of characters, from comic to serious. Many of these roles are shared with the *Spielbass*, although a specialist in this *Fach* would have a deeper, richer vocal tone.

The character Gianni Schicchi, in Puccini's opera of the same name, is a delightful example of this *Fach*, as he outwits the scheming relatives of a dead man and ends up with the disputed inheritance for himself.

Another example is Daland, a Norwegian sea captain in Wagner's *Der fliegende Holländer*, whose daughter Senta is enamored of the mythical Dutch sea captain (yes, two different captains). Basses love singing these roles, which demand maturity, exquisite technique, and effortless stamina.

Examples of *Schwerer Spielbass/Schwerer Bassbuffo* Roles

- Rodrigo, *Lulu*, Berg
- Abul Hassan, *Der Barbier von Bagdad*, Cornelius
- Plumkett, *Martha*, Flotow
- Mama Agata, *Viva la Mamma*, Donizetti
- Méphistophélès, *Faust*, Gounod
- Gianni Schicchi, *Gianni Schicchi*, Puccini
- Daland, *Der fliegende Holländer*, Wagner
- Baron Ochs, *Der Rosenkavalier*, R. Strauss
- Osmin, *Die Entführung auf dem Serail*, Mozart
- Falstaff, *Die lustige Weiber von Windsor*, Nicolai

Serious Bass/Deep Bass (C–f1), *Seriöser Bass/Tiefer Bass*

A mature voice with a rich, dark color and powerful low notes.

Also called a German black bass (*Schwarzer Bass*), this is the lowest of the male voices and usually the one with the most vocal color. A truly beautiful voice, this *Fach* demands a statuesque physique and a commanding presence on stage. Often, but not always, this category is portrayed by the older singer who has developed his technique and acting abilities and is able to easily portray complicated personalities with a commanding tone and physical stance.

The Russian bass Michael Litmanov is an example of this *Fach*, having worked his way from bass-baritone roles to portrayals of the kings and princes representative of this *Fach*. In an interview in 1984, Litmanov credited his success to his study at the Tchaikovsky Music Conservatory in Moscow, where he was told he would study voice as a bass. As a result his career progressed, first through many dramatic baritone roles, and culminated in his becoming a full *Seriöser Bass* in his fifties.[10]

There are many leading roles for this *Fach*, especially those in Verdi and Wagner operas. The characters portrayed are often kings or wise older men but include enough scoundrels, giants, doctors, and generals to make the acting assignments challenging and fulfilling. Some of the solos these gentlemen sing are so beautiful they simply stop the action of the opera, such as Prince Gremin's lush aria in Tchaikovsky's *Eugene Onegin*, a paean to the beauty and goodness of his young wife, Tatyana; or Sarastro's fervent aria in Mozart's *Die Zauberflöte*, invoking help from the gods Isis and Osiris for the young prince Tamino, who must endure some severe ordeals in order to marry Pamina.

Examples of *Seriöser Bass/Tiefer Bass* Roles

- Rocco, *Fidelio*, Beethoven
- Orovist, *Norma*, Bellini
- Sarastro, *Die Zauberflöte*, Mozart
- Colline, *La bohème*, Puccini
- Trulove, *The Rake's Progress*, Stravinsky
- Banquo, *Macbeth*, Verdi
- King Philip, *Don Carlos*, Verdi
- Ramfis, *Aida*, Verdi
- König Heinrich, *Lohengrin*, Wagner
- Hagen, *Götterdämmerung*, Wagner
- Fasolt/Fafner, *Das Rheingold*, Wagner
- Gurnemanz, *Parsifal*, Wagner
- Prince Gremin, *Eugene Onegin*, Tchaikovsky

NOTES

1. Gian Carlo Menotti, *Amahl and the Night Visitors* (Milwaukee, Wis.: G. Schirmer, 1997).

2. Gustav Kobbé, *The Definitive Kobbé's Opera Book*, rev. and updated (New York: G. P. Putnam's Sons, 1987), 81.

3. Puccini, *Turandot*, Bodisches Staatstheater, Karlsruhe, Germany: Ghena Dimitrova (1941–), dramatic soprano, as Turandot, March 17, 1996.

4. Daniel Taylor, "An Introduction to Singing Technique and a Short History of the Countertenor," *La Scena Musicale* 7, no. 7 (April 2002).

5. Klaus Schultz, *Intendant*, Aachen, Germany, 1991 lecture to University of Illinois voice students.

6. *Kobbé's Opera Book*, 487–489.

7. Homepage for Wolfgang Brendel, http://www.wolfgang-brendel.de/eng/eng.htm.

8. *Kobbé's Opera Book*, 951.

9. Ibid., 134.

10. Conversation with Michael Litmanov in Kassel, Germany, 1984.

3

Using *Fach* to
Train Young Voices

In chapter 1, *Fach* was described as voice + range + size + timbre + physi-cal build + age and experience + desire + frequency of performance. As you can see by the formula, training the young voice involves learning about and developing a great number of things besides musical notes. All the elements of this formula contribute to a singer's *Fach*. Therefore, being familiar with the attributes that constitute each *Fach* category is an effective guide for training young voices.

The information in this chapter refers to three categories of young sing-ers, each of which could be considered a *Fach* category, although they are not listed as such in the Kloiber *Handbuch der Oper*. They are the child, young lyric (*Lyriche/Lyricher*), and the beginner (*Anfänger/Anfängerin*). Young singers who progress through these categories will have the basis for continued and successful training throughout a career.

FACH AND THE YOUNG VOICE

Even the youngest singer is already attracted to certain styles of music. A young soprano may already prefer singing connected musical lines. Another might have a natural affinity for many high, light notes. Some teens already have developed a mezzolike tone, with most of the color in the lower-middle range. A young man may already have the richness of voice in the middle range to indicate baritone, and a few have the full low notes that would indicate a bass range.

Young singers who enjoy classical music can be attracted to operas and opera arias because of the beauty of the music and the obvious artistry and prestige of the people they hear singing. The real danger is that young voices who try to sing opera do not yet have all the elements necessary for a particular *Fach* and may try to copy a particular sound. It is important to guide them and study only arias in a *Fach* that are within their capabilities. These young singers are already showing their natural tendency to sing a certain *Fach* repertoire. A teacher needs to encourage this budding opera singer to learn music that suits her or his age and present vocal abilities.

Learning the Basics

Patience, patience, and more patience is required for the careful preparation of a future operatic voice. Getting through the notes is not the main point of singing. Singing easily and expressively is.

The problem of how to train young singers involves more than communicating effective methods of vocal technique. All voice teachers strive to teach the basics of good singing: breath support, range, resonance, and an absence of tension.

There are many fine publications addressing the teaching of young voices. Some of the most interesting statements, however, come from the old masters, such as baritone and music educator Manuel Garcia (1805–1906). In his 1894 book, *Hints on Singing*, Garcia lamented the lack of training young voices for flexibility, what teachers and vocalists know as the bel canto, or beautiful-singing, style. He wrote: "At the present day the acquirement of flexibility is not in great esteem. . . . This is to be regretted, for not only must the art suffer, but also the young fresh voices, to which the brilliant florid style is the most congenial."[1] His advice is as applicable today as it was one hundred years ago.

In addition to the basics of bel canto singing, teachers must teach coloratura singing (the ability to use runs, trills, and other embellishments in vocal music), as well as how to sing a correct forte (loud) without forcing the voice, and a correct pianissimo (soft) without using falsetto. Many of these vocal techniques are accomplished by the correct use of breathing and control of the breath during singing.

Another old master, Giovanni Battista Lamperti (1813–1892), was a great proponent of singing without forcing. He had the following to say regarding breath: "The foundation of all vocal study lies in the control of the breath."[2] Lamperti went on to write, "The language best suited for the study of singing is Italian, because it is the only one without aspirates. The music which I prefer for vocalists is that of the masters Rossini, Mozart, Bellini, Weber, Donizetti, et al."[3] Lamperti's methods are still used today to promote singing in a full, clear tone.

Too Much Too Soon

It is important for the teacher to guide the young singer, especially a teenager, not to sing too much too soon. This can remain a problem well into a student's early twenties. An exception would be a young soubrette soprano, who could be perfectly trained at eighteen. *Soubrette,* in French, literally means "a waiting-maid, especially an intriguing, coquettish maid."[4] These sopranos tend to have youthful, flexible voices to begin with.

A young future dramatic tenor is wise to sing lyric as long as possible. It is more practical, and usually a better career move, to sing not only lyric repertoire, but also character and acting tenor roles, for as much as fifteen to twenty years, until the voice matures and the singer has the experience needed for dramatic tenor roles.

Also, a young soprano with the potential to be a *Jugendlich* (young) dramatic soprano should not be regularly singing arias in the *Fach* until her mid-twenties at the earliest, and thirty would be even better. The key word is "regularly." Soprano Lilli Lehmann (1848–1929) also expressed concern about young singers trying heavy roles too early. In her book *How to Sing*, she advised, "Long-continued exertion should not be exacted of the voice at first; even if the effects of it are not immediately felt, a damage is done in some way. In this matter, pupils themselves are chiefly at fault, because they cannot get enough, as long as they take pleasure in it. . . . No woman of less than twenty-four years should sing *soubrette* parts, none of less than twenty-eight years second parts, and none of less than thirty-five years dramatic parts; that is early enough."[5]

An interesting side note: Another German soprano with a similar name was Lotte Lehmann (1888–1976). It is said that while in Salzburg in 1936, she discovered the Trapp Family Singers (of *The Sound of Music* fame) and persuaded them to make their first public performance. She left Europe just before Austria was annexed by Germany in 1938 and emigrated to the United States, where she sang at the San Francisco Opera and the Metropolitan Opera until 1945.[6]

LEARNING TO SING

The teacher and the student must focus first on the process of learning to sing and the technical knowledge to protect the voice throughout the performing lifetime. This is sometimes frustrating for students who want to have a "product" they can immediately use and want to enjoy using their voice in the most dramatic way possible. The truth is that most singers have to study for many years until the vocal technique comes together with the physical and mental development. Only then can certain roles be regularly performed and a career built and sustained.

Junior high and high school choral programs can be a boon to voice teachers whose students participate. These preteen and teenage students are learning repertoire, theory, ear training, sight singing, and other musical and stylistic elements necessary for any future career as a singer. At the same time, the choir's "one of many" atmosphere encourages young singers to work on their contribution to the group.

Participation in school musicals is also wonderful for a young singer's confidence, whether as a choral or solo singer. Such performances provide early training in acting, stage deportment, and character study. Students learn the most essential tool for acting while singing, which is to use the emotion of the music to shape facial and vocal expressions.

The only negative would be if a young singer tries to imitate a role from a recording. It is a delicate balance for the voice teacher to train a young voice, encourage performances, and still preserve the vocal health of the student's voice. As Lamperti said, "The maltreated voice will, with time, become old and tired."[7]

To avoid this happening, several simple steps can be used to help a young classical voice develop without either damaging future potential or interest in the classical music fields. These include the following:

Determine Innate Aptitude and Abilities

A voice teacher can determine a student's natural affinity for a particular range and vocal style after just a few lessons. It will soon become obvious whether a young singer is more comfortable singing long lyric lines or enjoys rapid, energetic passages. The initial attraction of the young student to a certain type of music can indicate the most effective repertoire to use when training this voice and ensure that the student will enjoy the process.

Select Vocalizes and Roles to Match the *Fach*

Vocalizes, or vocal exercises, enhance the study of each *Fach* category, and an endless variety of exercise books is available. The teacher can select specific exercises for range, flexibility, resonance, support, and other factors pertinent to the development of roles within a particular *Fach*.

Many great teachers have suggested vocal exercises, especially for the young voice. Manuel Garcia, famed nineteenth-century teacher of bel canto, wrote the following regarding teaching vocal flexibility: "The acquirement of agility . . . [is to be obtained] by the study of diatonic scales, passages of combined intervals, arpeggios, chromatic scales, turns, shakes, light and shade . . . it renders the organ flexible, even mellow, besides strengthening and preparing it for the florid style."[8] Joan Frey

Boytim, voice teacher and editor of numerous anthologies for young singers, put it bluntly: "Even singers with naturally beautiful voices must learn technique to survive."[9]

Some interesting classical exercises are suggested by the legendary soprano Lilli Lehman and can be found in her book *How to Sing*.[10] She has the following suggestion for young voices: "In order not to weary young voices too much, it is best to begin in the middle range, going upward first, by semitones, and then, starting again with the same tone, going downward. All other exercises begin in the lower range and go upward."[11]

More complicated and varied vocalizes can be added to match the abilities of the singer and the music being studied. Again, having knowledge of the *Fach* categories can lead the singer and teacher to a selection of effective vocalizes.

Select Appropriate Music Using *Fach* Criteria

It is always possible to find opera music appropriate for a young singer's age and experience. (See appendix D, "Opera Roles for Children, Young Lyrics, and Beginners.") Selecting music to match the student's abilities will encourage successful study and facilitate a natural progression to more difficult music as the student becomes increasingly knowledgeable. Nothing sells like success. It is far preferable to have a student easily sing "Evening Prayer" from Humperdinck's *Hänsel und Gretel* than struggle through Papagena's patter duet from Mozart's *Die Zauberflöte*. Save the latter for the young soubrette. The songs for children and young singers are usually short and of a restricted range. Sometimes they are even assigned the predominant theme of the opera, such as the "soprano" voice in act 4 of *Aida*, who sings the beautiful temple theme music.

Define How and When to Practice

A brief word about practicing is appropriate at this point. As all voice teachers are aware, the beginning student often has no concept of how to practice or how often. Quite often, new students rely on the voice lesson to learn songs and exercises and seldom practice by themselves. As soon as possible, communicate clearly that the best practice sessions are daily and short. This can be for as little as fifteen minutes.

Even though young singers have the ability to sing without even taking time for normal warm-up exercises, daily practice—including warm-up—is an excellent habit to establish.

Lilli Lehmann said that practice was "the great secret of those singers who keep their voices young till they reach an advanced age. Without it all voices, of which great exertions are demanded, infallibly meet disaster.

Therefore, the motto must be always, practice, and again, practice, to keep one's power uninjured; practice brings freshness to the voice, [and] strengthens the muscles."[12]

Learn Elements Separately

Professionals have learned to study the music "off the page." This means they first analyze the rhythm, style, and dramatic development of the piece, and then speak the text as a poem. Only then do they learn the notes as slowly and carefully as possible. Professionals know that if you learn music incorrectly, it remains the basic version for your entire career.

Encourage Acting Techniques to Support Character Study

Every performance experience by the young voice student can lead to an understanding of acting as communication. The student must realize, as soon as possible, that all forms of singing are simply communication with a listener or listeners. Even art songs can be studied as stories by making up a story suggested by the art song's words. Young students have tremendous imaginations, and living in the "what if" world of acting comes naturally to them. When students are encouraged to move from the "I am singing" to the "I am telling a story" mode of performing, they are already learning good acting techniques. All performance experiences are valuable and will help young singers learn acting techniques that will enhance their singing. The teacher is an important guide and a critically important interpreter of these experiences.

Avoid Copying

Young singers sometimes rely on recordings to teach them the music. There are problems with listening to a recording or even watching a video before studying a piece of music. The young singer could be learning mistakes, not just from the vocalist on the recording, but also by the ensemble, orchestra, or even the conductor—especially with live recordings. Also, the vocal style or musical style of the recording might not be an accepted norm today. Copying the stylistic or vocal characteristics of another singer is not always advantageous. Rina del Monaco, wife of tenor Mario del Monaco and herself a vocal teacher, said of a young soprano who was singing in a Rossini opera in the Rossini Theater in Pesaro, Italy, "She is trying to sing like Maria Callas. But she is only copying all of Callas's bad habits."[13]

TEACHING THE YOUNG LYRIC

When teaching the young lyric, the teacher should follow the same steps as have been previously described, with the following additions:

Translate Text

The young lyric singer who is learning the Italian art songs and simple arias should be encouraged to translate these songs and arias word for word rather than depend on the English written below the Italian. The English is meant only as a text to sing when performing in English and is not a literal translation. Knowledge of what each word means actually makes the song easier to sing with appropriate emotion. Translating the words also builds knowledge of a language even before formal study.

An interesting phenomenon related to the above: In Italy the Italians often notice that American opera singers sometimes speak an archaic Italian, rather than the modern. They will ask, "Are you a singer?" and when the singer answers "Yes, how did you know?" the Italian will laugh and say, "It is because you are speaking seventeenth-century Italian." This is because so many American singers learn much of their Italian from the various collections of Italian art songs, rather than from formal language study.

Sing within Current Abilities

The young lyric voice usually has the good fortune to be cast in lead roles in musical theater productions in high school and college. Sometimes these singers have opportunities to sing an operatic role in a university or with a regional opera company. Both singer and teacher need to be sure that the role matches the present capabilities and training of the singer. If the music does not match the age and development of the singer, the opportunity to perform is not worth the risk of damaging a promising young classical voice.

The difficulty still remains in persuading young lyric singers to accept roles that will not put excessive demands on their voice but will still enhance their experience and acting abilities. As the singer matures, encourage the study of formal acting technique as opportunities become available. There is really no such thing as a singer who doesn't act. Even art songs can be acted using facial expressions and some body movement.

Listen to Recordings

Listening to recordings is generally interesting to the young lyric singer who has already learned the basics. Recordings can also be used to demonstrate the historical development of voices and how vocal styles have changed. Taping your students also gives them a unique perspective on how they actually sound.

Young lyric singers may be eager to sound like their favorite singer and to sing the more dramatic and powerful and, yes, showy roles they might hear on recordings. Unfortunately the singers engaged to do these recordings are usually age thirty-five and up, and most are mature singers in their forties and fifties. Remind the young lyric to sing easily, lyrically, and with good technique and a lack of tension. The dramatic roles will come later.

Sound Young

One of the teacher's most difficult tasks is to convince young lyric students that they should sound young. They should also be able to easily sing arias that enhance flexibility—a requirement for a lyric voice. Magda Olivera (1910–), a soprano known for her expressiveness, and who was still singing in her nineties, addressed this problem in an interview with American bass Jerome A. Hines (1921–2003) for his book *Great Singers on Great Singing*: "We must have respect for our limitations," she said. "Take care of what you have to the point of not overdoing, not going beyond your natural capability, like singing wrong things. One should be able to sing hours and hours without fatigue."[14]

Avoid Vocal Fatigue

Avoiding vocal fatigue, especially during a performance, is important. Three safeguards should be kept in mind. First, learn the music so well that you do not even have to think about technique in order to support the breath and sustain the sound. Second, warm up appropriately. Don't overdo the warm-up if you know that your voice will be fatigued at the end of two hours of singing and the performance is two hours and a half. And third, control your emotions when singing. Nothing will drain the voice faster than becoming too emotionally involved in your role. Remember, acting is just that—acting. It is fine to "feel" the emotion of a song, but keep it in control so that the throat doesn't tighten up and the vocal quality disintegrate.

Lilli Lehmann also wrote about the importance of avoiding vocal fatigue, using soprano Adelina Patti (1843–1919) as an example: "Everything [for Patti] was united—the splendid voice, paired with great talent for singing, and the long oversight of her studies by her distinguished teacher, Strakosch. She never sang roles that did not suit her voice; in her earlier years [Patti made her debut at age sixteen[15]] she sang only arias and duets or single solos. . . . She spared herself rehearsals which, on the day of the performance, or the day before, exhaust all singers, because of the excitement of all kinds attending them, and which contribute neither to the freshness of the voice nor to the joy of the profession."[16] Good advice even today.

Continue to Develop the Basic Voice with Carefully Chosen Repertoire

The process of analyzing a singer's vocal skills and ability to sing specific repertoire must be ongoing. The teacher might assign an aria, or a reduced version of an aria, from an opera representing a heavier *Fach* as a learning and motivational tool. But students should primarily work on arias they can sing easily, even if these represent roles that are not as emotionally attractive as those with more dramatic or demanding music. Students should resist the temptation to sing music that is not age appropriate and that their current vocal skills will not support.

During a conversation following a singer's audition at the National Theater in Munich in 1979, conductor Heinrich Bender stated that in the past conductors would hear a young voice and send the singer out to a small opera house to sing all the small and medium-size roles, so that the singer could accumulate experience and stamina without the pressure of a huge opera house. They would then watch the development and invite the singer back to Munich to reaudition when the singer was ready for bigger roles. But Bender admitted that conductors no longer had time to do this.

Soprano Magda Olivera observed the newer practice of opera directors hiring young singers, encouraging them to sing dramatically, and then, when the voice became damaged, letting them go and hiring new singers: "I have seen opera management push a young singer to do roles too heavy for him . . . and then when he collapses under the load he is dropped from the roster instantly."[17]

ROLES FOR YOUNG SINGERS

There are many opera roles for young singers. They are often listed as a voice type—"soprano" or just "voice," for example—or by function, such as "messenger," "priestess," "peasant," "shepherd," "soldier," or "lady."

The time they spend singing is usually limited, and any solos are short and of limited range.

Important in the selection of roles for the young singer, whether a child, lyric, or beginner, is how performing the role will support the continued development of the singer's voice. The four elements of vocal training that can be supported by opera roles are lyric singing, vocal flexibility, extension of range, and encouragement of expression and dramatic singing.

The teacher also needs to be careful, however, about the length of the role if the student is learning the complete opera. For example, while all young sopranos can benefit from learning the main arias from roles listed under lyric, the longer roles in this category would usually be beyond the stamina or acting abilities of most singers until the middle to late twenties.

Choose roles that are short, such as Barberina in Mozart's *Le nozze di Figaro*. This type of role will give the young singer the chance to become acquainted with this opera and Mozart's style. Serpetta in Mozart's *La finta giardiniera* is another excellent choice for the young lyric soprano.

Roles for young singers could include one of a vocal group, such as the three attendants of the Queen of the Night in Mozart's *Die Zauberflöte*, or the trio of women in Richard Strauss's *Ariadne auf Naxos*. For men, these are usually the character or "acting" roles—the sidekick instead of the hero—or one of the comedic characters in a Mozart opera.

With increased experience and training, young sopranos can select roles from the soubrette soprano *Fach*, such as Barbarina in *Le nozze di Figaro*. A young soprano with a flexible voice and developed range can select music from the lyric coloratura *Fach*, such as Blonde in Mozart's *Die Entführung aus dem Serail*.

Again, many of these roles are listed in appendix D, "Operatic Roles for Children, Young Lyrics, and Beginners."

Following are some additional examples of child/beginner roles that can enforce the elements of lyric singing, vocal flexibility, extension of range, and encouragement of expression and dramatic singing:

Child/Beginner Roles to Reinforce Lyric Singing

- Child, *L'enfant et les sortilèges*, Ravel
- Shepherd boy, *Tosca*, Puccini
- Priestess, *Aida*, Verdi
- Love pair duet, *Il tabarro*, Puccini
- Strawberry girl, *Porgy and Bess*, Gershwin
- Sandman, *Hänsel und Gretel*, Humperdinck
- Soprano voice/tenor voice, *Il tabarro*, Puccini

Child/Beginner Roles to Reinforce Vocal Flexibility

- Three boys, *Die Zauberflöte*, Mozart
- Amahl, *Amahl and the Night Visitors*, Menotti
- Zephyrus, *Apollo et Hyacinthus*, Mozart
- Squirrel, *L'enfant et les sortilèges*, Ravel
- Four bridesmaids, *Der Freischütz*, Weber

Child/Beginner Roles to Extend Range

- Forest bird, *Siegfried*, Wagner
- Voice of the falcon, *Die Frau ohne Schatten*, R. Strauss
- Spirit, *Dido and Aeneas*, Purcell
- Bat/nightingale, *L'enfant et les sortilèges*, Ravel

Child/Beginner Roles to Encourage Expression and Dramatic Singing

- Amahl, *Amahl and the Night Visitors*, Menotti
- Cobweb, *A Midsummer Night's Dream*, Britten
- Harry, *Albert Herring*, Britten
- Cricket/frog/fly, *The Cunning Little Vixen*, Janácek
- Owl/frog, *L'enfant et les sortilèges*, Ravel

Having young singers learn these roles provides an introduction to the world of opera while encouraging light, easy, and expressive singing. At the same time, children can be taught the elements they will use later. Making it fun at the same time should be the goal of every teacher of young voices. While the voice is developing in size and strength, and the actor is accumulating performing experience, these roles facilitate a continual learning process and ensure that the voice will not be forced into overly dramatic singing at a young age.

HOW AND WHEN TO MOVE FROM *FACH* TO *FACH*

The single answer to the above implied question is to move from *Fach* to *Fach* when the voice and the level of experience indicate the singer is ready. The basic rule in the teaching world, and the performance world as well, is to start a young voice with lighter, more lyric repertoire using selections that are age appropriate.

Once a young singer has tried out short roles in the beginner *Fach* categories and is studying the lyric categories successfully, it becomes possible to begin combining some of the repertoire from other categories.

This depends on the training, experience, range, and the vocal ease and sound that are most comfortable for each singer. The suggested progression of young voices into adulthood could be charted as follows but is by no means typical of every voice:

A Typical Vocal Progression

Soprano: child—beginner soprano—soubrette—lyric—lyric coloratura—*Jugendlich*-dramatic—*Hoch*-dramatic

Mezzo: child—beginner mezzo—lyric—coloratura mezzo—dramatic mezzo

Tenor: child—beginner tenor—lyric—buffo/*Spiel* tenor—*Jugendlich*-dramatic

Baritone: child—beginner baritone—lyric—cavalier—*Helden*/dramatic baritone

Bass: child—beginner bass—buffo/*Spiel* bass—heavy bass/buffo—serious bass

All young voices will eventually progress into a *Fach* that best suits them. Not all voices become dramatics, and very few ever become a true *Hoch*-dramatic soprano, *Helden* tenor, *Helden* baritone, or a serious bass. However, there are enough opera roles for children, young lyric, and beginner singers to make them an exciting beginning to a career in opera.

NOTES

1. Manuel Garcia, *Hints on Singing*, trans. Beata Garcia (New York: E. Ascherberg & Co., 1894), iv.

2. Giovanni Battista Lamperti, *Vocal Wisdom*. Transcribed (1931) by William Earl Brown, trans. Lillian Strongin (New York: Taplinger Publishing, 1957), 5.

3. Ibid., 7.

4. C. O. Sylvester Mawson, *Dictionary of Foreign Terms*, 2nd ed. rev. and updated by Charles Berlitz (New York: Thomas Y. Crowell, 1975).

5. Lilli Lehmann, *How to Sing*, trans. Richard Aldrich (New York: Macmillan, 1929), 108.

6. Beaumont Glass, *Lotte Lehmann: A Life in Opera and Song* (Santa Barbara, Calif.: Capra Press, 1988).

7. Lamperti, *Vocal Wisdom*, 3.

8. Garcia, *Hints on Singing*, 19.

9. Joan Boytim, *The Private Voice Studio Handbook* (Milwaukee, Wis.: Hal Leonard, 2003), 56.

10. Lehmann, *How to Sing*, 186–208.

11. Ibid., 186.

12. Ibid., 9.

13. Conversation with Rina del Monaco, Pesaro, Italy, 1986.

14. Jerome Heines, *Great Singers on Great Singing* (New York: Limelight Editions, 1988), 205.

15. John Frederick Cone, *Adelina Patti: Queen of Hearts* (New York: Hal Leonard, 2003).

16. Lehmann, *How to Sing*, 11.

17. Heines, *Great Singers*, 205.

4

The European Opera House

Once the well-trained and experienced young singer has an understanding of the *Fach* categories and the *Fach* system, he or she is ready to audition in Europe. Often young singers have stars in their eyes and unrealistic hopes of appearing at prestigious houses such as Covent Garden in London, Munich's National Opera, or La Scala in Milan. However, the world of European opera is surprisingly extensive, and before singers set off it is important for them to learn about the value of an opera house to a European community, as well as the different kinds of European opera houses and how they are financed. This will help singers understand where they have the best chance of starting their career.

THE OPERA HOUSE AS A CULTURAL CENTER

Europeans acknowledge work as only one part of their lives. Cultural activities and some sort of physical sport or exercise are other components. This exercise could be something as simple as an evening stroll through the neighborhood, window-shopping on days that stores are closed, or a simple walk in the park.

In Europe the opera house is the cultural center of the city, and music is the primary cultural experience. Understanding this will add to your enjoyment of being an opera singer in Europe.

In addition to the opera house, musical performances of all types are held everywhere—in churches, parks, abbeys, restaurants, museums, and courtyards. American bands, choral groups, instrumental groups, folk dancers, mimes, opera, theater and ballet, flower shows, art displays—all have their enthusiastic fans.

Many churches use their beautiful spaces and wonderful acoustics for almost daily noontime concerts. When performing in this venue, it is not unusual to have a fluid audience that comes and goes as people finish their lunch hour and return to work. These concerts are so popular that most performance groups deliberately limit their music programs to forty-five minutes to an hour to accommodate the lunchtime audience.

In Europe all cultural experiences are equally valued. One person may prefer classical opera to any other type of musical event and usually has a preference as to composer or style. For example, fans of Wagner's operas might seek out and attend virtually all these performances. These are so popular that the Wagner operas performed at the Wagner Festival in Bayreuth, Germany, can be sold out years in advance.

Other people might prefer operetta and attend only performances such as Sigmund Romberg's *The Student Prince* or Gilbert and Sullivan's *H.M.S. Pinafore*. Even American musicals, such as *Wicked* and *The Lion King*, are often presented as part of a normal opera house season, and some theaters, such as the Theater des Westens in Berlin, specialize in this genre.

There is no stigma about "going to the opera." Europeans go because an evening in the theater is enjoyable and because it adds to the variety and value of their lives. There is no required attire. Except for a major opera premiere, most attendees show up in everyday dress and often come right from work. Students throng to the opera dressed in their usual casual or creative fashions. In American regional and small-city opera houses, this is becoming more the norm as well.

Europeans are justifiably proud of their opera houses. From the beautiful small opera houses in many Italian cities, to the medium-size opera houses in the heart of Germany, such as the Staatstheater Kassel, to the huge national opera houses throughout Europe, such as La Scala, Covent Garden, the Opéra Garnier and Opéra Bastille in Paris, and the Munich National Opera (Bayerische Staatsoper)—all are equally valued for the impact they have on the local quality of life.

Opera houses provide a cultural heart to a city, attract new residents, and also lure new business to the area. Addressing University of Illinois opera students, *Intendant* Klaus Schultz of the Aachen Opera, Germany, described the European view: "Any city calling itself a city would have a theater. The theater indicates that there is something to do in the evening."[1]

In Europe, businessmen and manufacturers often won't consider moving into a city unless it has a functioning opera theater. Their assumption is that a town unable to financially support even a small opera house is not large enough to support the development of new business. They also reason that a town without a theater has no focus for the cultural activities that add polish to a well-rounded life. In Europe, life is enhanced and partially defined by the cultural center of the city—the opera house.

FINANCIAL SUPPORT

One of the most obvious differences between the American and European opera systems is their financial support. European houses are supported first by taxes and then by ticket sales. American opera houses are just the opposite, supported first by ticket sales and the remainder with gifts and grants and, in some cases, taxes. Many small city opera companies in the United States depend almost entirely on ticket sales to cover costs, with only a small amount of money coming from contributions and other organizations such as Allied Arts and the National Endowment for the Arts.

Adequate funding is the primary reason that European opera houses have the financial security needed to offer a regular schedule of performances and hire an ensemble of singers who can expect to work at that opera house for at least three years—the normal length of a contract. This security also gives the opera artistic directors the ability to plan long range, employ full-time ensemble and staff members who are assured of a job (along with retirement and health insurance), and provide all the necessary support personnel and materials for professional opera productions. The *Deutsches Bühnen Jahrbuch* for 2006 lists 25,920 artistic personnel just in the country of Germany. This annual yearbook (referred to as the "Red Book" by Americans), contains over a thousand pages and also lists the addresses of theaters (opera houses) in Germany, Austria, Switzerland, and of the other major theaters in Europe.[2]

Due to their level of financial support, European opera houses also have the luxury of regularly scheduling premiers of new compositions. As a condition of tax support, it is understood that part of the responsibility of the theater is to offer new creative works to their audiences. Even if the new composition is not successful, at least six performances will be offered of the work. The staging of *Vincent* at the Kassel Opera in the early 1980s is an example. The opera received such poor reviews, weak attendance, and even violent behavior from the few audience members who attended (rotten fruit and vegetables were thrown at the stage) that the production was canceled after the sixth performance.

OPERA HOUSE FACILITY

An opera house complex is normally made up of a group of theaters. There is the main theater, which has the largest stage and auditorium area; a smaller stage; and often other performance spaces. Singers, actors, dancers, and other artists and theater personnel are engaged as members of the performing ensemble.

In each opera house complex the largest stage is used primarily for opera, operetta, and musical theater performance. The one or more smaller stages are used for other purposes, including plays and ballet. A good example is the mid-size opera house in Kassel—a state theater (*Staatstheater*). Kassel has five performance spaces: the opera house (*Musiktheater*); the drama theater (*Documenta-Halle*); the foyer of the *Documenta-Halle*; the Small Theater Space (*tif*); and the foyer of the *tif*.[3]

Of the several stages within each opera house complex, the large stage (*grosse Bühne*) is where most opera performances take place. It is usually larger and has more staging capabilities, such as trapdoors, revolving sections of the floor, and elevators beneath the stage, than do the smaller stages in the opera house. This main stage is used primarily for opera or musical performances and sometimes for a performance of a major ballet.

Each *grosse Bühne* is made up of the main stage area visible to the audience and a large area on both sides where additional set pieces are stored for subsequent acts. There is an area at the back of the stage that is as large as or larger than the stage itself and can be opened up to provide tremendous illusions of distance, such as a street that disappears into the distance in the *La bohème* café scene. A *grosse Bühne* will have multiple traps set into the floor, which can be opened to allow characters, or a special effect, to pop suddenly up onto the stage or disappear just as quickly. In a Munich Opera production of Richard Strauss's *Daphne* (starring American soprano Julia Conwell), a tree "grew up" through the stage to a height of fifteen feet.

The middle of many *grosse Bühnen* stages can be raised and lowered to suggest caves or ponds or other special effects. For the Munich Opera's production of Dvorak's *Rusalka* in the 1980s, the entire middle of the stage was dropped down to create the illusion of a pond, allowing the water spirit Rusalka to "swim around" with other water spirits. She then "swam" out of the water, climbed up a tree, and stretched out on a limb to sing her song to the moon. Opera stages can also be "raked" (set at an angle slanting up away from the audience) or can revolve (*Drehbühne*), facilitating set changes.

Each opera house might also have one or more areas somewhere else in the city that could be used for performances or rehearsals. Again, the National Theater in Munich is a good example. In addition to the same types of areas listed for the Kassel Opera, Munich also has performances in two other theater buildings: the *Prinzregententheater* and the *Cuvillies-Theater*. (For more information on the individual performance spaces, see chapter 9, "Life in the Opera House.")

Regardless of where the opera is performed, all the areas are managed by a large staff of artistic directors, managers, secretaries, and technical personnel. All opera houses are organized in the same manner and have the same function in their cities—that of cultural center.

TYPES OF OPERA HOUSES

City Theater (*Stadttheater*)

The *Stadttheater* is representative of the first level of opera house in Europe, and there are approximately 250 of these kinds of theaters just in Germany.[4] Its primary financial support is from city taxes. For an American, this may be the most accessible house for that first engagement as an opera singer and is an ideal setting in which to learn roles, polish languages, and become comfortable with a European lifestyle. Representative theaters are those in Aachen, Bielefeld, Bremerhaven, Coburg, Essen, Freiburg, Heidelberg, Lübeck, Magdeburg, Oberhausen, and Regensburg.

Being employed at a *Stadttheater* brings the same level of respect from opera fans as employment in the larger opera houses. A *Stadttheater* presents the same ten-and-a-half-month season of operas, ballet, and musicals, as well as theatrical performances. Musicians are highly respected, and the development of new young singers is eagerly followed and appreciated. Opera performances in this level of theater were originally presented in the audience's native language, as opposed to the original language of the opera. However, even in *Stadttheatern*, many more operas are now produced in original languages and on an impressive artistic level.

Regional Theater (*Landestheater*)

The next level of opera house is the regional theater, or *Landestheater*. There are fifty-six *Landestheatern* in Germany,[5] and they are supported financially by the cities in the theater's immediate area, as well as by the city in which the theater is situated. This opera house has a larger financial base than the *Stadttheater*, with a correspondingly larger ensemble and the funding to produce more complex productions. The orchestra will also have more members, as will the chorus, theater, ballet, and technical areas.

There is no difference in the organization of the performance schedule, the number of performances during a season, or the pride of the people of the area for their opera house. Some of these regional theaters include the

Landestheater Detmold, the Landesbühne Hannover, the Landestheater Schleswig-Holstein, the Theater der Altmarkt Stendal, and the Landesbühne Wilhelmshaven.

Unfortunately, many Americans consider both *Stadttheatern* and *Landestheatern* less important than the larger houses. This can be a mistake, as all opera houses in Europe are equally important to the development of a career. These houses are also wonderful opportunities to get that first job, learn the system, learn and polish roles, and develop a reputation. Once the requisite experience has been accumulated, it will become possible to move on to a larger opera house.

State Theater (*Staatstheater*)

The *Staatstheater* is the third level, and it is also supported financially by the cities within that state, as well as the specific city in which the opera house is located. There are sixty-five state theaters in Germany.[6] Some of the best known of these are the opera houses in Berlin, Braunschweig, Bremen, Darmstadt, Dresden, Hamburg, Hannover, Karlsruhe, Kassel, Mainz, Nürnberg, Gärtnerplatz in Munich, Saarbrücken, Stuttgart, and Wiesbaden.

Without question these *Staatstheatern* are some of most prestigious and desirable houses in which to perform. Houses of this size have excellent financial support, offer correspondingly more performances of new compositions, employ a larger number of people, and present operas on a larger scale. A performance of Wagner's *Tristan und Isolde* could be presented because these houses would have a large enough orchestra to play the music effectively. These houses might also have a heavy dramatic soprano (*Hochdramatischer Sopran*) under contract to sing Isolde and not have to bring one in as a guest. There would be the funds to support more elaborate costuming and sets, and soloists would have the opportunity to perform a greater variety of roles.

Although many singers have a fine career at the *Stadttheater* and *Landestheater* levels, any who progress to a *Staatstheater* can be very proud of this accomplishment.

National Opera Houses (*Staatsopern*)

National opera houses are the epitome of success when it comes to prestige and popularity. The national opera houses in Germany, especially those in Munich and Berlin, are considered international-level theaters along with the Vienna Opera, the Metropolitan Opera, Covent Garden in London, the Paris Opera, the Rio De Janeiro Opera, Sydney Opera, La Scala in Milan, and the summer season in Verona, Italy. Although national theaters have resident ensemble performers, the emphasis is on the international guest "stars" and the elaborate productions.

Staatsopern are supported financially by the entire country, as well as the local area or county and the city in which they are located. These are the most important houses, with the largest financial base and the most elaborate productions, and are the ultimate goal of any opera singer. They are where you will see the superstars of opera performing. In Germany there are four national opera houses: Staatsoper Berlin, Staatsoper Dresden, Staatsoper Hamburg, and the Bayerische Staatsoper in Munich, also referred to as the National Theater.

Opera singers will not usually perform in a house of this size until they have received extensive experience and developed a national or international reputation. An exception would be someone who is engaged in a national opera house as a beginner (*Anfänger* or *Angängerin*) to fill small roles, or is hired for the *Staatsoper*'s opera studio. Studio ensemble members receive extensive operatic training and are also featured in their own performances, as well as performing small roles with the opera house ensemble.

The number of singers engaged at these national houses is impressive. At the National Theater in Munich, their 2007–2008 *Spielplan* (season plan) lists eighty-seven singers in the chorus, seventy-five female soloists and guests (*Solisstinnen und Gäste*), and ninety-three male soloists and guests.[7]

National opera houses can afford to hire internationally known singers as guest soloists, such as the legendary singers Mario del Monaco, Luciano Pavarotti, Renata Tebaldi, and Maria Callas, as well as today's stars, such as Placido Domingo, Juan Diego Flórez, Leo Nucci, Roberto Frontali, Barbara Henderson, Cheryl Studer, and Renée Fleming. This level of opera house also has the money to fund new productions for these stars. The national houses also offer summer seasons, such as the Strauss festival in Munich or the Mozart festival in Salzburg, Austria.

Many European opera houses are magnificent buildings with their own architectural and cultural merit. Young singers should take the time to learn the history of their new place of employment.

A lovely example is the Vienna State Opera house, which opened on May 25, 1869, with a production of Mozart's *Don Giovanni*. The building is a massive structure, built in the neo-Renaissance style and covering an area larger than an American football field complex. The opera theater's auditorium takes up only a small portion of this huge, ornate complex—less than one-tenth. The remaining public areas are the equivalent of a luxurious museum with tearooms, saloons, and a lobby filled with artwork, tapestries, sculpture, and silk hangings. The other half of this magnificent complex is made up of the backstage areas for set construction, storage, costume and makeup, dressing rooms, rehearsal stages, and offices.

From the Vienna State Opera's main entrance, a grand marble staircase is embellished with statues of the seven liberal arts (including Music and Dancing) and reliefs of opera and ballet. When the opera house was bombed in l945, the city felt it as a symbolic blow and rebuilt it with the latest stage technology, reopening in 1955 with a production of Beethoven's *Fidelio*.[8]

Other Opera and Touring Companies

There are many other opera companies in Germany. These include private theaters with their own facilities and personnel (279), theaters without a regular ensemble (143), and touring companies (90). All together, there are 920 performing companies just in Germany.[9] Add to this number 63 summer festivals, and the employment opportunities for performers and artists of all types seem limitless.

THE PRESS AND THE OPERA HOUSE

The European press actively supports its opera houses. Whether it is an article in a hometown newspaper, or reviews and notices in opera and theater magazines, the press gives a significant amount of time to reporting events in each opera house. If the theater is a national opera house, a greater number of magazines or newspapers likely will feature articles about the singers and performances; but all opera houses receive excellent coverage. The important opera magazines, such as *Opern Welt* and *Orpheus*, list the repertoire of small as well as large houses, print reviews, provide information about singers, and list the performance schedules.

This is great news for Americans developing their careers. Even performances in the smallest houses in Europe provide a constant stream of reviews, photos, articles, and even personal interviews. Schedules of performances, for all opera houses, are published regularly, displayed on posters, and sent to all the agents. A performer in a small opera house is just as noticeable as a soloist in the largest and has regular access to all the publicity materials needed to develop and maintain a career.

NOTES

1. Klaus Schultz, *Intendant*, Aachen, Germany. Lecture to University of Illinois students, February 13, 1991.

2. *Deutches Bühnen Jahrbuch* (Hamburg: Genossenschaft Deutscher Bühnen-Angehöriger im Verlag der Bühenschriften-Bertriebs-Gesellschaft mbH, 2006), 14.

3. Ibid., 325.

4. Ibid., 12.

5. Ibid.

6. Ibid.

7. *Bayerische Staatsoper Jahrevorschau* 2007–2008, 141–142.

8. *Vienna*, Eyewitness Travel Guide (New York: DK Publishing, 2004), 140.

9. *Deutsches Bühnen Jahrbuch*, 14.

5

Opera House Organization

Before one applies for a job with any business or organization, it is important to know how it is organized and functions. This is true of a European opera house as well. Having knowledge of all its pieces, parts, and personnel, and how they relate to one another, can be valuable in finding that first job in the opera world, as well as maintaining that job well into the future.

When people attend an opera, they see only a small number of those individuals dedicated to the realization of an artistically valid and successful opera performance—the conductor, soloists, chorus, orchestra, dancers, actors, and extras. The number of people not seen is far greater—the administrative staff, artistic directors, technical directors, musical directors, set and costume designers, lighting, sound, publicity, secretarial, and facility support personnel.

Using a *Staatstheater* as an example, such as the one in Kassel, Germany, the top of this organizational pyramid would be made up of a vocal ensemble of approximately thirty-five soloists and forty chorus members, plus several conductors, an eighty-member orchestra, fifteen ballet dancers, several prompters, and twenty-five actors employed by the drama house (*Schauspielhaus*). Additional personnel are engaged as needed for specific operas, such as extra string bass players for larger orchestrations, additional chorus members, or extras for nonsinging assignments.

Again, in order to know exactly who's who in the European opera world, an important resource to have is the *Deutsches Bühnen Jahrbuch*, known as the Red Book because of its red cover. Updated and published annually, this thousand-plus-page book contains lists of all opera houses in the German-speaking countries (Germany, Switzerland, and Austria), along with their current ensembles and staff.[1]

There are three main areas involved in the organization of an opera house: first, artistic management/historian (*Intendanz/Dramaturgie*); second, administration (*Verwaltung*); and third, the numerous music house (*Musikhouse*) personnel. Aspiring opera singers need to understand each of these areas, memorize the associated terms, and be aware of how each position in these three areas can be helpful to the development and maintenance of a career.

ARTISTIC MANAGEMENT/HISTORIAN (*INTENDANZ/DRAMATURGIE*)

The artistic management/historian area includes the people who have direct control over the artistic endeavors of the opera house. These people include the opera house artistic director (*Intendant*), the music historian (*Dramaturg*), and all those who work in the artistic management office (*Künstlerisches Betriebsbüro*). This also includes the set designers, costume designers, and secretarial services. Primary responsibilities include planning the season; engaging soloists, choir, orchestra, actors, dancers; the scheduling of all rehearsals and performances; and all other technical components of planning a successful season.

Artistic Director (*Intendant*)

The artistic director or *Intendant* is considered the head of the opera, and he or she is the most important person associated with the opera house. The *Intendant* is responsible for the overall artistic control of the house, which includes engaging soloists, conductors, and coaches, and overseeing all other artistic management personnel. This person also oversees all administrative and support staff, including the technical and design personnel.

The *Intendant* is also the most important person at house auditions, usually accompanied by a committee made up of the general music director (GMD), a stage director or two, and some of the other personnel such as coaches or costumers. (See chapter 6, "Auditioning," for more information on the *Intendant*'s role in auditions.)

Music History (*Dramaturgie*)

The *Dramaturg* is the person in charge of the opera house's music history (*Dramaturgie*) office, an important function of artistic management. The *Dramaturg* is responsible for all historical research pertaining to the opera, up to and including preparation of the musicological notes for the programs. This office also prepares posters used for publicity, hires photographers for the premiers of each production, organizes interviews with singers and other house personnel, and coordinates all publicity.

Artistic Management Office (*Künstlerisches Betriebsbüro*)

The artistic management office is of supreme importance in an opera house. These professionals have the responsibility for planning all aspects related to performances. The director of this office is called the *Betriebsbürodirektor* and is an extremely important person. He or she directs a large staff and has a bewildering amount of details to organize. If this director also has the title *Referenden des Intendants,* then he or she also has the ear of the both the *Intendant* and the general music director and often acts as the *Intendant*'s agent, facilitating all plans should this person be out of town.

It is important to set up a good relationship with the *Betriebsbürodirektor* as soon as possible. This is the first person the singer goes to when requesting a role or protesting a proposed role or schedule. This is also the person who gives permission for a singer to be away from the house and approves or denies requests for extra vacation time or to perform as a guest for another opera company.

The first thing this office does is create a performance plan. It decides which operas will be produced in the coming year and anywhere from two to five seasons in the future in the larger houses. This involves coordinating the schedules of all soloists offered a contract, in order to make sure each soloist's personal and performance schedules will match the proposed operas. Another important detail handled by this office is determining which opera could be substituted if for some reason the scheduled opera cannot be performed.

Once all the soloists, conductors, and directors have been hired, and the remaining staffing is confirmed, an official season plan (*Spielplan*) is printed in booklet form for the public. These are often fifty to a hundred pages long and will feature all the planned productions for the coming year, as well as their casts and staff.

Example 1 is a combination of pages 21 and 37 of the Bayerische Staatsoper (Munich Opera) *Spielplan* for 2007–2008. It shows the new productions (*Neuinszenierungen*) and the established productions (*Repertoire*) that will be presented.

Example 2 is also from the 2007–2008 Munich Opera *Spielplan* and shows the cast and principal staffing for the operas *Luisa Miller* and *Madama Butterfly.* Note that when the leads are double cast, dates are given to indicate who is singing when. (Fans are very loyal to their opera stars.) "N.N." indicates the second-cast soloist had not yet been selected.

Munich Opera *(Bayerische Staatsoper)* *Spielplan* for 2007-2008

NEUINSZENIERUNGEN (New productions)	REPERTOIRE

NEUINSZENIERUNGEN (New productions)

[37]

EUGEN ONEGIN
Peter I. Tschaikowsky
Nationaltheater
Premiere am Mittwoch, 31.10.2007

NABUCCO
Giuseppe Verdi
Nationaltheater
Premiere am Montag, 28.01.2008

TAMERLANO
Georg Friedrich Handel
Nationaltheater
Premiere am Sonntag, 16.03.2008

DIE BASSARIDEN
Hans Werner Henze
Nationaltheater
Premiere am Montag, 19.05.2008

IDOMENEO
Wolfgang Amadeus Mozart
Cuvilliés-Theater
Premiere am Mittwoch, 18.06.2008

DOKTOR FAUST
Ferruccio Busoni
Nationaltheater
Premiere am Samstag, 28.06.2008

ARIADNE AUF NAXOS
Richard Strauss
Prinzregententheater
Premiere am Donnerstag, 24.07.2008

REPERTOIRE

ALICE IN WONDERLAND
ARABELLA
ARIODANTE
UN BALLO I N MASCH ERA
IL BARBIERE DI SIVIGLIA
LA BOHEME
LA CALISTO
CARMEN
CHOWANSCHTSCHINA
COSÌ FAN TUTTE
ELEKTRA
DIE ENTFUHRUNG AUS DEM SERAIL
DIE FLEDERMAUS
DER FLiEGENDE HOLLANDER
DER FREISCHUTZ
DAS GEHEGEjSALOME
HANSEL UND GRETEL
KONIGSKINDER
LUISA MILLER
MADAMA BUTTERFLY
DIE MEISTERSINGER VON NURNBERG
NORMA
LE NOZZE DI FIGARO
ORPHEE ET EURYDICE
PARSIFAL
I PURITANI
ROBERTO DEVEREUX
DER ROSENKAVALIER
TOSCA
LA TRAVIATA
TRISTAN UND ISOLDE
IL TURCO IN ITALIA
WERTHER
DIE ZAUBERFLOTE

Example 1. Munich Opera (Bayerische Staatsoper) *Spielplan*, 2007–2008, pages 21 and 37. Printed courtesy of the Bayerische Staatsoper.

Example 3 is from the calendar section of the 2007–2008 Bayerische Staatsoper *Spielplan* and shows what was planned for July 2007. It includes several different types of concerts (*Konzert*) and vocal recitals (*Leiderabend*), as well as the operas being staged that month. The "location codes" indicate where the event is taking place and include churches,

LUISA MILLER

Giuseppe Verdi -Musik

Salvatore.Camlnarano, Libretto

nach Friedrich Schillers „Kabale und
Liebe"

Musikalische Leitung Massimo Zanetti

Inszenierung Claus Guth
Biihne und Kostiime Christian Schmidt
Licht Michael Bauer
Chore Andres Maspero
Dramaturgie Sophie Becker

Il Conte di Walter Carlo Colombara

Rodolfo Massimiliano Pisapia 30.03/02.04/.05.04.

Ramon Vargas 06.07/10.07.
Federica Anna Kiknadze
Wurm Steven Humes
Miller Paolo Gavanelli
Luisa Miller Krassimira Stoyanova 30.03/02.04/05.04.
N.N.06.07/10.07[6]

In italienischer Sprache mit deutschen Dbertiteln

Nationaltheater
So 30.03.2008, Preise K
Mi 02.04.2008,Abo Serie 32, Preise K
Sa OS.04.2008,Saison-Abo Serie 20, Preise L
So 06.07.2008
Do 10.07.2008

MADAMA BUTTERFLY

Giacomo Puccini-Musik
Luigi Illica, Giuseppe Giacosa Libretto

Musikalische Leitung Vjekoslav Sutej

Inszenierung Wolf Busse
Biihne Otto Stich
Kostiime Silvia Strahammer
Chore Andres Maspero

Cio-Cio-San Liping Zhang 12.01./17.01./19.01.
Patricia Racette 24.05-12.05.

Suzuki Heike Gr6tzinger 12.01./17.01./[l]9.01.
Daniela Sindram 24.05·/27.05.
B. F. Pinkerton Andrew Richards 12.01./17.01./19.01
Kamen Chanev 24.05./27.05
Sharpless Anthony Michaels-Moore 12.01./[l]7.01./19.01.
N.N.24.05-/[l]7.05.
Coro Nakodo Ulrich Ress
Yamadori Christian Rieger
Onkel Bonzo Steven Humes
Yakuside Rudiger Trebes
Der Kaiserliche Kommissar Nikolay Borchev
Der Standesbeamte N.N.

In italienischer Sprache mit deutschen Dbertiteln

Nationaltheater
Sa 12.01. 2008, Preise I
Do 17.01. 2008,Abo Serie 11, Preise I
Sa 19.01.2008,Familienvorstellung, Preise I
Sa 24.05.2008, Familienvorstellung, Preise I
Di 27. OS.2008,Abo Serie 31, Preise I

Example 2.   Munich Opera *Spielplan*, page 48. Printed courtesy of the Bayerische Staatsoper.

schools, and other venues that stage operas. If no location code is listed, then the opera is being performed in the National Theater (*Nationaltheater statt*)—the main stage of the Munich Opera House.

Once opera seasons have been decided and contracts issued to performers, directors, conductors, and others, then the artistic management office creates rehearsal plans (*Probeplans*) and weekly rehearsal plans (*Wochenplans*) for the current season. These are very detailed and include the names of all ensemble members involved and where the rehearsals take place. These are given to all singers, so there is no excuse for not knowing where one has to be, and when.

These plans also reflect details like who is on vacation or singing as a guest somewhere else and which singers are in town and available should

Munich Opera Performance
Schedule for July 2007

Di 01.07. Der Sturm *
         | Idomeneo, C
Mi 02.07. | La traviata
Fr 04.07. |Tristan und Isolde
Sa 05.07. | Norma
So 06.07. | Luisa Miller |
         Idomeneo, C
         | Liederabend Anja Harteros, P
Mo 07.07. |Doktor Faust
Di 08.07. La Bayadere *
Mi 09.07. | Eugen Onegin
Do 10.07. |Luisa Miller
Fr 11.07. |Norma
Sa 12.07. | Festspiel-Konzert, Oper fur alle, MP
So 13.07. | EinfUhrungsmatinee:
         Ariadne auf Naxos, MJS |
         Eugen Onegin
Mo 14.07. |Nabucco
Di 15.07. |Tamerlano
Do 17.07. |Nabucco
Fr 18.07. |Tamerlano
Sa 19.07. | Die Bassariden
         iLiederabend Vesselina Kasarova, P
So 20.07. |Der Rosenkavalier
         | Festspiel- Duorecital, AH
Di 22.07. | Liederabend Dorothea Riischmann, P
Mi 23.07. | Arabella
         |FestspielKammerkonzert,AH   Do
24.07.|AriadneaufNaxos   Premiere, P
         | Werther
Fr 25.07. | Elektra
Sa 26.07. |Das Gehege/Salome
So 27.07. |Festspiel Kammerkonzert, AH
         Werther
         | Ariadne auf Naxos, P
Mo 28.07. |Festspiel-Konzert
Di 29.07. |Das GehegefSalome

Mi 30.07. | Cosi fan tutte
         | Ariadne auf Naxos, P
Do 31.07. | Die Meistersinger von Nurnberg

(Location codes)

SPIELORTE: P = Prinzregententheater, C = Cuvilliee-Theater,
AH = Allerheiligen Hofkirche, MP=Marstallplatz,
AP=Alte Pinakothek, PM = Pinakothek der Moderne,
ASK = Bayerische Akademie der Schonen Kunste,
MJS = Max-Joseph-Saal
Falls nichtt anders angegeben, finden die Veranstaltungen im
Nationaltheater statt.

PREISKATEGORI E: siehe Preislisten S. 182-188

#- Karten sind nur erhaltlich bei den Freunden des
Nationaltheaters e.v. unter T +49.(0)89.531048
* =Abonnement-Vorstellung. F Familienvorstellung
HBs=Karten sind nur erhaltlich bei der Heinz-BoslStiftung
unter T +49.(0)89.33 77 63

Example 3. Munich Opera performance schedule for July 2007. Printed courtesy of the Bayerische Staatsoper.

someone in the cast cancel or become ill at the last minute. Just the simple detail of planning which production will rehearse where and when is overwhelming when considering all the related details and actual number of people involved. (For more information on *Probeplans* and *Wochenplans*, as well as examples, see chapter 9, "Life in the Opera House.")

Technical Department (*Technische Abteilungen*)

The technical department is another area that falls under the artistic management. This includes set construction, costume, makeup, wigs, and shoemaker, stage management, lighting, and sound. Each of these areas has its own director. In a state house there can be more than 130 personnel involved in the technical department.

Set Designer (*Bühnenbildner*)

The *Bühnenbildner* has the same responsibilities as does a set designer in America—to design a set that will enhance the stage director's concept for the opera. Set designers in Europe are also the lighting designer for a production, as this position does not exist independently. Designing a set is a long process, with a considerable time spent studying the score with the director of the opera to achieve a consensus for the general artistic design for the production. The effects created by a good *Bühnenbildner* can be truly stunning. If this person has also studied acoustics, the results are not only visually magnificent but can act as a means of magnifying the singers' voices.

An example of the *Bühnenbildner*'s skill was featured in *Intendant* Giancarlo del Monaco's production of *Il tabarro* at the Kassel Staatstheater in the early 1980s. The set featured a wall across the stage about two-thirds of the way upstage, with a tunnel in the middle extending even farther upstage. Anyone singing in the tunnel was amplified as if singing through a megaphone. The rest of the wall acted as a sound shell, acoustically throwing the voices forward.

Costume Designer (*Kostümbildner*)

The costume department is a major part of every opera house. With the director and set designer, the costume designer plans the overall concept for costumes to match the set and the time period of the opera. The *Kostümbildner* is usually present at auditions, as his or her input on the physical appropriateness of a soloist for a particular role is important and is carefully considered by the audition panel. The general costume design is then assigned to the costume department staff, *Kostümabteilung*, which will then construct the costumes.

Costumes in European houses are stunning. If they look like silk, they are made from silk. Opera houses have large storage areas in which to keep costumes, which are reused or made over for subsequent productions. Costumes are created with beautiful materials, such as silk and taffeta, with hand beading and embroidery. They are not only representative of the historical era of the opera, but are beautiful artistic creations in their own right. Sometimes costumes from operas are also used by the drama theater (*Schauspiel*) for their productions.

In most houses, costumes are made for each major performer, even though there is a huge storage area with costumes of every possible period and style. The latter is normally relied upon for the chorus and singers in supporting roles. Costumes designed for the individual soloists are constructed specifically to their measurements. For example, if there are three sopranos in the ensemble who could be singing Leonora in *Il trovatore*, and five costume changes are required, then fifteen complete outfits are made for that one role alone. Costumes also include shoes, which in most houses are handmade for the performers, as well as wigs, also made by hand.

As a singer, you should take care to treat the designer and the costume personnel with great respect. They will then quickly learn your particular needs and design the costumes to help you sing and act appropriately. Occasionally singers can purchase costumes from a production, unless the costume is needed for a future production. These gowns, such as the second-act ball gown in Puccini's *Manon Lescaut*, or the gown that Roselinda wears in the second-act party scene in *Die Fledermaus*, make marvelous formal concert dresses. Some guest soloists, who specialize in a particular role, such as Butterfly in *Madama Butterfly*, have their own costumes.

In addition to set design and costuming, the technical department is responsible for all the theaters—that is, all the stages within the opera house facility—as well as the makeup, wig, and shoe departments.

Makeup Department (*Schminke*)

The makeup department has its own area and assigns a specific time in the *Probeplan* schedule for each singer to receive his or her makeup for the performance that evening. Singers usually change first into costume or go to makeup in a dressing gown. Singers provide their own false eyelashes and underwear. All other costume items—wigs, shoes, and even decorative items such as jewelry—are provided by the opera house.

Wig Department (*Maske*)

The wig makers have their own suite of rooms. As with shoes, wigs are made to the individual head size using head forms. When possible, wigs are made from real human hair, usually from Asia because it has more body and is easier to style. Several strands are carefully hand-hooked into a fabric base, similar to making a hooked rug. After the appropriate length and layers are created, the wig will be cut, styled, dyed, or decorated, depending on the demands of the role. The singer is sometimes allowed to purchase wigs for personal use following the end of the production, again only if the wig is not needed for future productions.

Shoemaker (*Shoemacher*)

This is one of the most delightful areas of the opera house. Many opera houses hand make period shoes for the performers. These rooms always seem to be warm and comfortable and filled with the mellow smell of new leather. Even if shoes are not made by a shoemaker, the opera house provides all footwear for each production. When a singer finds a really good pair of shoes, especially boots, it is sometimes possible to purchase these following the production, especially if the singer anticipates singing the same role elsewhere. Bringing personally fitted shoes to sing a performance as a guest will ensure that the singer's feet, at least, are comfortable.

Get to know the people involved in the technical departments as soon as possible. Compliment them on their contributions—a lighting designer on the illumination of an opera; the set designer for the artistic design of the set; the stagehands, makeup, and costume people—all need to be acknowledged and thanked. These technical personnel have heard many phenomenal voices, even in the smaller houses, and are not easy to impress. A simple acknowledgment of whatever this person does to make a performance more efficient will result in their personal interest in the singers and more effective productions. This carries over into a general awareness within the house that a soloist is something special, and perhaps a future great singer.

OPERA HOUSE ADMINISTRATION (*VERWALTUNG*)

The day-to-day organization and functioning of the opera house falls under the opera house administration (*Verwaltung*) office. This area includes finances, human relations, payroll, ticket offices, all the secretarial staff (*Secretariät*), the artists' entrance guards (*Pförtner*), as well as the people who work in the dressing rooms.

The opera house administrative director is the *Verwaltungsdirektor*. This person oversees the administrative function and is also the representative of the *Intendant*. He or she is also the director of finance. Responsibilities include the opera house budget and managing any extra money supplied by the city when necessary to hire guests. Although the *Intendant* hires and fires singers, this decision is supported, or not, by the *Verwaltungsdirecktor*. This person knows how much money the house can offer for specific contracts and will not allow the *Intendant* to go over budget.

The value of secretarial office workers (*Secretariät*) should not be overlooked by singers. Remember that movement within the opera house support staff positions is fluid, and people try to move up in the hierarchy the same as one would in any other business. A general office worker might become the assistant to the *Betriebsbürodirektor* or the *Intendant*'s personal secretary or even the new administrative director. The *Betriebsbüro* assistant might move up to the position of *Betriebsbürodirektor* and be the one who assigns soloists to important premieres.

The care and attention given to all the secretarial and office personnel should be based on interest in a shared profession. Extend an awareness of others beyond those in obviously influential positions such as *Intendant*, *General Musik Direcktor*, or *Betriebsbürodirektor*, and relationships can be developed to the benefit of all concerned. Soloists need to create professional relationships with these people as well as everyone in the house.

MUSIC HOUSE (*MUSIKHOUSE*)

The third area of an opera house is the music house (*Musikhouse*), comprising a great number of personnel who contribute to the actual presentation of the opera. These people are of immense importance to the solo singers. Besides the solo singers, they include the coaches, conductors, ballet directors, choreographers, chorus directors, stage directors, assistant directors, stage managers, prompters, director of the extras, and the orchestra, the ballet, and the chorus.

Soloists (*Soloisten*)

Soloists actually have the most precarious position of any member of an opera house. Solo contracts are always for a specific length of time. This is usually only two or three years at a time, which corresponds with the length of time an opera is normally presented in the house. Longer contracts are offered only to soloists who are of unusual value in some way. There is no guarantee that a soloist will be employed any longer than the length of time stipulated in his or her contract.

For various reasons, a contract can sometimes be terminated before the stipulated date. The most obvious reason would be the failure of the singer to meet any terms of the contract. Another scenario could be the arrival of a new *Indendant*, who might prefer to bring in singers with whom he or she is most familiar. When this happens, any existing contracts are allowed to lapse, and soloists must look for new engagements. Sometimes, however, a new *Intendant* will simply add his or her favorite soloists to the roster of the opera house, or bring them in when possible as guest soloists. (For more information on contracts, see chapter 7, "Contracts and Casting.")

General Music Director (*Generalmusikdirektor*)

Of the music house staff, the most important person is the conductor with the title of general music director (*Generalmusikdirektor*), usually just referred to as the GMD. The GMD does not necessarily conduct more often than the other conductors in the house but has the prestige of helping to organize the season and select the operas he or she wishes to conduct. This person also has a major say in the hiring and firing of soloists and is usually present during auditions for soloists.

The GMD is also often the conductor for performances of major symphonic repertoire presented by the opera orchestra. The GMD also has a performance schedule that allows her or him time to conduct for other venues, such as concerts and oratorios, and can engage opera soloists for these events. The GMD is an important person to get to know.

Conductors and Coaches (*Dirigenten und Musikalische Einstudierung*)

Conductors and coaches are valuable people to know and will often help soloists learn roles. A state-level opera house would have a total of approximately eight conductors and coaches. Conductors seeking a position in an opera house must go through interviews and auditions. During the audition they conduct one or more performances, and then the orchestra recommends their choice to the *Intendant*. The GMD is the only conductor that the *Intendant* might hire without the consent of the orchestra.

Conductors have the right to refuse to conduct specific singers for the operas they have been assigned to conduct. This does not happen often, but it does happen. If a conductor does not respect a singer's voice or performance ability, the conductor could either refuse to work with that singer or withdraw as conductor if that soloist is included in the cast. On the other hand, conductors can also ask that their performances include their favorite soloists and therefore can be a great help in the building and maintaining a singer's career.

The relationship between the conductor and the singer is a delicate one. Based on musicality, preparation, and performance effect, there is an indefinable trust that must be carefully nurtured and projected during all aspects of rehearsal and performing. Each must respect the other's needs and requirements. A successful performance is a synthesis of the entire musical, physical, interpretative, and practical aspects of opera production. Without a true awareness and respect between conductors and soloists, this would be almost impossible.

An excellent example of a highly respected opera conductor would be the late Alexander Sander (1940–1999). Impeccably trained, he conducted from memory. Musically and technically demanding, he was almost supernaturally aware of the needs of the singers on the stage, as well as the dramatic requirements of the music. He knew how to follow the singer's phrasing, how to direct the orchestra to support the singer's dangerous high notes, and he encouraged soloists on to higher creative and emotional levels without ever making them feel unsure or ineffective. He was the first to beam enthusiastically when the phrasing worked and the first to passionately push the orchestra to add that extra bit of energy that enabled the soloist to soar on the orchestral sound.

An eighth-note fanatic, Sander was also aware that the indefinable elements were what truly created the magic on stage and was always looking for these things within himself, the orchestra, and the performers on stage. Many of his performances were acknowledged with the orchestra tapping their stands in applause, something that seldom happens in an opera house and is thrilling to all who are lucky enough to be present. On many occasions his brilliant conducting of an opera's overture brought the audience to their feet in monumental applause.[2]

First Associate Conductor (*Erste Kapellmeister*)

The first associate conductor (*Erste Kapellmeister*) is of next importance in the house after the GMD, representing the GMD if necessary. This person is often, but not always, the *Studienleiter*—the director of the coaching staff. The *Erste Kapellmeister* is given more premieres and more choice of singers and performances than the other conductors except the GMD, and also contributes in the organizational planning of the season. A second associate conductor (*Zweite Kapellmeister*) would be third in line in the organization of conductors and their responsibilities within the opera house.

Director of the Coaching Staff (*Studienleiter*)

The director of the coaching staff (*Studienleiter*) organizes the schedules of all coaches and accompanists. This person assigns individual and ensemble rehearsals for each soloist, organizes the scheduling of all ensemble rehearsals, and is responsible for ensuring all singers have adequate preparation in diction, language, musical accuracy, and style.

The *Studienleiter* is a *Fach* expert and has the most immediate experience working, sometimes daily, with soloists. This person is often the first to notice if soloists have been assigned a role in an inappropriate *Fach* and could help them be released from this responsibility. The *Studienleiter* is also sometimes asked by the *Intendant* to suggest soloists that best match the *Fach* needed for operas projected for coming seasons. Therefore, this person can be of immense help in determining career decisions and development.

Even if a soloist already has performed in a role elsewhere, it is wise to ask the *Studienleiter* for coaching sessions so the role can be restudied to ensure any criteria of the current conductor and director are met. There are always details that can be improved, and a request for these extra sessions will add to the general perception of the soloist as a professional artist.

Coach (*Repetitor*)

A coach (*Repetitor*) is an excellent pianist who coaches the soloists. This person has the expertise to show soloists how to perfect the language, integrate the correct musical styles, and polish the operatic role to match the production requirements. This might be a very young conductor who has not yet received the chance to conduct.

Coaching sessions are planned first with individual soloists, and then with other soloists in any ensembles. Coaching sessions could also take place when the opera is revived in the second season. The coach could be a solo coach (*Solorepetitor*), one who works with soloists only, or a chorus coach (*Chorrepetitor*), who works with the chorus. The relationship between coach and soloist is critical, not only to make the learning process fun, but because there is always the possibility of being brought into a production later, when the coach has become a conductor of note. Many coaches in European houses have gone on to international careers as conductors. One such example is Arthur Fagan, who went from coach/conductor in Germany to the position of assistant conductor at the Metropolitan Opera. He now has a worldwide career as a conductor.

Many of the preeminent conductors within a house prefer to coach the soloists of operas they will be conducting. This could be during informative auditions, as a way to actually select soloists, or during actual coaching sessions later to ensure that the soloist will match their stylistic and vocal expectations. A conductor could choose to be the coach throughout the opera's learning process or only when a soloist has already learned the role and will soon be in ensemble or orchestral rehearsals. Any chance to work in any way with coaches or conductors is valuable, so take full advantage of any such possibility.

Prompters (*Souffleusen*)

Prompters (*Souffleusen*) are often retired singers, ballet dancers, or anyone with considerable musical experience and an enhanced rhythmic sense. These are well-paid positions and critical to the success of opera performances. The prompter needs excellent rhythmic skills and a voice that carries easily to soloists on the stage but is inaudible to the audience.

   This is an extremely difficult assignment. The prompter needs to be able to notice if the singer needs prompting and when. It is not a given that the prompter is continuously reading the libretto out loud. On the contrary, a good prompter knows that to some singers this is a distraction.

   If needed, the prompter speaks critical text soon enough to allow the soloist to pick up those words and continue with the song. Usually only the first word or two of the line is critical. If said too soon it is distracting, or the singer has to wait several beats and forgets the rest of the sentence. Too late and the singer has moved on. If a prompter does not respect a soloist, it is easy for this person to undermine the performance in subtle ways without jeopardizing his or her own position. On the other hand, when a soloist and the prompter respect each other, that extra bit of attention at the right time assures a secure and effective performance.

Orchestra (*Orchester*)

The size of an orchestra varies according to the size of the house. In a state-level house such as Staatstheater Kassel, the orchestra is composed of approximately 130 ensemble members. The orchestra is often augmented by extra players in the case of Wagner or Strauss operas, or if a special instrument is needed and is not covered by one of the orchestra members under contract.

   Although Americans often assume that the biggest opera houses have the best orchestra players, this is not necessarily true. There are many tremendously gifted players in even the smallest of opera house orchestras who have, for whatever reasons, remained in that position. Sometimes the sound of the orchestra is determined by the fact that the opera house owns many of the instruments. The larger houses would have the budget for more expensive instruments for their players to use, thus enhancing the sound of that orchestra.

   Orchestra members in a European opera house enjoy well-paid, respected positions. They have a set schedule and are permanently hired after their first try-out year (*Probejahr*). Often they are also members of the city's symphonic orchestra. If they are members of a large house orchestra, they also tour with the opera, make recordings of the operas (both televised and recorded), and have considerable vacation time.

   The historical division between orchestra players and singers still exists. Orchestra members are still considered by some singers as accompaniment, and some orchestra members resent the visibility and publicity given to individual soloists. This misunderstanding can be corrected by the elementary act of building respect.

   Get to know your orchestra members and let them know if they have made a significant contribution to the success of a performance. When the orchestra members respect a new soloist, this totally changes the mood of a performance. They play much more precisely and enthusiastically when they have a personal interest in what is happening on stage and can make performances extraordinarily successful and exciting by their enthusiasm and attention.

Like the stagehands, costume, and makeup people, the seasoned orchestra members have heard many singers, usually over an extremely long time. They are not easy to impress and can be judgmental of new soloists. The simple expedient of acknowledging these people and their artistic gifts provides a frame for mutually supportive relationships.

Concertmaster (*Konzertmeister*)

The concertmaster is the first chair violinist and the one who leads the tuning of the orchestra. The *Konzertmeister* also has organizational responsibilities within the orchestra and often serves as the organizer of orchestra auditions. He or she also has a major influence on who is hired or fired for the orchestra. There are also times when the concertmaster becomes the "acting conductor" during performances. This can happen if the actual conductor is a last-minute guest, or an inexperienced conductor is conducting the performance.

During a 1993 interview with John La Montaine, Pulitzer Prize–winning composer and conductor, he talked about an experience he had while he was a member of the NBC Symphony, with conductor Heitor Villa-Lobos. La Montaine described Villa-Lobos as "loving his music so much his arms would wave like a windmill. I had to play four quarter notes for maybe eight bars. And I turned to the guy, sitting next to the flute player in the orchestra, and I said, 'what shall I do? I don't know where the beat is!' And he said, 'Look around you. Do you see anyone else looking at him?' He said, 'Play with whoever's playing loudest.'" La Montaine said he never had any trouble after that![3]

If necessary, the *Konzertmeister* will indicate the tempi with bowing, or set the style and expression of the performance with body language. Sometimes even the conductor relies on this to successfully get through the performance. At other times conductors are blissfully unaware that the *Konzertmeister* is actually holding the performance together. In either case, soloists should be as aware of the concertmaster as they are of the conductor.

Opera Chorus (*Chor*)

An opera chorus, at the state opera house level, usually numbers around forty to forty-five members. This can be augmented with extra singers as the opera demands. To be a chorus member in a European opera house is not only a position of respect and importance but, after the first-year probationary period, a guaranteed job until retirement.

Ballet Company (*Ballett*)

A ballet company is part of the ensemble of an opera house, although they also have a separate schedule of performances that are eagerly attended by their fans. These dancers must be able to perform in all styles, and they have the same opportunities to guest-perform, and the same privileges and vacation schedules, as soloists, the chorus, and the orchestra.

A state-level opera house will have approximately twelve to fifteen dancers under contract. To be an ensemble dancer in an opera house is a wonderful career. Many of them start their careers at the age of fifteen and dance well into their thirties. Many careers within the house are still open to them when they decide to stop dancing. They often become prompters because of their intense musicality and rhythmic gifts. Those that can sing join the chorus or sing small roles. Others establish professional dance studios, or become choreographers. Any one of these dancers, not just the choreographer, can help the singer rehearse stage movement and learn any dances in the season's productions. Any training a soloist can find and take advantage of will improve career longevity.

OTHER COMPONENTS OF THE OPERA HOUSE

Other components of the opera house include the extras (*Statistiere*), the house photographer (*Theaterphotographie*), the drama theater (*Schauspiel*), and even the cantina (*Kantina*).

Extras (*Statistiere*)

The *Statistiere* are any extra personnel needed on stage to make a production effective. These extras usually assume nonspeaking or nonsinging roles and generally are in a group or crowd scene in an opera. Often they come from the *Schauspiel* or could even be ordinary citizens who enjoy being part of an opera.

Extras might be used to enlarge the group of soldiers in an opera like *Il trovatore* or be the palace guards in the opera *Salome*. In European houses, extras can be as young as fifteen to eighteen years of age. Hired on an as-needed basis, extras allow a production to look like it has a cast of hundreds.

Photographers (*Theaterphotographie*)

Each opera house contracts with photographers to document performances. Photography enhances opera productions in several ways. A portrait of each singer, in costume, is made to keep as examples of hair and makeup for the production so that the look can be duplicated for guest soloists or for the following season's performances. Photos can be purchased from the official house photographer to use in a portfolio, but they are usually quite expensive. Instead, have a trusted colleague take a photo, which can be used for publicity.

Photographs are taken during the final rehearsals of an opera (*Hauptproben*) and again during the dress rehearsal (*Generalprobe*). A house photographer takes photos not only of the set and the individual performers on stage, but of the general action during the opera. These are the photos that the house uses for posters, publicity, and reviews. They are also featured in programs and in the other publicity materials generated by the house, such as brochures and posters.

Soloists who are singing as guests can invite the house photographer to document their performance, and the photographer would stand at the back of the auditorium or on the side of the stage to take photos. They will sometimes do this without charging for their time, since a fee is charged when printing the photos, and they retain the copyright.

Drama Theater (*Schauspiel*)

The drama theater (*Schauspiel*) has an organization and personnel similar to the opera house. For example, it also has a director of music for the ballet, musicals, or for the occasional music used in plays.

One of the best ways to become fluent in the native language is to attend plays. Actors in the *Schauspiel* can be valuable to the American opera singer, if the singer can find an actor willing to assist with dialogue or in refining correct pronunciation. And of course, invaluable acting and directing tips can be learned from attending their performances.

Café (*Kantina*)

Even the *Kantina* (a restaurant, lunchroom, or café) in an opera house is an important area. Certain groups within the opera house ensemble have a favorite table (*Stammtisch*) for lunch or rehearsal breaks. Sometimes the *Kantina*, such as the one at the Kassel Staatstheater, is at the side of the house on the ground floor, with an outside area where employees can relax when the weather permits. Other houses have *Kantinas* that seem to need a guidebook to find them. At the Munich Opera it is necessary to go downstairs, around the lower level of the stage, downstairs again, down several halls, with a final turn into the far corner of the house complex. In any case, *Kantinas* are great places to relax for a few minutes between rehearsals, to visit with colleagues, or even to have a chance encounter with an interested *Indendant*, conductor, or director.

NOTES

1. *Deutches Bühnen Jahrbuch* (Hamburg: Genossenschaft Deutscher Bühnen-Angehöriger im Verlag der Bühenschriften-Bertriebs-Gesellschaft mbH, 2006). This book can be ordered online at www.buehnengenossenschaft.de\dtbuehnen buch.htm.

2. Alexander Sander was *Erste Kappelmeister* in Kassel, Germany, in the 1980s and went on to conduct worldwide until his death in 1999.

3. Pearl Yeadon McGinnis, *The Solo Vocal Music of American Composer John La Montaine: Compositions for Voice on Piano* (Lewiston, N.Y.: Edwin Mellen Press, 2004), 34.

6

Auditioning

Learning how to audition effectively is obviously one of the most important elements in finding a job and is invaluable later on in maintaining a career. There are many different kinds of auditions. Auditions that lead to that first job in European opera will be discussed in this chapter, and those that will help in maintaining a career will be discussed in chapter 10, "Maintaining a Career."

Many aspects of auditioning can be identified and learned beforehand, to help one audition effectively. There are other aspects that are more difficult to define, such as the ability to express personality and project an air of quiet authority and confidence.

The singer must learn to enjoy the process of auditioning, as if it were a chance to perform an actual role. Opera house directors and managers hire confidence even before voice, looks, or acting skills, so learn to be confident. After all, each individual is the only one who has that particular combination of talent, intelligence, personality, and desire.

AUDITION ARIA CRITERIA

Before auditions are even requested and arranged, the singer must prepare a selection of audition arias. Since an audition might only be long enough to present one aria, be extremely careful with this choice. The following criteria will help in the selection of the first audition aria—and all others, too.

Prepare *Fach* Representative Arias

Select arias that best represent your *Fach*. The most dangerous thing to do is to sing selections from a *Fach* category inappropriate for your age, skill level, and experience. The selection of arias should represent roles that the singer could perform immediately or with very little rehearsal.

If your arias are in a *Fach* other than the one the audition panel is seeking to fill, the audition itself could still be successful. Agents remember, even after many years, what was performed and the result of the audition. If the initial audition is successful with an agency, this could lead to a future audition with that agency or an opera house when an opening in the correct *Fach* becomes available.

Prepare the Well-Known Arias

Arias from the lesser-known operatic works may be fine for concerts, or as preparation for some future performance possibility, but are uninteresting to agents and opera houses at auditions. They would rather hear ten sopranos sing "Un bel di" from Puccini's *Madama Butterfly* than have someone perform "Suicidio" from Ponchielli's *La Gioconda*, an opera that is rarely produced. Agents and opera houses want to compare each new singer's voice, physical attributes, personality, and *Fach* appropriateness with everyone else. This way they can see which person would have the best chance to compete for a specific role, such as Mimi in Puccini's *La bohème*, for example.

In the following example of audition selections, the soprano is auditioning first in her primary *Fach* as a lyric soprano. Then, since it is also acceptable to offer a few arias in one or more neighboring *Fach* categories, she has listed some of the *Jugendlich*-dramatic and lyric coloratura roles and representative arias.

Primary *Fach*: Lyric Soprano

"Signore, ascolta," Liù, *Turandot*

"Ach, ich fühl's," Pamina, *Die Zauberflöte*

"Marietta's Lied zur Laute," Marietta, *Die tote Stadt*

Heavier *Fach*: Young (Jugendlich) Dramatic Soprano

"Dove sono," Countess, *Le nozze di Figaro*

"Wie nahte mir die Schlummer," Agathe, *Der Freischütz*

"Si, mi chiamano Mimi," Mimi, *La bohème*

Lighter *Fach*: Lyric-Coloratura Soprano

"No word from Tom," Anne, *The Rake's Progress*

Several things are immediately noticeable about the soprano who would list the above arias for her audition. By choosing selections from *Turandot*, *Die Zauberflöte*, and *Le nozze di Figaro*, she is announcing a mastery of lyric, long-line singing. Also, Marietta's solo in *Die tote Stadt* requires the expertise to float exquisite lines. Her choices of the arias sung by the Countess, Pamina, and Liù also suggests she prefers more tragic-elegant personalities rather than comic-energetic. Mimi's aria from *La bohème* suggests that she can sing the long-line lyric passages and is comfortable acting passionate scenes.

By listing Anne's aria from *The Rake's Progress*, this soprano is indicating that she has a flexible, agile voice capable of effective coloratura passages.

By listing two arias from operas containing significant dialogue—*Der Freischütz* and *Die Zauberflöte*—she is also indicating that she is comfortable with spoken German. And she hasn't even sung yet.

Make It Sound Easy

A major consideration when selecting the first audition arias is that they must appear to be easy to sing. This statement is more complex than it seems. Dr. Nandor Domokos, opera coach in Los Angeles and former director of the Opera Department at St. Louis Institute of Music in 1949, advised, "Sing whatever it is that you can sing if someone wakes you up at midnight and you have to leap out of bed and sing immediately."[1]

Easy to sing does not necessarily mean that the aria would technically be the easiest aria. But it needs to sound like it was easy. A wonderful example of this was lyric-coloratura soprano Judith Blegen. While singing at the Metropolitan Opera from 1970 until her retirement in 1991, Blegen frequently appeared on *The Tonight Show* with Johnny Carson. She always sang, and Carson always remarked how easy she made it sound.

The first audition aria needs to be one that has been prepared carefully. If long, lyric lines are your forte, select this type of aria. If it is easy to sing high notes but not comfortable to remain in a high tessitura, then select an aria that has a few high notes to show range but has the bulk of the aria in the middle or lower range of voice. Although no single aria can show everything about an individual voice, careful selection of the initial aria can help make auditioning pleasurable and successful.

Keep It Short

Short arias are best for auditions. Be sure, however, that the aria is long enough to demonstrate the voice's particular skills and range and has enough drama to imply potential as an actor. The short aria "Di rigori" from Strauss's *Der Rosenkavalier* is often criticized as a poor choice for an audition aria, because just as soon as the tenor gets going, it is over. On the other hand, the beautiful strophic aria for tenor from Massenet's *Werther*, "Pourquoi me reveiller," although only two verses, lasts long enough and demands enough passionate vocalism and high notes to be a convincing first audition aria.

The soprano aria "Ah forse lui" from Verdi's *La traviata*, plus the cabaletta, is considered a long aria and not usually recommended for agent auditions. However, it is effective as an audition aria for an opera house because its vocal dangers are well known. This is because it contains both a lyric/passionate section and the dramatic fireworks of the cabaletta. A soprano who can sing this aria effectively and easily would be demonstrating her expertise in the dramatic coloratura *Fach* and would probably have an excellent chance of being hired.

Make It Enjoyable

Having fun singing the aria is also of utmost importance. Many singers pick an aria because it is impressive or technically difficult. Instead, always select an aria that is enjoyable to sing and one where the voice feels as fresh at the end as at the beginning. If it is obvious at the end of the aria that the singer is vocally or physically tired, the audition will not be successful, no matter how well the aria was performed.

Agents and opera houses are looking for soloists who can sing for long periods of time. The comfort level demonstrated while auditioning, especially when performing more than one aria, will go a long way to convincing the agent that the voice can be maintained throughout an entire season.

An example was a young soprano's first audition in Vienna for Herr Docktor Raab of the prestigious Raab Agency. After the soprano had sung four *Jugendlich-dramatischer* arias in a row, Dr. Raab said she had sung a wonderful audition. But then he added that he wouldn't know if she could "really sing" until she had performed at least thirty Agathes (*Der Freischütz*), twenty-five First Ladys (*Die Zauberflöte*), and thirty Toscas every year for at least two seasons. He was correct. Singing a few arias does not prove one can survive a season.[2]

Have the Role Prepared

This magical first aria also has to represent a role that could be performed immediately and often. By singing that first aria, the singer is announcing that this is the preferred *Fach*, the favorite role in that *Fach*, the preferred tessitura, and the most enjoyable style, as well as something that could be performed now. If the audition is successful, it could lead immediately to an offer to perform that role.

Portray It Dramatically

The aria should be portrayed in a manner to suggest that the role has been performed on stage, even if that is not yet the case. *Intendant* Klaus Schultz, in a lecture to University of Illinois voice students, pointed out the limitations of auditions: "There are no arias specifically composed for auditions that would show the range of voice, personality, and acting abilities. Auditions don't show how one can act or move on stage."[3] Therefore, auditioning singers should do their best to demonstrate their acting ability as they sing their audition aria, but this does not mean that everything is "acted out" or pantomimed. However, the actions of the singer while performing the aria have to clearly indicate what drama is taking place. For example: Siebel in Gounod's *Faust* can pantomime picking a flower or dipping her fingers in a bowl of holy water. Manon in Puccini's *Manon Lescaut* does not have to lie down on the floor to successfully dramatize the aria "Sola, perduta, abbandonata," which is usually staged with Manon prostrate and dying. However, during an audition this state of exhaustion and desperation can be portrayed through body posture and the emotion conveyed by the voice. Schultz cautioned, "What is most important in an audition is to introduce your voice. Don't try to act too much, but show temperament whenever possible."[4]

Demonstrate Confidence

The final criteria to having a successful audition is to pick a first audition aria that will project confidence. This comes from selecting an aria that is easy to sing and allows the musical and vocal qualities of the voice, as well as the singer's personality and energy, to show. Agents know that opera houses seek confident, secure soloists and look for this quality in the singers they choose to represent.

A colleague, who sang fabulously, was asked to sing twelve arias in a row for an opera house audition in Germany. After the twelfth, she finally asked the panel, "Is this an audition or a concert?" (*"Singe ich ein Vorsinger oder ein Konzert?"*) She was hired.

Obviously, being asked to sing multiple selections indicates the panel was interested. She found out later that the house audition panel initially did not like her physical appearance but was obviously impressed enough with her voice, and her confidence, to have her sing that many selections.

Be Able to Sing It Frequently

The final factor in selecting audition arias is whether the roles listed could be performed frequently without taxing the voice of the singer. For example, a lyric soprano who auditions with *erste Partien* arias from *Turandot*, *Der Freischütz*, and *The Rake's Progress* and is hired could be performing all three during a one-week period. *Turandot* might be the Monday night performance, *Der Freischütz* on Wednesday, and *The Rake's Progress* on Saturday. Fortunately, soloists seldom perform more than three leading roles within one week and are not required to sing operas on back-to-back evenings.

To summarize, use the following formula in selecting the first audition aria:

Fach appropriate + well known + easy to sing + short + enjoyable + represents a prepared role + is dramatically portrayed + shows confidence + can be frequently sung.

TYPING IN OR OUT

Of course, the first impression the audition panel has about a singer is based on what they see—the singer's looks, including his or her height and weight. As a result, the auditioning opera singer is often "typed in or out" of a role almost as rigidly as typecasting in musical theater.

A singer may meet vocal requirements of her or his primary *Fach* category but may not possess the physical attributes implied by the role, nor meet the director's conception of the part. The agent or the committee, which often includes the costume designer, is always thinking about how the singer would portray the role, wear the costumes, and move on stage. Therefore, it is not wise to sing one of Mimi's arias from *La bohème* if significantly overweight. Klaus Schultz also addressed this issue in his lecture when he said: "Weight is a definite problem. During an audition I often think, how would I cast that voice?"

Gone are the days that led to the stereotype of the full-figured female opera singer in a horned helmet with a spear in her hand. As David Glockley, general director of the San Francisco Opera, said in a 2006 interview, "We find ourselves in an increasingly visual driven age."[5] As a result, some very famous opera singers have been told they must lose weight to continue being cast in their favorite roles. Soprano Deborah Voigt is a good example and a recent success story. Fired by London's Royal Opera because she was too large for her costume in Richard Strauss's *Ariadne auf Naxos*, she lost 150 pounds before starring in the San Francisco Opera's

2006 production of Verdi's *Un ballo in maschera*.[6] Soprano Maria Callas (1923–1977) was very heavy before she lost weight and subsequently became the mistress of Aristotle Onassis.

Typing in or out is not restricted to simply the singer's height and weight. It is the overall impression by the audition committee that a singer does not match the implied physicality of the *Fach*. That is to say, a soubrette soprano should look like a sweet young thing. This is a very hard thing for a six-foot-tall, full-figured soprano to pull off, and even some more petite singers might not project the desired attributes.

A colleague with less-than-petite physical attributes, auditioning at a city opera house in Germany for a role as a dramatic soprano in an Italian opera, was told that she had sung quite wonderfully. However, they said they were "seeking someone more Italian looking." She quite coolly looked at the assistant and replied, "Don't you make wigs in your house?"

Agents, too, are acutely aware of the physical impression a singer will make when they send them to an opera house audition. The following translation of a passage in a letter from a German agent illustrates this point, which is as pertinent today as when the letter was written:

"How is your figure? It is known to you that today in the German stage world, they are looking for young, slim people, and only a very few full-figured voices are hired. . . . In your profession . . . the way you look is very important."

It is unusual for an agent to take even this much interest in a young singer and to offer personal advice of this sort. Agents will usually just move on to the next singer in the *Fach* category who more closely meets the physical criteria the house is looking for.

Exceptions

There are always exceptions to "typing in or out." Singing beautifully, passionately, easily, and with confidence is sometimes enough, and there are many success stories that attest to this. The late tenor Luciano Pavarotti is a well-known example of a singer who struggled with his weight. Fortunately for Pavarotti, and those who love opera, his size was no deterrent to his career.

That first impression, to the agent, audition panel, and even to the audience, is less important as a singer becomes known in the business for his or her portrayal of certain roles. By that time the performer's ability to put together a vocal and dramatic presentation becomes more important, even if the singer is not the typical shape or size for that role. Again, Pavarotti is a good example.

PUBLICITY MATERIALS

Publicity materials are an important part of preparing for an audition. Standard publicity materials include a one-page résumé, listing all pertinent information and experience, and a good photo. Although a publicity photo in the United States is eight by ten inches, in Europe these photos are the size of a typical postcard, approximately four by six inches. Black-and-white photos or color are both acceptable. The photo can be either a head shot or a performance photo. What is most important is that it show personality, energy, and confidence.

The résumé should ideally be one page long and include, first, the phone number where one can be reached at all times, and then the address. It is not necessary to list height, weight, and hair or eye color. List operas performed and where, roles in preparation, and musical education, including names of important vocal teachers or coaches. Oratorio roles and concert repertoire can also be listed.

Sample Résumé Information

Name
Telephone, fax, e-mail
Permanent address
European address (if applicable)
Opera companies (list as paragraph)
Opera repertoire (* if a world premiere)

(composer)   *(opera)   (role)

Oratorio and symphonic repertoire

(composer)   (composition)   (role/voice)

Conductors (significant conductors: opera, symphony, oratorio)
Stage directors (significant stage directors: opera, musicals)
Recordings/CDs (if applicable)
Voice teachers and vocal coaches

AUDITION REQUEST

Now that the audition arias and publicity materials are prepared, it's time to request an audition. Start with established agencies first. (See appendix A, "Agencies.") Communication can be by e-mail, fax, or letter; however, many agencies will not respond to an e-mail or fax, other than to state the requirements to put in your letter and information as to whether they are listening to auditions at that time.

The letter does not have to be long. It should include your request for an audition; a statement of your primary *Fach*, plus a list of a few roles that you have performed; information on how long you plan to stay in Europe; and the best week or weeks to audition for that specific agency. Be sure to include all the contact information, including a permanent address and, if possible, an address where you could be reached in Europe. This communication should be in English, unless you are fluent in German.

Include publicity materials (résumé and photo) with the letter. When sending a request for an audition, do not send a video, CD, or cassette, unless specifically requested to do so. The opera house's website will often have information regarding what they will or will not accept.

Send your audition request four to six months in advance of when you hope to go to Europe. Auditions are held all during the opera season, which runs from September until early July. When planning to audition in Europe during the fall audition season, a request letter should be sent to agencies by the beginning of the previous May at the latest. Agencies take summer vacations and have a reduced number of personnel in the office during this time. If an agency does not receive the request for a fall audition until August or later, it might not be able to accommodate the singer.

A self-addressed envelope for the agency's reply should be included. Agencies will send a postcard or letter as an answer, with the date and time of your audition.

Synopsis: Audition Request Letter, Fax, or E-mail

- Your name, telephone number, American address, European address (if applicable), fax, and e-mail
- Your primary *Fach*, plus a brief description of roles performed and roles studied
- Your vocal training, names of coaches, and any important conductors
- Length of time you will spend in Europe
- Week of preferred audition

THE AUDITION TOUR

An American considering an audition tour in Europe should concentrate on the German-speaking countries of Austria, Germany, and Switzerland, because these countries are the most receptive to hiring nonnative opera singers. Although auditions take place during the entire season, the autumn months attract the most aspiring singers. The most effective audition tour would be between August and December.

Allow plenty of time for the audition tour, as much as two months. It can sometimes take a week just to audition for several agencies in one city. For example, if you were planning on auditioning in Vienna one week, your next week's auditions could be scheduled for Munich, the following week Frankfurt, then Düsseldorf, then Hamburg, and perhaps Berlin that same week. Two months go by very rapidly when attempting to sing for all the agencies even within one country such as Germany.

An audition schedule is helped by the fact that agencies in the same city do not hold their auditions on the same day—that is to say, their "open auditions" would not be on the same day. For example, if an audition can be arranged for the Stoll agency in Munich on a Monday and the Hilbert agency in Vienna on Thursday of that same week, there would still be time in between to audition for some of the private agents in these areas.

Travel plans need to stay flexible. Any one audition for an agency demands at least a couple of days' time. Travel to the audition at least the day before. The audition may take most of a day, and then you will need time to travel back to your home base or on to the next city or area. An important tip: if at any time you are offered an audition in a house, accept and change any other plans for agency auditions that would conflict with the house audition.

TRANSPORTATION, LUGGAGE, CLOTHES, MUSIC, DOCUMENTS

If planning on auditioning primarily in the German-speaking countries, Frankfurt or Munich would be the most efficient destination for an airline ticket. Flights to these airports are often the least expensive tickets because of the high volume of traffic. All other destinations in Europe are easily accessed by train from either of these airports.

The most efficient way to travel within Europe is to purchase some form of Eurail train ticket. For a relatively small amount, you can travel easily and comfortably with a ticket designed to match your length of stay in Europe. For additional information on Eurail tickets, see chapter 11, "Living in Europe," or access "Eurail tickets" online.

Resist the temptation to take too much luggage, but a raincoat and umbrella should be included. Include two audition outfits and casual clothes with comfortable shoes for travel. One medium-size rolling suitcase is plenty, especially when this has to be lifted in and out of trains and carried up and down stairs.

Place audition arias in a folder in your suitcase, and be sure the music is legible and easy to read for the accompanist. Anything else that might become necessary can be purchased during the tour.

Be sure to arrange for a passport well in advance of any trip, and make sure your existing passport is valid for six months beyond your return date. This is a new requirement since 9/11/2001. Make a copy of the passport and all other personal documents, and keep these in a place other than a suitcase, briefcase, or purse. In case the passport is stolen or lost, the copy will help get a replacement quickly. Hotel desks have safes, as do many rooms.

Visas are not necessary in any of the European Union countries. For a list of countries that require a visa, ask the passport office.

When you get to Europe, the ideal situation would be to stay with a friend and use this as a home base. Otherwise, a bed-and-breakfast hotel (pension) will have the best prices. An easy way to find a hotel room is to go to the hotel office at the train station. They will also book it for you and show you on a map how to find it. It is also possible to sleep in a train while traveling, although not very comfortably.

Synopsis: The Audition Tour

- Send requests for fall auditions by May 1.
- Audition for agencies first, unless a house audition is offered.
- Secure passport, airline ticket, Eurail ticket.
- Pack audition outfits, comfortable shoes, and clothes for travel.
- Pack folder of audition arias.

AUDITION ATTIRE AND APPEARANCE

What is worn to that first audition is part of the impression a singer makes on the audition panel. The best advice is to wear something simple, moderately dressy, and which focuses all the attention on the face.

For women this should be a dress of one color that flatters the figure without being too tight or obviously sexy. A dress that falls just below the knees is preferred, but not full length. A dress with sleeves is best. Sleeveless is not recommended, since the attention is then directed to the upper arm instead of the face. A simple neckline, not too deep, is best, as this also focuses attention on the face and eyes.

Shoes should be comfortable low heels or flats. If the first aria is successful, it might be necessary to perform three or four or more arias in a row, so being able to stand comfortably for a long period is important. The same care should be given when selecting jewelry. Remember that anything too decorative, such as a brightly colored belt on a dark dress, or a fancy collar, attracts attention and detracts from your face. However, wearing one piece of obviously good jewelry, a ring or watch or pin, can add to the general impression of confidence and style.

An exception to the dress rule would be mezzo-sopranos or lyric coloratura sopranos specializing in pants roles (*Hosen Partien*). These sopranos can successfully audition wearing loose slacks color-coordinated with a blouse or sweater, since it suggests the roles in this *Fach*. An outfit should still be selected that sets off, rather than conceals, the waist.

Men have a choice between auditioning in a casual suit or in slacks and a nice shirt or a sweater. A tie is optional and depends on the singer's comfort level. Most singers do not like any sort of pressure around the throat when they sing.

Generally speaking, jeans and scruffy shoes and shirts are not indicative of a professional singer. However, every rule has exceptions. A friend, who is a well-known tenor, wore baggy, ripped jeans, old tennis shoes, and an old shirt to an audition for an important German house. In this case, even before he sang, the *Intendant* turned to the general music director and said, "That's my tenor!" The friend was never sure if this was because the *Intendant* thought his tall and robust build matched the *Fach* he would be performing, or because dressing in such a casual manner projected confidence. (It was probably the former.) Although in this case he was hired, as a general rule the sloppy, unkempt look is not recommended.

Synopsis: Audition Attire

Women

- Simple, below-the-knee dress with sleeves
- Simple neckline
- One color
- Comfortable flats or low heels

Men

- Suit or slacks and nice shirt
- Tie optional
- Nice, comfortable shoes

The first rule of hair, for both men and women, is to style it so the face and expressions can be clearly seen. This is very important! Hair should not cover the eyes or part of the face in any manner. The audition committee wants to see dramatic expression in the face and eyes when the singer is auditioning and be able to imagine different styles of makeup and costuming.

Makeup can be used to enhance the appearance, especially when auditioning for a house and the audition is taking place on stage. However, it should never be obvious. It should only help make one look fresh or healthy. Even men could benefit from a bit of base makeup to even out their complexion so they don't look pale under the stage lights.

Note: the fake-eyelash look for women is never used in Europe for auditions.

AGENT AUDITIONS

Agencies in Europe have open auditions on specified days each month. Some agencies have an audition date each week, although most do not. Each agency needs to be contacted separately with an audition request. As opera singers in Europe have contracts facilitated by more than one agent, it is necessary to audition for as many agencies as possible, especially during the first audition tour. Auditions must be set up in advance, several months before a proposed audition tour.

The first audition for a new singer in Europe should be for an established agency. In Germany, one of the most important agencies is the Stoll agency in Munich. Stoll prefers that new singers have not yet sung for other agents. As a general principle, it does not matter which agency is contacted or in what order, except for this agency. They want to be first! In addition to the Stoll agency, there are many other agencies and private agents in Munich, so if possible spend the first audition tour week in this lovely city.

Be honest with agents if asked whether an audition has already taken place for another agency. Agents remain in constant contact with one another. They often cooperate with an agency that is the primary agent for opera houses in another area and share information about new singers. Sing for agents first.

Punctuality

Be on time! The agency will have suggested either a specific time slot or indicate that auditions begin at a certain time. In this latter case, an individual appointment time can be secured when arriving at the agency. Anyone who is late to an audition risks losing the chance to audition on that day. Professionals are expected to be on time. Be sure to build in enough time in the travel schedule to allow for problems, and make every effort to be early.

Prior to the audition it will be necessary to fill out an information sheet for the agency. Unless fluent in the language of the country, use English. Fill out all the forms in English, with the exception of listing *Fach* with the correct German title. Be careful of what is listed on the form, because this becomes a permanent file. If there is a charge for the accompanist, it is paid at this time. After the requisite forms are filled out, return these to the assistant and then wait patiently. Do not leave the building or the waiting area.

The Waiting Room

There are no spaces to warm up at an agency. The restroom should not be used as a warm-up space. This will bring an angry secretary out of the office and produce a strong admonition to be quiet. Professionals are expected to be already warmed up prior to reaching the agency and to be ready to sing, even after having waited several hours without making a sound.

During an agency audition there will be many other people also waiting, and everyone can usually hear the auditions taking place. Resist the temptation to speak or chat with the other singers. This could tire the voice and create an atmosphere of tension and competition. As much as possible, stay quiet, read, or simply focus on audition preparation. After the audition it will be possible to talk to new acquaintances, if desired. It is fun to meet fellow Americans, even in these situations. These might become future colleagues.

The Audition

Auditioning at an agency usually takes place in a small room that has an upright piano and one or more people sitting at a desk. Acoustics are usually poor. Some agents sit with a window at their back or a lamp behind them, which makes their expression hard to see. This is deliberate. The agent wants to be able to study the singer's expressions, physical technique, and breathing. Agents come into these positions from within the business and are often former singers, so they are well aware of which singers are secure vocally and technically.

The agent, and any others in the room, will give the singer their entire attention. This is a serious business and represents a future investment on the part of the agent. Sometimes the assistant agent will be the one in the room, while the primary agent listens from an adjoining room. This is done to see if the voice carries at a distance and to see if the voice retains power and beauty even through walls and doors. The vocal impression a singer makes when only a few feet away from the agent is often a false one. A voice that is large and beautiful close up may not carry across the stage, through the orchestra, or to the farthest reaches of the house.

When it is time to audition, give the agent the photo and résumé and a list of audition arias. Sometimes the secretary or assistant has collected this material prior to the audition and will hand it to the agent or the panel. Then give the music to the accompanist. This person is usually provided by the agency, or the singer could bring her own. Even though the agent now has the materials, introduce yourself and announce which aria will be performed first. Be prepared to sing several arias without a break or even a drink of water.

Language

Unless fluent in German, speak English. Short, polite phrases are acceptable, such as *vielen Dank* (thank you) or *Wiedersehen* (good-bye), or even introducing an aria in German. For example, "Ich möchte zuerst 'Un bel di' singen." ("I would first like to sing 'Un bel di.'") Be careful with this, because the agent might then begin speaking German to you, and you would need to be prepared to reply somehow or other.

It is not necessary, nor any kind of an advantage, to speak fluent German when auditioning. It is only important that you can *sing* in fluent German, Italian, or French, or whatever the language is of the arias you choose.

Sometimes, when the primary agent is listening from an adjoining room, the phone will ring, and the agents will confer with each other while the singer continues performing. This could be at any time during the audition. This will not be a business call from outside the agency, as the other people in the office will handle such calls during auditions. The call will be from the primary agent in the other room. Assume it is positive interest and keep singing.

Most agents do not like to be watched during the audition, so do not look at the agents while singing. Look elsewhere or over the agent's head. The singer's job is not to see if the agent is paying attention but rather to pretend to be on stage, in costume and makeup, actually performing an opera. The agent's room becomes the set, the walls disappear, and the singer visualizes the action.

If an agent likes what is being presented during the audition, his or her first thought likely is, "How long can I represent this singer?" All other factors being equal—looks, voice, presentation, and experience—agencies want to represent the most confident person and the most representative of any *Fach* opening. Agencies also tend to be more interested in unknown singers who are young, under thirty-five, because this means there will be a longer period for the agency to earn money through this singer and a greater chance that this person will develop into a highly paid performer in great demand.

After the Agency Audition

When an audition for an agent is completed, the first question singers will be asked is how long will they be in Europe. The agent might immediately produce a list of dates and times for opera house auditions, or might tell the singer to get back in contact with the agency later. Never assume that the latter is a brush-off. It could just be that there are no house audition possibilities at that time.

It is sometimes impossible to tell if an agency audition was successful. Agents usually will not offer any kind of critique or review of the audition and will have no comments other than to possibly offer an opportunity to audition for a house.

After the audition, formally thank the agent for the opportunity to sing and also thank any assistants and secretaries. And don't forget the accompanist. Go to this person, shake his or her hand, and offer your personal thanks. Not only is this an indication of professionalism, but one never knows if this person is a coach in an important house, perhaps even a conductor, or even another agent.

Professionalism is demonstrated by the way the singer handles the audition, as well as the acknowledgment of the time and trouble the agency personnel have taken to listen to a new person perform. Any future relationship with an agency depends partially on building a successful relationship with these people. Politeness goes a long way in the business!

The Successful Agency Audition

If the agency audition is successful, the agent will give the singer a list of potential house auditions. This could be in the form of a card or list you sign for, which obligates you to accept auditions in those houses only through this particular agent. It may simply be a form with the house listed, the *Fach* or role listed, or a specific audition date and time. Or the agent might ask the singer to call back later to get the specific time.

A successful agency audition might result in a more immediate additional audition, called an "informative audition," which takes place in an opera house. This could be for one of two reasons: either there is a vacancy for the singer's *Fach* in that house, or the agent has an agreement with the *Intendant* to arrange these informative auditions for potential singers to determine the actual size of voice and effectiveness of the singer on a real stage. In that case the *Intendant* will report these details back to the agent.

If there is an actual vacancy in the opera house, the agent will give the singer a note or letter with a date and a time for the house audition. Accept any such offer and change any previous plans. If there are other obligations that conflict with this day and time, *do not mention or discuss these with the agent*. Informative opera house auditions through an agency are rare, so accept and deal with the other obligations later.

Follow-up

If asked by the agent to contact the agency again, do so on a regular basis. It is a good idea to stay in touch, not only to ask if there are any new audition possibilities, but to build a relationship. Even if the agent or secretary seems to be irritated by frequent calls, keep in contact. Persistence is another key to success in the opera world.

Synopsis: Agent Auditions

- Be on time.
- Fill out required forms carefully in English.
- Come warmed up.
- Wait quietly without chatting.
- Give résumé, photo, and audition list to the agent or panel.
- Pay the accompanist, if applicable.
- Sing *Fach*-appropriate repertoire as if on stage.
- Thank the agent or panel and the accompanist.
- Thank the assistants and secretaries.
- Follow any instructions for informative house auditions.
- Stay in contact with the agency.

State Agency Auditions

The German State Agency (Zentrale Bühnen Vermittlung), usually referred to by the initials ZBF, has a complete list of opera house vacancies as they come open. ZBF is usually the last agency to be visited by Americans and often the first to offer a new singer an opportunity to audition for a house. This is the agency that handles all chorus, orchestra, and accompanist openings, as well as soloists. It has the same ability to offer a singer a job opportunity, though not considered as important or as prestigious. All the agents in this agency are polite, interested in Americans, and helpful. The audition process is the same as for the well-known agencies.

Private Agents

There are a number of private agents in Europe. These agents have their own individual relationships with specific houses. Some of these agents specialize in concert performances, a venue that should not be overlooked when looking for a job and additional experience on your résumé. The audition process is the same. Also, if the audition is successful, some of the private agents might have more time to discuss the audition with the singer, as well as any career possibilities. The American seeking a first job in Europe should consider every opportunity to audition, including these private agencies. (See appendix A for a listing of agencies.)

Agents' Fees

The agent who arranges a contract with an opera house has the right to receive 12 percent of the singer's salary for up to a year. Fifty percent of this is paid by the house and fifty percent by the singer. The singer's half is withheld from the singer's paycheck, by the theater, and sent in as part of the total 12 percent. This is the usual fee for Germany, Austria, and Switzerland. There is one exception—at the Vienna State Opera, singers pay the total fee to the agent.[7]

Agencies can ask for as much as 15 percent of the salary for an engagement as a concert soloist or as a guest for an opera house. The singer pays the whole fee. If the singer arranges contracts through a private agent, the actual amount of agent's fee is negotiable. Private agents don't arrange contracts for chorus positions. If contracts are obtained through the ZBF, no fee is assessed.

OPERA HOUSE AUDITIONS

Opera houses most often arrange their auditions through agencies. Certain agents have more influence than others with specific houses. However, even some of the largest houses will invite singers directly to their informative auditions if they are interested enough in a potential soloist's letter and résumé. This does not mean that they are actively interested in finding someone in the representative *Fach* at that time. However, if the roles indicated in the singer's résumé are of interest for future seasons, an opera house might invite that person for an audition. Therefore, if your performance experience is impressive enough, it is certainly worthwhile to contact opera houses directly, in hopes of receiving an invitation to one of these informative auditions.

The singer is expected to cover all costs for this type of house informative audition, including travel, hotel, and food during the stay in that city. The accompanist will be provided by the opera house. However, if an agent made the appointment for the opera house audition and has prearranged for the singer to be paid for all or part of the expenses, this will have been communicated to the singer prior to the audition. If this is the case, the singer must report to the appropriate house business office following the audition to collect the reimbursement.

A specific time for the audition is usually assigned through the agent. But if the audition time is not individually assigned, it is possible to sign up for a specific slot when you arrive at the opera house. If you have a specific time slot, be on time! This cannot be stressed enough. If you arrive late for any reason, the audition time might be given to someone else, and the agent will be notified. A professional is expected to show up early enough for the audition to allow for any adjustment in audition times.

When you arrive at the opera house, there will be someone assigned to show you where to warm up and how to find the stage or wherever the audition will take place. Give the photo, résumé, and list of audition arias to the assistant. (Note: the singer does not usually receive any of the forms or photos back, so make sure you have enough copies.)

The assistant will take each person auditioning to a rehearsal or practice room. You will not usually have a chance to work with an accompanist before the audition. Warming up is the only chance to exercise the voice prior to the audition, so use this time wisely. Sometimes the actual audition will be as much as several hours away.

The Waiting Area

Once you have warmed up, you will be directed to a waiting room or area. In an opera house, this could be a room close to the main stage, filled with all the other people who are auditioning on that date. It could also be the hallway right outside the stage.

A friend was invited to audition in Düsseldorf, Germany, for a dramatic soprano role. When she was taken to the waiting area, she realized that dramatic baritones were also being auditioned. At least twenty-five dramatic sopranos and dramatic baritones were wandering up and down the hall, mumbling to themselves and making strange gestures and sounds while waiting to audition. Everyone ignores everyone else.

Chatting among singers would be unusual, as all are seeking the concentration and energy to perform effectively. Waiting in the wings and watching the other auditions is not allowed. Sometimes a singer will be told to go to the stage while the prior person is still singing, in order to make the audition process more efficient for the audition panel. Wait quietly just offstage until announced or requested to go on stage.

It might be necessary to remain in the waiting room or hall for a considerable amount of time—as long as five hours. It is not proper procedure to
leave this area to go eat, get a drink, or warm up again. Bring water with
you. Restrooms are usually in the immediate area, but any other absence
will be considered a cancellation of that audition.

The Audition Space

Opera house auditions are usually, but not always, held on the main
stage. The stage could be bare or could contain the set for a rehearsal or
a performance. Other people from the opera house could be standing
in the wings listening to the audition. Sometimes some of the audition
panel is backstage or in the wings to check demeanor, nerves, and professionalism. If a singer is a "bitch" or otherwise unprofessional backstage,
everyone will know this immediately.

The *Intendant* is almost always present, as well as the general music
director. Often the panel will also consist of other conductors, coaches,
and possibly stage directors, as well as costume and makeup personnel.
This is especially true if the audition is in a huge house such as Vienna
or Munich.

One benefit of singing on stage is that it is easier to simulate an actual
performance. Although a stage audition is usually limited to standing in
one place and performing with limited movement, the larger space makes
it easier to create the feeling of an actual performance. Another comfort-
ing fact is that the singer has already been preselected for this audition by
an agency and knows the house is already interested.

The Audition

After giving the assistant the music to take to the accompanist, walk to
the middle of the stage. If the singer is expected to give the music to the
accompanist, this is a good chance to shake his or her hand and offer your
thanks. Remember, the accompanist could be one of the major conductors
in the house. Also, if you are hired, this will be a new colleague, so it is
wise to begin a professional, respectful relationship as soon as possible.

Find a space on stage that seems comfortable, but not too close to the
edge of the stage. Somewhere just behind the proscenium arch is best. If
stage lights are on, seek out the best light and stand in the hot spot.

At the end of the first aria, someone in the panel will say "Thank you,"
at which point, if there are no follow-up questions or requests to sing an
additional aria, respond with your own "Thank you" and leave the stage.

A reminder about language: as with agent auditions, if you are not fluent in German, use English. Trying to speak in German will only invite

the *Intendant*, or anyone else on the panel, to respond in German with questions about your length of stay, travel plans, arias prepared, and so on. *Intendant* Hellmuth Matiasek told the following story to anyone who would listen:

> A young man was auditioning for an opening and introduced himself in German. At that point I asked the singer [in German] how long he would be remaining in Europe. The singer answered in poorly accented German. I continued to ask questions, which the young man attempted to answer in increasingly fractured German. Finally, after an uncomfortable pause, I said *vielen Dank* [thank you very much], and my assistant led the bewildered singer off the stage. He never got to sing a note.[8]

If German is used by the audition panel during an audition and not understood, simply admit that you are still learning German, and everyone will switch to English. Never pretend to speak a language or pretend to understand what is being asked of you, because this won't be successful.

After the House Audition

If the panel was sufficiently impressed with the audition, the singer might be asked to wait. If so, someone from the house will be sent to talk to the singer with comments about the audition, a request to return for another audition at a later date, or an invitation to go to the *Intendant*'s office to discuss a contract. If the opera house has an opera studio, and the singer matches the age range for participation—usually only up to age thirty—an offer to join the studio might be extended.[9] Even if the singer leaves without a contract, the audition could have been successful. This will be communicated to the singer later, through the agent.

Experienced singers always allow for some time in their schedule following any audition, in case they are asked to stay. Even if there is no contract offered, a member of the panel might have questions or specific comments about the audition. This kind of attention is a good sign. Report all details back to the agent. There is every possibility that the opera house will be interested in another audition at a later date.

Following the house audition, make sure you contact the agent or agency and give them all the details about the audition, such as how many arias were performed and if there were any follow-up comments or questions.

The Successful House Audition

If the *Intendant* has decided to offer a contract, the singer will be invited to follow the assistant to the *Intendant*'s office or a meeting room. Any contract offer will be described, including the type of contract and length of time, such as a contract in the lyric soprano *Fach* for two years. Possible roles will be communicated. No mention of money is made at this point.

Resist the temptation to immediately sign a contract. Verbally accept the offer, thank the *Intendant* and any others present, say politely that your agent will be in touch, and then leave. There is no worry that the offer will be withdrawn. In Germany, an oral offer is as good as a written contract. After leaving, contact your agent immediately with the good news. The agent will then contact the *Intendant* and work out all the details and send the contract to the singer to sign. Then all the singer has to do is show up at the new house at the specified date and with the role or roles already learned. Congratulations!

Synopsis: House Auditions

- Be on time.
- Fill out any required forms carefully.
- Warm up carefully.
- Wait.
- Give résumé, photo, and audition list to the assistant or panel.
- Sing *Fach*-appropriate repertoire
- Thank the *Intendant* or panel and the accompanist.

If Not Asked to Wait:	If Asked to Wait:
Thank everyone, and then leave	Wait in indicated space
Report back to the agency with all details	Enjoy any discussion
	Verbally accept any contract
	Contact agent
	Celebrate!

OTHER TYPES OF AUDITIONS

Guest Contract/Time Contract (*Gastvertrag/Teilvertrag*)

Sometimes an agent will send a singer to a house to audition as a guest singer for a specific role (*Gastvertrag*) or to fill a needed *Fach* category for a specified time (*Teilvertrag*). The procedure is almost the same as for an informative house audition, with only a few exceptions. The audition will probably be for the stage director and the conductor of the opera or operas for which they are seeking a soloist. The audition may be on the main stage but often is in a rehearsal room. The audition committee will expect to hear an aria or arias from the opera or operas being cast.

These *Gastvertrag* auditions are to select the singer who best fits the role. The stage director and conductor already know the competing singers have the required *Fach* for the role. They now are looking for the ideal face, figure, and actor for the role—that is, "the complete package." Sometimes other singers, already cast in roles in the opera, are present at the audition. They might be asked to sing one of the duets from the opera or to stand next to the person auditioning, so that the stage director can check height and physical build with the potential partner. But sometimes there are exceptions to the above.

An example of one such audition took place at the Ulmer Theater, Ulm, Germany, for the role of Manon in Puccini's *Manon Lescaut*. After auditioning, the tall and somewhat overweight soprano overheard the stage director say to the conductor, "The opera doesn't say anything about size, only that Manon is beautiful." The tall, overweight soprano received the role. Later the stage director told her that the conductor had actually liked the voice of one of the other singers better, but that she had been the most dramatic and convincing actress during the audition. In this case, beauty and acting ability trumped the other *Fach* considerations.

Following an audition for a specific role, the same degree of professionalism is expected. Be sure to thank everyone for the audition opportunity and report all details of the audition back to the agent.

Opera Studio Auditions

Opera studio auditions are sometimes an unexpected result of a house audition. As was mentioned earlier, following a successful audition, a contract for the house opera studio might be offered to a singer who is less than thirty years old. For a singer with limited performance experience, this position would be a tremendous opportunity. Singers in opera studios have the opportunity for advanced training in language, style, diction, repertoire, and all other aspects of performing opera. They also perform small roles in the regular productions in that house and are featured in their own productions in special performances. And while under contract to the house opera studio, a singer can always continue to audition for a *Fach* contract.

Auditions for opera studios can be arranged by writing a house directly and asking when they are auditioning for studio singers. Many houses, such as the Munich Opera (Bayerische Staatsoper), often referred to as the National Theater, post these audition dates online. Agents, understandably, are much more interested in securing a *Fach* contract for their client than a studio contract, as the former pays more; but any chance to get into the opera system in Europe should be taken. If the age requirements match, and there are no house contracts in sight, an opera house studio would be the best opportunity for that first contract.

AGE CONSIDERATIONS

This issue needs to be discussed, as age is a critical factor in both agency and house auditions. Age is also a factor when considering someone for a specific role. Houses will normally not hire a singer who looks too old to sing a role requiring a very young-appearing singer. Makeup can only do so much.

Agents consider age when they make the choice as to whom to represent between singers of equal merit. Even *Intendants* don't like to hire new unknown singers if they are over thirty-five, with an exception being the dramatic categories. They will usually choose a younger singer. The implication is that "something is wrong" with singers who waited until their late thirties to audition in Europe.

Americans are seldom ready to go to Europe to audition until their mid-twenties or later. Generally speaking, the lighter the *Fach*, the earlier one can seek a career in Europe. Dramatic voices will still be seriously considered by agencies into their late thirties, and a full dramatic baritone or low bass is just beginning his best years at forty to forty-five. Opera studios also normally hire singers who are no older than thirty.

Given the weight attributed to a singer's age, some aspiring singers will subtract a few years. This must only be done during the first audition in Europe, because agencies communicate with each other constantly, and every detail recorded on that initial agency form becomes available to all other agents. Once a birth date is listed at an agency, this is the one that must be given during any house auditions the agent arranges.

Whether or not years are subtracted during the first audition is partially dependent on the singer's *Fach* and the quality of the voice. For female singers in their twenties there is no need to subtract years. On the other hand, a lyric coloratura soprano in her early to mid-thirties would be wise to take off a few years at that first audition. This may sound dishonest and may be a pointless endeavor if the vocal quality does not match that of a younger singer. But it is often done.

An exception would be a singer who is a true low bass or is one of the dramatic categories. This voice usually needs years to gain its full sound. But such singers could be hired even at a young age if their performance experience backs up the vocal sound.

The only time years can be subtracted with impunity is when someone develops an international career. It is almost expected that famous singers will release publicity giving ever-younger ages, and no one cares—

especially in America, where the youth culture carries over into the opera field. On the other hand, many fabulous artists have never altered their ages. Bass baritone Hans Hotter (1909–2003) was not only teaching in his eighties but also still performing on stage. Astrid Varney has been an internationally recognized Wagnerian soprano since her mid-twenties and only recently stopped performing, after more than fifty years. Luciano Pavarotti continued to perform until a few years before his death at age seventy-one.

CHANCE OF SUCCESS

There is no way to predict success. There are usually only a few openings for new ensemble soloists each season. Vacancies are often filled by soloists moving from one house to another, either to a larger house as they gain experience or to one offering better roles. Movement between houses is more common than a sudden opening where a house would be seeking an unknown singer. However, these openings occur often enough to give every voice type that chance for a first job—especially tenors. There are always fewer tenors auditioning than other *Fach* categories. Even *Intendant* Klaus Schultz remarked, "The only sure way to be successful is to become a tenor."[10]

NOTES

1. Conversation with Dr. Domokos, 1979.
2. Author's experience, 1981.
3. Klaus Schultz, *Intendant*, Aachen, Germany, lecture to University of Illinois students, February 13, 1991.
4. Ibid.
5. Carolyne Zinko, article in *San Francisco Chronicle*, Sunday, September 3, 2006.
6. Schultz, February 13, 1991.
7. Interview with *Intendant* Alexander Senger, founder and artistic director of Operamobile/Kleines Musiktheater, Niedersachsen, Germany, and *Operette Sich Ver Kann* at the Staatsoper, July 3, 2006.
8. Conversation with Hellmuth Matiasek, *Intendant* of the Staatstheater am GärtnerPlatz, Munich, Germany, 1984.
9. Senger, July 3, 2006.
10. Schultz, February 13, 1991.

7

Contracts and Casting

European opera houses use the *Fach* system as a guide when considering which singers to hire. The artistic and administrative directors are vitally interested in being able to cast roles with the minimum number of singers under contract and yet have enough voices in each needed *Fach* category to be able to produce an effective season. Each house likes to have two or three singers who could sing the same *Fach* roles, providing a double and sometimes a triple cast for each opera. By using the *Fach* system as a guide, it is possible to accomplish this.

The different types of contracts reflect not only the *Fach* categories the opera house is seeking, but also how these singers will be used during the season. Opera houses engage singers not just for their voices, appearance, or acting abilities, but for a *Fach* that can be used throughout the entire season in a great variety of roles.

This chapter will discuss the types of contracts normally offered to an ensemble singer. See chapter 10, "Maintaining a Career," for information on types of contracts offered to the seasoned, experienced singer who is not currently engaged with a house.

BEGINNER AND CHORUS CONTRACTS

The easiest first contract for a young singer to get is a beginner contract (*Anfängervertrag*) or a chorus contract (*Chorvertrag*). Both of these have their advantages and are a good place to start a career.

Beginner Contract (*Anfänger/Anfängerin Vertrag*)

The beginner contract is a contract for a young singer, usually one who has not yet performed in Europe or accumulated many roles elsewhere. With a beginner's contract, a singer can expect to perform almost every evening. For example, a soprano could sing the woods bird (*Waldvogel*) in Wagner's *Siegfried* one evening, one of the trio in Strauss's *Ariadne auf Naxos* the next, or any short song or section described by its title such as "messenger," "glassblower," or "prisoner" in the following evening's performance.

These roles, often called *comprimario* roles in the United States, provide stage experience and the chance to listen to and learn from the more established singers.

Chorus Contract (*Chorvertrag*)

The other way to break into the opera business in Europe would be to accept a chorus contract. For the young opera singer, this provides a guaranteed income and enough time and experience to learn the language and opera repertoire while preparing to sing solo roles.

Many opera singers choose to be a chorus member for practical reasons. First of all, many excellent singers with beautiful, powerful voices, and more than enough talent to be hired as soloists, prefer singing as a part of a group. Then, once the tryout period (*Probezeit*) is successfully completed, a chorus member is guaranteed this job until retirement, something that is not true of a soloist. This provides the job security to establish and enjoy a family life and develop vocal and performance skills without the uncertainty of having to renegotiate contracts every two to three years.

In a large opera house, such as the National Opera in Munich, the chorus also participates in world tours, extra performances with symphony orchestras, and other events that feature the opera chorus, thus providing extra income. Chorus members also receive extra compensation for participating in any filming or recordings of operas. A chorus member has until the age of thirty-five to move up from a small opera house to a larger one. After that, opera houses usually will not hire new members for their chorus. There are two types of chorus contracts: a chorus-solo contract (*Chor-Solovertrag*) and a solo-chorus contract (*Solo-Chorvertrag*).

Chorus-Solo Contract (*Chor-Solovertrag*)

A *Chor-Solovertrag* stipulates that the singer is hired primarily as a chorister but will be guaranteed small roles on occasion. Examples could include the dance master in Puccini's *Manon Lescaut*, one of the love pair in Puccini's *Il tabarro*, or even the shepherd boy in Puccini's *Tosca*.

Solo-Chorus Contract (*Solo-Chorvertrag*)

A solo-chorus contract means that the singer is hired primarily as a soloist for small roles but must also sing as a member of the opera chorus. Many of these small roles are delightful both in their acting and vocal demands. In the smaller opera houses this could mean singing both small roles and in the chorus in the same performance.

As with a chorus-solo contract, this singer is guaranteed employment until retirement but also has the opportunity to be heard and seen as a soloist. Either contract should be carefully considered by the beginning singer.

CATEGORY CONTRACTS (*FACHVERTRAG*)

A *Fach* category contract is the goal of all opera singers who consider themselves soloists. Every opera house hires at least one solo specialist in each *Fach* required by the season's *Spielplan*, either as an ensemble member or as a guest. All scheduled roles belonging to that *Fach* category become the soloist's primary performance responsibility for that opera house.

There are four different types of *Fach* category contracts (*Fachvertrag*): normal contract (*Normalvertrag*), guest contract (*Gastvertrag*), piece contract (*Stückvertrag*), and time contract (*Teilvertrag* or *Teilspielzeitvertrag*).

Normal Contract (*Normalvertrag/Festvertrag*)

The *Normalvertrag* or *Festvertrag* is a solo contract for an ensemble member of an opera house. It will stipulate the *Fach* and also the length of time the singer is to be engaged. For beginners, the usual length of the contract is from two to three years; for more experienced singers, it is from two to five years. There is no rule about the maximum length of time that can be offered in a contract.[1]

Any other conditions stipulated in a contract are negotiable via the agent. There can be some unusual restrictions, such as "no skiing." Seriously! No one wants to see a Mimi on crutches or a Tristan in a wheelchair.

The *Normalvertrag* states exactly which *Fach* category or categories the opera house expects the singer to perform. When this contract is accepted, the soloist is accepting the responsibility of singing all the roles listed in this *Fach*. As most contracts name two or more *Fächer*, this allows the opera house to double and sometimes triple cast roles. For example:, a *Jugendlich*-dramatic soprano, hired to sing Agathe in Weber's *Der Freischütz* and Leonore in Beethoven's *Fidelio*, could also have lyric soprano in her contract. This means she would be obligated to sing any roles in both categories. This would allow the house to cast her as Pamina, daughter of the Queen of the Night in Mozart's *Die Zauberflöte*, which is listed in two *Fach* categories, young dramatic and lyric soprano.

With a *Normalvertrag* contract, both the singer and the opera house assume certain responsibilities. The singer assumes the responsibility of performing any role in the *Fach* categories stipulated in his or her contract and must perform at least two performances of each role. Singers asked to sing extra roles outside their *Fach* contract can refuse or require an addendum to their contract, which would stipulate exactly what was being asked of them for each individual extra role (*Partien nach individualität*). Or they could even ask for a new contract. Accepting any extra roles also obligates the singer to two performances of each role. If a singer does not wish to sing more than the two performances, he or she must negotiate this with the house as soon as possible.

Many soprano roles overlap in their vocal requirements, leading to many possibilities for casting roles. An opera house might have three sopranos who all sing the *Jugendlich*-dramatic soprano roles. However, each soprano would have a slightly different contract, as shown in the following:

> Soprano 1: *Jugendlich-dramaticher Sopran und Dramatischer Sopran, Partien nach individualität*
>
> Soprano 2: *Lyrischer Sopran und Jugendlich-dramatischer Sopran, Partien nach individualität*
>
> Soprano 3: *Dramatischer Koloratursopran und Lyrischer Sopran, Partien nach individualität*

As you can see, these *Fach* description are quite explicit and protect these soloists from being forced to accept roles inappropriate for their experience or vocal abilities. And it also assures the opera house of having at least one soloist with the primary responsibility for each *Fach*. Apply this method of determining role assignments, by using *Fach* categories, to the approximately thirty to forty soloists in a medium-size opera house and it becomes obvious how it is possible to produce many operas with only a relatively small core group of ensemble members.

The opera house must also schedule the *Normalvertrag* singer for two premieres per season in the singer's *Fach*. This could be the first premiere (*erste Premier*); the second performance, referred to as the "B" premiere, which features the second cast; or the first performance of the opera in the following season (*Wiederaufnahme*).

Two exceptions to having to perform roles in the *Fach* stated in a contract are age and experience. A young soloist who has accepted a contract as a young dramatic soprano (*Jugendlich-dramatischer Sopran*) and as a dramatic soprano (*Dramatischer Sopran*) could refuse the heavier dramatic soprano roles such as Isolde or Brünnhilde and plead her age and a lack of experience (and the corresponding stamina). In this case, a contract specifying roles by individuality (*Partien nach individualität*) is worked out between the singer and the *Betriebsbüro* director, with input from the *Intendant*.

Guest Contract (*Gastvertrag*)

A *Gastvertrag* soloist is hired for a specific role or roles, as well as for a specific length of time. This is very advantageous to do once a soloist has enough experience and has developed a reputation for performing specific roles. (For more on this type of contract see chapter 10, "Maintaining a Career.")

Soloists can be an ensemble member of one opera house and, with the permission of their *Betriebsbüro*, perform as a guest in a specific role for another house. Singers occasionally complain that the *Betriebsbüro* director doesn't want them to accept guest contracts. But they have to remember that the director's responsibility is to assure the smooth running of his or her own opera house, and he or she simply doesn't have to let the singer go. Guest contracts can still be arranged if the singer has a good relationship with the *Betriebsbüro* director and there are other singers in the house to cover any performances that would be missed. In this instance, the singer would be responsible for paying his or her substitute.

An ensemble member could even accept a *Gastvertrag* in his or her own opera house for a role that is outside of the member's original *Fach* contract. A general recommendation, and one emphasized by *Intendant* Klaus Schultz, is to spend from three to four years as an ensemble member to acquire the roles, experience, publicity, and reputation necessary to sustain a guest career before taking on any guest contracts.[2]

Piece Contract (*Stückvertrag*)

The *Stückvertrag* is a contract for a specific role that might cover more than one season. The *Fach* would be stipulated by the role assignment, although the singer would *not* be expected to sing any of the other roles in that *Fach*, unless a separate contract was negotiated for each role.

Specified Time Contract (*Teilvertrag or Teilspielzeitvertrag*)

If a solo singer is needed for just a short period during a season, then a *Teilvertrag* contract, which states a defined amount of time, is offered to a guest singer. This usually happens when an opera is being presented that contains a *Fach* that cannot be covered by a member of the ensemble, or a soloist needs maternity leave or has to be absent for a particular length of time for health or other reasons. This type of contract differs from a regular *Gastvertrag* (guest contract) in that the singer is usually employed only as needed, rather than as a prior planned *Gastvertrag* singer who could be in residence for the whole season.

A *Teilvertrag* conveys on this type of guest singer all the rights and privileges of that specific *Fach* or roles defined in the contract and provides the luxury of a guaranteed income for a specific length of time, as well as the freedom to seek other contracts.

THE USE OF *FACH* TO PLAN SEASONS AND CAST ROLES

Planning the Season

The *Intendant* is primarily responsible for planning the season or seasons. He or she receives suggestions and recommendations from the conductors in the house, primarily the general music director (GMD) and sometimes from stage directors who have specific requirements for the protagonists in their particular production. *Intendant* Alexander Senger stated that by law the *Intendant* has total control of who is hired or fired. However, in most opera houses the true power lies with the general music director—the GMD.[3]

The *Intendant* will have discussions with the GMD, other conductors, the *Betriebsbürodirektor*, stage directors, and often the *Studienleiter* (who is also a conductor) in order to decide what *Fach* assignments will be necessary for coming seasons. This group also decides which singers in the present ensemble should have their contracts extended, and who should be let go. The results of these deliberations are communicated in individual meetings with soloists. If it is decided that there will be a vacancy in one or more of the *Fach* categories for the next season, this information will be given to agents.

The *Intendant* and the committee will first determine if they have the proper soloists under contract to fill each *Fach*. It is preferable to have at least two in each category, which provides more than one cast (*Besetzung*) on each role. If there is a role that is too dramatic to be sung by anyone in the ensemble, a guest will be engaged. An example of a role that might need a guest, especially in smaller houses, would be any of the heavy Wagner opera dramatic (*Helden*) tenor heroes, such as Siegfried or Tristan, or the most dramatic of the soprano roles, such as Brünnhilde or Isolde.

Once it is determined that each *Fach* is covered by ensemble members, the *Betriebsbüro* director, with the input from the committee, will put together lists of cast members for each role. This system seems to operate without problems and guarantees that an opera is always cast with more than one singer to a role and that the singers are never asked to sing a role inappropriate for their voice or abilities. The magic phrase *Partien nach individualität* ensures that the opera house as well as the singer has considerable flexibility in the definition of what constitutes a *Fach* role assignment. The need to regularly reevaluate roles and *Fach* assignments, as singers mature in voice and experience, is also the impetus for frequent conversations about role assignments.

Casting the Roles

Although each singer has a right to roles listed under his or her *Fach* designation, the person who actually sings the role, especially the premiere, is determined by other people or factors, especially when each opera house has more than one soloist who could sing a particular role. This decision is based not only on vocal skills but on which singer might best portray the role physically or has the best facility in the language of the opera, such as a role in Italian with recitative.

When several singers are possible for any one role, the stage director makes this choice with input from the *Intendant* and the conductor of the opera. Remember, conductors have the right of refusal for any singer with whom they don't want to work, for whatever reason. Stage directors also have their own concept of what the singer should look like or how the singer should move or act. The *Betriebsbürodirektor* will also have input and keeps track of which singer has a right to that particular role or must be assigned a premiere of a particular *Fach*.

The first cast (*erste Besetzung*) for roles in an opera will usually be the soloists that the stage director prefers in the roles, supported by the conductor, who would have his or her own ideas about the ideal voices and musical abilities required for the roles. The second and third cast would be the soloists also assigned to that particular *Fach*. The reason any one opera can be performed over several seasons is that more than one singer has the right to learn the role and rehearse and perform it. Sometimes during the rehearsal process, or during the first few performances, a third *Besetzung* soloist, who was not originally considered ideal for that role, will turn out to be the singer who best portrays the role both dramatically and vocally and will wind up with most of the performances.

An additional consideration when casting is the length of the role. Roles are listed in Kloiber's *Handbuch der Oper* in three categories: main role (*grosse Partie*, or *gr. P.*), medium role (*mittlere Partie*, or *m. P.*), or small role (*kleine Partie*, or *kl. P.*). These designations refer to the actual length of the role in relation to the length of the opera. A soloist singing a role designated as *grosse Partie* would be performing a role critical to the development of the plot and would be on stage for most or for a major part of the opera. For example, a role defined as a *grosse Partie* in Leoncavallo's *Cavalleria rusticana*, a one-act opera with a running time of approximately one and a quarter hours, would not seem comparable to a *grosse Partie* in Wagner's *Lohengrin*, which lasts approximately four hours. However, the proportion of time actually singing on stage would be about the same in both operas.

This same type of organization is assigned to the individuals in a chorus, depending on the length of involvement the chorus has in each production:[4]

- Large chorus role, or *grosse Chorpartie* (*gr. Chp.*): lengthened chorus role that lasts for a significant time during the opera or throughout the entire opera
- Large role, or *grosse Partie* (*gr. P.*): leading solo role; a role that lasts throughout the entire opera, or for the major part of the opera; musically demanding
- Medium chorus role, or *mittlere Chorpartie* (*m. Chp.*): medium-length chorus role that takes place during a significant length of time during the opera but not throughout the entire opera
- Medium role, or *mittlere Partie* (*m. P.*): medium-length solo role presented during a significant length of time during the opera but not throughout the entire opera; sometimes this character will perform in major ensembles with the lead roles
- Small chorus role, or *kleine Chorpartie* (*kl. Chp.*): small chorus role that is limited to one scene, or several short appearances.
- Small role, or *kleine Partie* (*kl. P.*): small solo role that is limited to one scene or several short appearances

The practical result of this sizing of roles is another added dimension to the assignment of roles by the opera house. Although most of the roles performed by a soloist with a normal contract would be large or main roles (*grosse Partien*), there are occasions when leading singers would be assigned the medium or small roles. An important festival such as the Salzburg *Festspiel* is an example where even the smallest roles are assigned to recognized singers.

Within an opera house a small role (*kl. P.*) will usually be assigned to a beginner, *Anfänger* or *Anfängerin*, or sometimes to a chorus singer, if a soloist isn't available. If the small role is critical to the drama or needs to be sung by an imposing voice, then one of the major singers in the house will sing this role. An example of a small role that would almost always be cast with a major singer is the hermit in Weber's *Der Freischütz* or the Italian singer in Richard Strauss's *Der Rosenkavalier*.

Medium roles (*m. P.*) are often assigned to the major singers and are considered as important to the drama and overall development of the opera as the *grosse Partien*. Examples of these roles would be the first, second, and third ladies of the Queen of the Night in Mozart's *Die Zauberflöte*; Valentin, Marguerite's brother in Gounod's *Faust*; Kuno in Weber's *Der Freischütz*; and Walter in Wagner's *Tannhäuser*.

SALARY AND SCHEDULES

Singers in Germany are paid the equivalent of a thirteen-month salary (*Gage*). They receive the extra month in two payments: two weeks as a bonus at Christmas and another two weeks' bonus before the summer vacation. In Switzerland this is a fourteen-month contract, with two extra months of pay.[5]

Salary for Opera Soloists

The minimum salary for an ensemble member in 2009 was approximately 1,550 euros per month. The average salary in a national opera house would be significantly higher.[6] Other factors that would add to this base salary would be payments for any performances over the maximum stated in the contract, which would be paid per performance, as well as any fees for appearances as a soloist with symphonies or oratorio societies and any fees from guest appearances in other theaters. Although this amount might seem low to Americans, the salary base is more than enough to live quite comfortably. And since the first contract provides retirement, health insurance, and other benefits, including a six-week paid vacation in the summer, even the smallest salary is more than acceptable.

More women than men enter the opera profession, and there are usually more roles for women in operas. This generally means the highest-paid singers in an ensemble are men, usually the dramatic tenors. There are not as many singers available in this *Fach* category, which also takes more experience and vocal expertise to develop. Opera director Stephan Minde put it this way: "If you shake the trees the sopranos fall out. But you have to be careful of tenors, mezzos, and low basses."[7] In other words, there are fewer of them.

Also, some voices seem to have an easier time finding work than others. The most common *Fach* among singers is the lyric, and the most unusual, the dramatic voices. However, if a singer has a well-defined *Fach*, he or she has every chance of becoming successful in the opera world.

Scheduling

The maximum number of performances a singer performs depends on the contract. Eighty performances during a season would be considered the maximum, and the normal amount is about sixty. However, if one accepted a contract as a beginner or without a *Fach* stipulation, it would be possible to perform as many as 120 performances a season, singing almost every evening in some short role or scene.

Singers can have a stipulation in their contract that states they are paid an extra amount if they exceed the normal amount of performances for the season. The amount agreed on would be paid per extra performance and would show up on the singer's monthly account. A singer's salary as an ensemble member of a European opera house is more than adequate to provide for a comfortable life, especially since the opera house pays half the health insurance and half the social security. Even though tax deductions are high—about a fourth to a third of the income, depending on the contract—the house salary, with extra money from concerts and guest contracts, makes opera a financially rewarding life.

Vacation Rights and Privileges

Opera houses close for an official six-week vacation during the summer. Generally this is from mid-June to the beginning of August. Summer vacations are a chance for the artistic personnel to simply rest, visit family, or perform in summer festivals such as the Strauss Festival in Munich or the Wagner Festival in Bayreuth.

Singers are guaranteed a six-week vacation during the time the opera house is closed. A soloist with an ensemble contract (*Normalvertrag*) will also have a number of days of official vacation (*offizielle Urlaub*) during the season. Ensemble members also have the right to ask to be absent for an unofficial vacation if they are not scheduled in rehearsals or performances. They must, however, give a telephone number where they can be reached in case the opera house substitutes performances or the singer is needed to substitute for a colleague who is ill. During an unofficial vacation, the singer is not allowed to be farther away than the time it would take to return to the opera house for a performance on the same day as the notification. If handled carefully, all the official vacation days, as well as the unofficial vacation possibilities, result in a lot of time off.

This is offset by the intense schedule of rehearsals leading up to a new production of an opera. These rehearsals can last for approximately two months and require the singer to rehearse from four to eight hours a day for the upcoming production and still perform the operas currently running in the opera house. During the season singers usually have Sunday off, but only if they have no performances on that day.

Canceling a Performance

If it becomes necessary for a singer to cancel on the day of a performance, this must be done, at least by telephone, by whatever time is stipulated by the *Betriebsbüro*. By law, this must be by noon, although some opera houses prefer an earlier time, if possible. This gives the *Betriebsbüro* staff enough time to notify a substitute singer in their own house or to call neighboring opera houses to request a singer to perform that evening.

If one or more of the singers in a scheduled performance cancel, and other singers for those roles are not available, it might be necessary to substitute another opera. All the artistic personnel for the new opera have to be notified, as well as the technical and support personnel, plus the orchestra, dancers, and chorus, with only a few hours' notice. This is an amazingly complex procedure, but because of the detailed organization of all schedules by *Betriebsbüro* personnel, even a sudden crisis can be solved.

Illness

Occasionally a singer must cancel a performance or miss rehearsals due to illness. If singers are ill for any reason, they are allowed to miss rehearsals and performances for three days without any formal proof of the illness. After the three days, an official note from a physician is required.

Although singers can be genuinely ill on occasion, it is not wise to be frequently absent from rehearsals or performances. Sooner or later the singer's contract will be allowed to lapse in favor of a singer who can remain healthy. Since soloists are allowed to rehearse by marking (singing lightly or singing in a lower octave), rehearsals are still possible with a cold or laryngitis, when such vocal use does not threaten the voice.

If a singer becomes ill and knows that it will not be possible to perform that evening, he or she notifies the *Betriebsbüro*, and the director makes other arrangements, as previously stated. However, if singers fall ill yet believe that the illness will not prevent them from singing or acting on stage, there are several options.

Options for Illness Prior to a Performance

Option 1: If the singer thinks if it is possible to get through the performance but is worried that the voice might show the illness, he or she can ask the assistant director to go out on stage prior to the performance and make an announcement (*Ansage*) such as the following: "Dame Swansong is indisposed but has agreed to perform." Audiences are very understanding of this situation, which usually results in enthusiastic applause at the end of the opera for the indisposed singer.

Option 2: If the singer does not want the audience to be worried about the performance, he or she can chose to perform until the point in the opera when the illness becomes noticeable and then send the assistant director out to make the announcement. In March 2008, soprano Deborah Voight had to leave a Metropolitan Opera performance of Wagner's *Tristan und Isolde* due to illness. She had told the general manager before act 2 that she was not well, and the cover singer was alerted. Near the beginning of the second act's love duet, Voight signaled she could not continue and hurried offstage. The curtain came down, an announcement was made, and fifteen minutes later the opera continued, with the cover singer substituting for Voight.[8]

Option 3: If the performance is a premiere, and the soloist is only slightly indisposed or has an illness that presumably will allow him or her to get through the performance without an *Ansage*, the soloist can ask that only the reviewers be told of the illness. This protects the singer's reputation if the reviewer notices something amiss during the performance. However, if the singer becomes noticeably ill during the performance, Option 2 can be invoked.

Illness during a Performance

If the singer becomes unexpectedly ill during a performance or is injured while performing the opera, there are also several options.

Option 1: If two-thirds of the opera has already been performed, the performance can be legally stopped and the audience must leave with no refund of money or offer of a ticket for a future performance. An example of this happening was a performance of Wagner's *Die Walküre* in Mannheim, Germany, which was canceled *before* the third and final act when an announcement was made that the Brünnhilde had suddenly become ill. A guest dramatic soprano with a reputation for jealous petulance, she had received only lukewarm applause during the act 2 curtain call, while the local mezzo, singing Fricka, had received a thunderous ovation. Thus the sudden illness! As there was no cover singer for Brünnhilde, the audience had to leave without seeing or hearing the famous "Ride of the Valkyries"—and without a rain check.

Option 2: If the opera is stopped after the first act of a three-act opera, or before two-thirds of the opera has been performed, and there are no substitutes for the singer who could jump in (*einspringen*), then the audience is sent home and allowed to exchange their tickets for a future performance. This can be a disastrous financial burden for the opera house, as everyone involved—singers, orchestra, technical personnel, and support personnel—still has to be paid.

In fact, if the opera is stopped for *any reason* prior to two-thirds having been performed, the same scenario applies. In 1991, prior to the beginning of a performance of *Il trovatore*, in Keil, Germany, the lead soprano was approached by the costume mistress and told to "take off your wig and costume and leave the building!" There had been a bomb threat, and everyone was evacuated and the performance canceled. The audience was given a rain check, and the opera ensemble and technical staff was still paid for a performance. A costly situation for the house!

Option 3: If the singer is suddenly incapacitated, but only vocally, and the opera house does not want to cancel the performance, the singer can be asked if he or she is capable of completing the performance without singing. If so, and another ensemble member who can sing the role can be found quickly, the substitute singer can sing the music from the orchestra pit, while the voiceless singer acts the role on stage.

Some of the options pertaining to canceling a performance due to illness are spelled out in the singer's contract, but not all. And all options are negotiable and should be discussed with the agent first.

Synopsis: Opera House Rights and Privileges

Both the house administration and the opera singers enjoy specific rights and privileges. These can be best be shown by the following:

Ensemble Member: Normal Category Contract (*Normal Fachvertrag*)

- The right to two premieres per season in a *Fach*-defined role
- The right to perform at least two performances within the singer's *Fach*
- The right to refuse roles in the singer's *Fach* if the role does not match the singer's abilities or experience
- The right to ask for performances in another *Fach*
- If allowed to prepare a role not in one's *Fach*, the right to two performances of this role

- Six weeks of vacation every summer
- Additional vacation days during the season as defined by the individual contract
- Additional time for guest opportunities, if released by the opera house
- Three sick days without doctor's note (illness/absence of longer than three days requires a doctor's note)
- The right to protest rehearsal or coaching assignments
- The right to be absent from the opera house if not rehearsing or performing
- The right to accept or refuse any extra assignments by the opera house
- The right, having accepted an optional assignment, to withdraw from the role after two performances

Ensemble Member: Beginning Contract (*Anfänger/Anfängerin-Vertrag*)

- The same rights as in the normal category contract (*Normal Fachvertrag*) but without the premieres or two guaranteed performances in the singer's *Fach*

Guest: Part-Time Contract (*Teilvertrag*)

- The right to as many performances of the opera or operas as is stipulated in the contract
- The right to any premieres as stipulated in the contract
- The right to be paid the full amount of the salary, even if the opera house cancels performances

Guest: Piece Contract (*Stückvertrag*)

- The same rights as the guest part-time contract (*Teilvertrag*)

CONTRACT RENEWAL NEGOTIATIONS

Although the agent will handle any details of a contract, it is helpful to understand the process involved in contract renewal and how to initiate contract changes. Keep in mind that ensemble members of an opera house are under continuous review, and contracts can be refined or changed at any time. This can be crucial to maintaining a career.

Contract Renewal Dates

As a general rule, contracts come up for renewal or renegotiation in the fall. Each contract stipulates how many years the contract will last and has a specific date stating when the contract is over. For singers who have been performing in the house for a period of less than eight years, the house has until October 15 to initiate a discussion with the singer about the contract. Following this discussion, the house has until October 31 to let singers know if they are going to have their contract extended (*Verlängern*) or are going to be let go (*Nichtverlängerung*). The wise singer will have met with his or her agent in advance of these dates and will certainly do so once notification is given so the agent has time to negotiate contract conditions with the house. Even though a singer might not have a contract extended, he or she would still be performing for the entire season and have that time to audition for new contracts.

If a singer has held a contract for more than eight years, then July 31 is the deadline to tell the singer the decision.[9] Singers then have all summer plus the full season to find new engagements. The same conditions apply if the singer decides not to extend a current contract. Contracts can be renegotiated at any time, although such a discussion usually happens prior to the date stipulated in the contract (*Nichtverlängerungstermin*).[10]

Contract Negotiation Meetings

It is useful to have some idea what might happen at the contract negotiation meeting. The meeting usually takes place with the *Intendant* in his or her office. Also present is the *Intendant*'s personal secretary, and possibly the financial director. The other directors, especially the general music director, have already had the chance to recommend, or not recommend, extending the contract.

Singers can bring a more experienced colleague with them to the meeting, or the union representative for the house, but not an agent. However, this is not recommended if the singer is a beginner (*Anfänger/Anfgängerin*). This first meeting is only informative. The singer should not sign anything at this time, but report all details back to the agent, who facilitates any proposed extension of a contract.

If the singer is told that the house wishes to extend the existing contract, the rest of the meeting might be the time to discuss future roles or any *Fach* changes. This could involve discussion about changing to a more difficult *Fach*, possibly of more use to the theater. A new contract might give the singer more premieres or extra performances, with the resultant extra fee for any performances over the maximum stated in the contract. Following the meeting, the singer must contact the agent who originally facilitated the contract. The agent will formalize the extension or work out any changes with the opera house. If the singer refuses a contract offer, the agent must still be contacted with all details about the meeting.

Even if the existing contract is not extended, the *Intendant* might offer one of the guest contracts, such as a part-time contract (*Teilvertrag*) for specific roles, or a piece contract (*Stückvertrag*). It is also possible that a lighter or less demanding *Fach* might be suggested. This sometimes happens in the final years of a career, when opera singers are no longer able to effectively portray young personalities or don't have the stamina to sing the longer, more dramatic roles, but the *Intendant* still wants to keep this performer in the ensemble.

Being offered one of these guest contracts is not a negative outcome to the meeting, as the fee from even two or three of these guest performances a month could be more than the former monthly salary as an ensemble member. A guest contract with one house also allows for the possibility of accepting similar contracts in other opera houses.

NOTES

1. Interview with Alexander Senger, *Intendant* of Operamobile/Kleines Musiktheater, Niedersachsen, Germany, and *Operette Sich Ver Kann*, July 3, 2006.

2. Klaus Schultz, *Intendant*, Aachen, Germany, February 13, 1991.

3. Senger, July 3, 2006.

4. Rudolf Kloiber, Wulf Konold, and Robert Maschka, *Handbuch der Oper* (Kassel, Germany: Bärenreiter-Verlag, 2006), xiv–xv.

5. Senger, July 3, 2006.

6. Information from Staatstheater Kassel, Germany, October 2009.

7. Conversation with Stephan Minde during auditions for the Portland Opera in Los Angeles, late 1970s.

8. Anthony Tommasini, "Reigning Wagnerian Tenor Returns to 'Tristan,'" *New York Times*, March 27, 2008.

9. Information from Staatstheater Kassel, Germany, 2009.

10. Senger, July 3, 2006.

8

Official Requirements

Once the audition tour is over and a contract with an opera house has been offered and accepted, a number of steps still need to be taken in order to formalize the contract and make it valid. This involves obtaining the permits required in order to live and work in a European country.

Using Germany as an example, go on the Internet to German Missions in the United States at www.germany.info for information about visa, residence, and work permits, as well as information about the country and its people.

PROCEDURES AND PERMITS

The Consulate or Embassy Office

Once you arrive in Germany, whether you are there to audition for several months or are coming to start your job in an opera house, it is advisable to register with the nearest U.S. embassy or consulate office. This is a free service and ensures that if any emergency happens, the U.S. embassy or consulate can be a source of assistance and information. If you are auditioning, it's a good idea to have an itinerary and to leave a copy with a parent or close friend in the United States and provide the embassy or consulate where you register a copy as well.

In Germany, the U.S. embassy is in Berlin. There are four consulate offices: Bremen, Frankfurt, Leipzig, and Munich. It is possible to register online by going to the U.S. Department of State's website at http://germany.usembassy.gov, and clicking the Travel Registration link.

Residence/Employment Permit/Visa (*Aufenthalserlaubnis*)

United States citizens need only a valid U.S. passport to travel to Germany for business, as a tourist, or to audition. However, they can only remain in the country for ninety days, after which a residence permit and an employment visa are required. For singers who already have an opera house contract and supply this information on the application for residency, an employment visa will be included in the residence permit. For information on the required documents and forms needed to obtain this residence/employment visa, access the website www.germany.info.

Application forms can also be obtained at the German consulates in Atlanta, Boston, Chicago, Houston, Los Angeles, Miami, New York, or San Francisco. It takes one to three months for the application to be processed.

Health Insurance (*Krankenversicherung*)

As an employee of an opera house in Germany, you are provided German government health insurance as a major part of your benefit package. This insurance covers regular doctor visits, hospital stays, and even maternity leave, and also applies to spouses and dependents. All employees below a certain income (approximately 85,000 euros in 2008) must be publicly insured. Above that amount an individual may opt for insurance from a private company. Since a new opera singer will not be making anywhere near 85,000 euros, having public health insurance is a good thing.

When a singer is publicly insured, the opera house pays half the cost of the singer's health insurance, while the other half is deducted from the singer's paycheck. The singer's only out-of-pocket expenses are small surcharges for prescriptions. With private health insurance, no money is deducted from a paycheck, and the full cost of the insurance policy is borne by the subscriber.

Social Security (*Rentenversicherung*)

The opera singer will also be paying into a pension insurance fund (*Rentenversicherung*), which is the German equivalent of U.S. Social Security. This is another automatic deduction each month from the singer's paycheck. Again, half is paid by the opera house and half by the singer. This *Rentenversicherung* pays for unemployment, retirement, and health insurance similar to Medicare, which goes into effect once the singer is retired.

If the singer is unemployed for some length of time, or is between guest contracts, a small fee can be voluntarily paid (*freiwillig*) to protect any future *Rentenversicherung* benefits.

When registering with this office, the singer will receive an insurance ID number (*Versicherungsnummer*) which is permanent, just like a social security number. Singers will also regularly receive a statement of contributions (*Versicherungsnachweis*). This is a permanent record and should be kept with other important papers.

The retirement system in Germany imposes the same types of conditions as in the United States as to when benefits can be withdrawn. Singers need to reach a specific age (*Altersgrenze*) and must have paid into the system long enough to be assured of benefits. Even after reaching the minimum age to retire, usually sixty-five, it is possible to continue to work and receive benefits later.

Stage Insurance (*Bühnenversicherung*)

An additional form of retirement insurance for opera singers is provided by stage insurance (*Bühnenversicherung*). With the first engagement in a German opera house, singers are automatically registered with the Stage Retirement Office. The intent of this office is to provide extra retirement coverage as well as some financial help if the singer is unable to work for an extended period of time (due to illness, for example).

EUROPEAN TAXES (*STEUER*)

In Europe, just like in the United States, taxes are paid on all earned income. When you are employed by an opera house, these taxes will be deducted from your salary. There are six levels of taxation in Germany, depending on the amount of income. The *Lohnsteuerkarte* (tax card) is the equivalent of the W2 form and will list the tax class.

If you are employed as an ensemble member, this tax card is filled out by the opera house with your yearly income (*Einkommen*), and then it must be sent to the local tax authorities (*Stadtverwaltung*). If the singer is working as a guest in various theaters, or is on unemployment, the card can be picked up from the opera house's finance office, or it can be mailed to the singer. The *Lohnsteurkarte* will state all earnings and other information necessary to determine taxes for the year. All employees must prepare a declaration of income (*Lohnsteuerjahresausgleich*), which is sent in with the tax card to the Financial Office (*Finanzamt*)

The easiest way to handle taxes is to hire a tax expert (*Steuerberator*), who will prepare a tax return and send it in to the proper authorities. The usual time to set up an appointment with a tax expert is in September, to prepare the paperwork for the prior year. The *Steuerberator* has until December to file the forms.

In order to prepare the report efficiently, and to take advantage of the many tax-free allowances (*Freibeträge*) and other allowable deductions, the *Steuerberator* will expect detailed receipts for anything related to singing. This includes office supplies, books and music, payment to coaches or voice teachers, and any clothing and equipment necessary for your profession. (Designer jeans would not qualify, but a new concert gown or tuxedo would.) When shopping, ask for a business-related receipt (*Steuerquittung*), which has a space to record the purpose of the purchase.

Some meals can be deductible, such as lunch with a coach or agent. Restaurant receipts have a space where the names of the participants of the meal and the purpose of the meal can be written. Singers are allowed considerable leeway with deductions, so be sure to keep accurate records.

UNITED STATES TAXES

United States citizens singing in a European opera house need to continue to file their U.S. federal and state income tax forms every year, even though they might only be earning money in Europe. Extensive tax treaties exist between the U.S. and European countries, and if certain requirements are met, the singer may qualify for "foreign earned income exclusions." For information on how to file for these exclusions, go to the U.S. Department of Treasury IRS website at www.irs.gov.

Even with any applicable exclusions, it is important to file U.S. taxes each year. If not, when returning to the United States after a wonderful career in Europe, you will have to file U.S. taxes on all earnings in other countries during the time you were absent. Once you are residing in the U.S. again and filing taxes, questions will immediately be raised about any missing years, and it is possible that you would have to pay fines, as well as any missing taxes. Filing every year eliminates this potential problem.

UNEMPLOYMENT (*ARBEITSLOSICHKEIT*)

Unemployment in Germany is a carefully regulated process. This is an additional deduction from the opera singer's monthly salary. Because many singers are temporarily unemployed when they are between contracts with opera houses, it is necessary to understand the process of applying for unemployment benefits. Any opera singer who has been employed for a minimum length of time and loses his or her job, usually due to nonrenewal of a contract, has the right to receive unemployment benefits. These benefits are managed by the German Federal Employment Office (Bundesanstalt für Arbeit). This office will arrange for unemployment benefits, provide detailed information about job openings (not necessarily in the opera field of work), and help the individual look for new employment. (It is sometimes necessary to take a job unrelated to singing while one reauditions for agents and opera houses in hopes of another opera house contract.) As soon as an individual has registered as unemployed, the basic fee for health insurance will be assumed by this office, so that all benefits will continue without a break in coverage.

No one is allowed unemployment benefits without actively seeking work. Benefits last only for specified lengths of time, as determined by law, and are in relationship to how long the applicant has worked. When benefits are approved, the money is simply transferred from the unemployment office (*Arbeitsamt*) into the singer's checking account. (It is recommended that the singer have an account in a local bank.)

The *Arbeitsamt* has only certain hours open for appointments. Double-check the hours and find out if any forms need to be filled out ahead of an appointment or what documents you must bring with you in order to apply for benefits.

This office is always very busy, so if the *Arbeitsamt* is scheduled to open at 8 AM, be there at 7 AM. If you're lucky, there might be only twenty or so people already in line. Exactly at 8 AM, not earlier and not a second later (Germans are known for their punctuality), the office will open. The *Arbeitsamt* employees are as fascinated by performers as are other Europeans and, after having the singer fill out a number of forms, may spend a good deal of the interview talking about opera and the singer's roles. Projecting confidence, a relaxed attitude, and a cheerful interest in the personnel in this office helps with the overall process.

A visit to the *Arbeitsamt* could also provide financial assistance. For example, when an audition has been confirmed, this office will give the singer an official certificate for travel, which is then traded in for a train ticket.

It is neither embarrassing nor awkward to be out of work from time to time. It is part of the performing business and simply one more experience to add to the European adventure. Detailed information on unemployment is available at www.bundesagenturfürarbeit.de.

AUTO LICENSE AND INSURANCE

Most of the time, having a car in Europe is not necessary and is more of a hassle than a convenience. Car insurance is expensive, and so is gas. Also, most people live in apartment buildings that do not come with garages, so any cars must be parked on the street, and these spaces are quickly taken. It is far easier and faster to take the very reliable forms of public transportation: buses, streetcars, trains, and subways. Even travel between singing engagements is best done by train. For more information on train travel in Europe see chapter 11, "Living in Europe."

For those Americans who decide a car is a necessity, their driver's license will be accepted in Germany, but only for the first six months. If staying longer than six months, but less than a year, it is necessary to go to the registration office (*Führerscheinstelle*) before the six months are up get an extension. Bring your American driver's license with an official translation (signed by the translator) and documentation of departure date from Germany within the year such as a plane ticket, or any form showing that any employment will be over by that time. Driving a car that is not insured is not allowed.

If you are staying in Germany for more than one year, then you will need to have a German license (*Führerschein*). Full details regarding the requirements of obtaining a German license can be found at http://germany.usembassy.gov/acs/drivers_license.html.

9

Life in the Opera House

Most American opera singers begin their international careers in an opera house in Germany, Switzerland, or Austria. In this chapter, a German opera house is used to illustrate life in an opera house during a typical season. This includes types of rehearsals, rehearsal etiquette, and performance tips.

To be an opera singer in Europe is something of a cross between a rock star and sports star in America. Opera singers receive instant respect. Fans send letters and notes to the performer and even write to the house to request that their favorite singer be assigned a particular role. Singers are recognized on the street, asked for their autograph, and regularly receive requests in the mail for publicity photos.

Many people in Europe, even if not specifically opera fans, are acquainted with the opera world. And those who appreciate opera also are familiar with the preeminent singers of the day, along with the famous teachers, conductors, and directors, as well as what it takes to enter this milieu. This level of respect extends to all professionals in the cultural and creative fields.

Most aspiring opera singers in the United States can only dream of a life where their only job is simply to sing. Many of them are primarily involved in the smaller regional and city operas and have to work at some other occupation in order to make a living. This is an astonishing fact to European opera singers, who have come through a rigorous training program and have a reasonable chance of immediately finding a job in their own country. They do not have to work part time and sing part time or, worse yet, hold down a full-time job while trying to perform as often as possible. An American who finds an operatic engagement in Europe has a job that provides security and respect, and allows a singer to do that one thing that makes singers truly happy—sing!

THE OPERA SEASON

There are almost 400 opera houses listed in the *Deutsches Bühnen Jahrbuch*, as well as 26 opera studios.[1] Each opera house presents operas, operettas, musicals, plays, and ballets during a ten-and-a-half-month season each year. This represents a tremendous number of productions available to the public during an opera season, and of course a great many opportunities for employment for aspiring opera singers.

Exciting seasons are presented even in the smallest opera houses, offering the opera-going public a choice of their favorite operas as well as lesser-known gems. The larger houses have an impressive repertoire and also present several new productions each year. Each opera is performed over a two- to three-year span while constantly being rotated with the other operas in the season plan.

For its 2007–2008 season, the National Theater in Munich (Bayerische Staatsoper) presented thirty-four operas from its repertoire and premiered seven new productions of established works. In the month of July 2007 alone, there were twenty-seven evenings of opera, two opera matinees, three *Leiderabend* (vocal concerts), and five *Festspiel* concerts.[2]

Each opera house season also features special performances on the smaller stages affiliated with the opera company. These could be authentically staged period productions of early Mozart operas, recital evenings by prominent singers, or performances by visiting musicians. For example, in 2008 the Munich Opera produced Mozart's *Idomeneo* at the Cuvillies-Theater and Richard Strauss's *Ariadne auf Naxos* at the Prinzregententheater.[3] If an opera house has an opera studio, the young artists are featured in their own productions of opera and operettas, often on the smaller stages.

REHEARSALS

A typical schedule for an opera singer includes rehearsals, opera performances, solo performances for orchestral concerts or oratorios, and performances as a guest for other opera houses. The singer receives individual coaching and ensemble coaching, and takes part in many types of final rehearsals for each opera.

Rehearsals for any one opera will take place over an approximately six-week to two-month period, which would be a luxury for most Americans in regional opera. Rehearsals of one type or another will generally take up as much as eight hours a day—four hours in the morning and four in the evening. During rehearsals, singers are excused for costume, shoe, or wig fittings.

However, if singers have an evening performance, they are usually only expected to rehearse in the morning. Singers are also allowed to "mark" (sing lightly or down an octave) for any rehearsals on these days, so that the voice can be saved for the performance. In addition, the opera house usually allows one free day of rest between the full dress rehearsal (*Generalprobe*) and the opening night.

Rehearsals for an opera are extremely detailed and cover enough time to ensure that everyone thoroughly knows his or her role. These include

- Solo rehearsals (*Soloproben*), for all ensemble members other than chorus members
- Ensemble rehearsals (*Ensembleproben*), for those sharing duets/ensembles
- First orchestra rehearsal (*Sitzprobe*), for full cast
- Blocking rehearsals (*Stellproben*)
- Sectional rehearsals (*Stückproben*)
- Stage rehearsals (*Bühnenproben*)
- Lighting rehearsals (*Lichtproben/Beleuchtungsproben*)
- Final rehearsals (*Hauptproben*)
- Dress rehearsal (*Generalprobe*)

Sometimes there will also be an explanatory rehearsal (*Verständigungsprobe*) for a guest assuming a role at the last minute or for a new cast member.

Rehearsal Plans (*Probeplan*)

There are several different types of rehearsal plans, which are very detailed and vitally important to the singer. The two most important plans are the weekly rehearsal plan (*Wochenplan*) and the daily rehearsal plan (*Probeplan*). These plans include the names of cast members and where each type of rehearsal is taking place, as well as details as to who is absent due to vacation or illness. Rehearsal plans are posted by the artists' entrance, and copies are given to each singer.

Example 4 is a portion of the weekly rehearsal plan (*Wochenplan*) for Monday, April 21, through Friday, April 25, 2008, from the Staastheater

Änderungen vorbehalten   Wochenplan 21. April 2008 bis 27. April 2008 KW. 17 // Nr. 35
Druckdatum: 15.04.2008 10.27

Opernhaus / Opernfoyer	Schauspielhaus / Schauspielfoyer	tif / tif-Foyer	Urlaubsanträge / krank	Opernhaus	Schauspielh aus / SH-foyer	tif / tif-Foyer
Vorstellungen	Vorstellungen	Vorstellungen		Proben	Proben	Proben
Mo 21.04 19.30 OF Resonanzboden 62 ...Praktikanten des Staatsorchesters Nobach, Gerke			?Buschmann?, ?Chor?, ?Costa?, Dusseljee, ?Engelke?, Fickenscher, ?Losaka?, ?Orch?, ?Preisinger bis 12.30?, ?WielandJoh.? Lis	Aufb Liebestrank Zuschauerraum 10-11 Orchesterfoto 19 BO 3 Liebestrank QF: 14-18.30 res. Strunz	18 Familienschlag er +Ton	tif-Foy 18 HPII Wanze Lehrer
Di 22.04			?Costa bis 18?, Dusseljee, ?Engelke bis 18?, Fickenscher, ?Holst ab 14?, ?Losaka?, ?SchmidtW?, ?WielandJoh.? Lis	10 BO 4 Liebestrank (+Charfoto) 14-18 Bel 19 BO 5 Liebestrank	10 Familienschlag er +Ton 13-18 Bel Korr. 19.30 HPI Familienschla ger	Aufb Schattenstimme n 18 Schattenstim men tif-Foy 11 GP Wanze
Mi 23.04 16-17 OF Einblicke	19.30 *KOSTPROBE* Familienschlager = öffentl. HP II Reiter, Noll, BeckM, BeckA, Weiser, Flake, Mann, Rohbeck, FischerH, Sprekelsen, RichterS, Watzke, Statisterie	11 tiFo Prem Wanze Scheuch, Steinbruch anschl. Premierenfeier	?Adam ab 14?, Dusseljee, Fickenscher, ?Losaka?, ?SchmidtW?, ?WielandJoh.? Lis	Zuschauerraum 10-10.45 Orchesterfoto 11-12.30 Vorsingen Stachow 14-18 Bel Liebestrank 18 HPII Liebestrank	10 Familienschlag er +Ton 13-18 Bel Korr. 19.30 s. ÖHP	18 Schattenstim men
Do 24.04 girls day			Dusseljee, Fickenscher, ?Losaka?, ?Preisinger bis 17?, ?WielandJoh.? Lis	14 Bel.Korr 19.30 GP Liebestrank QF: 8-9.30 + 13-14.30 res. girls day	10 Familienschlag er (+Ton?) 14 Bel 19.30 GP Familienschla ger	10 Schattenstim men 18 Schattenstim men
Fr 25.04 19.30 Jesus Christ *Misch-Freitag 8* Glennon, Zeiser Celesti, Küssner, Stachow, *ohne Whitford* Stanke, Merstein-MacLeo, Denkinger, Pabst, Appel, Georgopoulos, Ferreira, KimJW, Klages, Boksy, Bettenh., Gaik, Hüsgen, Rühl, Weweleisp, Hönig, Erkamp Clauder, Düllmann, BraunJa, Chang, Förste, Friedrich, Markstein, Roppel, Chor, E-Chor, Statisterie, CANTAMUS, Drücker, Pecher, Marstell, Rauch, von der Emde, Nauk, PapeH, Delano, Reinell, Mentel, Pfannsch.	19.30 Prem Familienschlager Reiter, Noll, BeckM, BeckA, Weiser, Flake, Mann, Rohbeck, FischerH, Sprekelsen, RichterS, Watzke, Statisterie anschl. Premierenfeier	20.15 Boxer SchulzeA, Bien, Drechsler, Lateika	?Adam ab 14?, Bitterlich **Sa 26.04** 19.30 Prem Li Baumann, Zeis Jurriens, Wohlr Chevalier, Heo Chor, Statisteri anschl. Premie **So 27.04** 19.30 Filmkon Baumann, Jur Holst/Hüß/Pfja , Dusseljee, Fickenscher, ?Losaka?, ?Ringborg ab 14?, ?Whitford?, ?WielandJoh.? Lis		18.30 Soundcheck	10 Schattenstim men

Example 4.   Weekly plan (*Wochenplan*). Printed courtesy of the Kassel Opera (Staatstheater Kassel).

Kassel in Germany. It indicates rehearsals (*Proben*) are taking place in the opera house (*Opernhaus*), the theater (*Schauspielhaus*), the theater foyer (TH-foyer), the small theater space (*tif*), and the tif foyer. On Monday, Wednesday, and Friday there are other productions (*Vorstellungen*) being rehearsed or performed as well. For example, on Wednesday there is a dress rehearsal for the play *Familienschlager*, and the premiere is on Friday at 7:30 PM (1930), competing with a performance of *Jesus Christ, Superstar* in the opera house.

The column labeled *Urlaubsanträge/krank* lists the names of cast and orchestra members who are officially absent—on vacation or ill.

Example 5 is a daily rehearsal plan (*Probeplan*) for Thursday, April 17, 2008. The first column indicates where the rehearsal or production is taking place. The second column indicates the time rehearsals begin and the names of ensemble members required for this rehearsal. In the Schauspielhaus, the small print opposite the term *"Maskenzeiten"* (makeup) labeled *Damen* (women) and *Herren* (men) indicates which soloists are to report to the makeup room, and when. Example: "60 minutes before beginning" (*60 Min. vor Beginn*). Note that singer Samantha Richter is to get her makeup applied in the men's makeup area before the men arrive. Perhaps she is playing a pants role (*Hosenpartien*).

This *Probeplan* also includes rehearsal plans for the chorus, ballet, and orchestra.

Probenplan für Donnerstag, 17. April 2008

	KL: Volk	VORSTELLUNG	BvD: Poschmann
Opernhaus	19.00	**KOSTPROBE** Der Liebestrank = öffentl. BO 2 *Fortsetzung vom Vormittag* Orch.wart: bitte Hammerklavier Chevalier, Heo, Brad, Ballard, Neidig, Chor, Statisterie (ZR: Klein, Ocsovai) anschl. *Stück von Beginn –andere Besetzung* dz. Savelsbergh, Heo, Brad, Klein, Neidig, Chor, Statisterie (ZR: Ocsovai)	**Baumann, Lee, Dapp,** Zeisei Celesti, Schmalöer, Küssner, Jurriens, Wohlrab
Opernfoyer	18.45	**Einführung** Kostprobe Liebe	Benzing,
tif	20.15	**Das Herz eines Boxers** *Hahlheger* Drechsler, Lateika	Schulze, Bien **KL:** KJT

MUSIKTHEATER			
Opernhaus	10.00	**Der Liebestrank** Orch.wart: bitte Hammerklavier BO 1 *Stück im Ablauf mit Auslassungen* Chevalier, Heo, Brad, Ballard, Neidig, Chor, Statisterie, ZR: Savelsbergh, Klein, Ocsovai, ~~Beleuchtungskorrekturen~~	Schmalöer, Küssner, Jurriens, Wohlrab, **Baumann, Lee,** Zeiser Celesti, 10.00-10.45 **Ward,** ab 10.45 **Dapp,**
	19.00	s. ÖBO 2	

SCHAUSPIEL			
Schauspiel- haus	10.00	**Familienschlager** +Ton *nach Ansage*	Heymann, Reiter, Noll, Beck, Möller,
	13.00	Beleuchtungskorrekturen	
	19.00	**HP 0** *Original Deko, Requ. Kostüm, Maske, Bel, Ton* **+Foto** für alle Beteiligten: Beck, Weiser, Flake, Mann, Rohbeck, Fischer, Sprekelsen, Richter, Watzke, Statisterie,	Heymann, Böing, Busch, Hartmann, Reiter, Noll, Beck, Möller,

Maskenzeiten

Damen (S. Richter siehe bei den Herren!)			Herren			
Schminkzeit	Anja		Schminkzeit	Georg	Andrea	
90 Min. vor Beginn	Agnes Mann		75 Min. vor Beginn	Hannes Fischer	Samantha Richter	
60 Min. vor Beginn	Christina Weiser		85 Min. vor Beginn	Matthias Flake		
			80 Min. vor Beginn		Andreas Beck	
			50 Min. vor Beginn	Uwe Rohbeck	Frank Watzke	
			40 Min. vor Beginn		Thomas Sprekelsen	

TuP O/1	10.30 anschl. 12.30 13.30	**Viel Lärm um nichts** *abends lernfrei* **2.3** Engelke, Wink, Link, Drechsler, **3.2** dz. Langel, **4.1** dz. Dörr,	Schlösser, Endreß, Martin,
TuP S/2	10.30 19.00	**Schattenstimmen** für alle Beteiligten: Elter, Leupelt, Richartz, Keller, Leest, *nach Ansage*	Bischoff, Hohlfeld, Bien, Ohta, Bischoff, Hohlfeld,

Example 5. Rehearsal plan (*Probeplan*). Printed courtesy of the Kassel Opera (Staats-theater Kassel).

tif-Foyer		**Die Wanze**		*keine Abendprobe*	Klinge, Vysotsky, Scheuch
	11.00	Steinbruch,			

PB 7	15.00-18.00	**Jugendclub (ab 16 Jahre)**	Cleven,Crnkovic	
extern	15.00	Senioren-Theatergruppe		

SONSTIGES				
kl. SiZi	10.00-14.00	**Personalrat**	10.30 + Intend.	
gr. SiZi	*09.00-14.00*	*res. Bibliothek*		

MUSIKPROBENPLAN				
Zi. +2.009		**Musikalische Probe**		
	10.00	Adam	WALKÜRE	**Dapp**
	10.45	Adam	PETER GRIMES	**Ward**
	15.00 res. Nava			
	17.00-19.00	*res. Einsingen LIEBESTRANK*		

CHORPROBEN			
Chor	10.00	ges. H-Chor incl. Neidig OH	BO 1 Liebestrank
	19.00	ges. H-Chor incl. Neidig OH	Kostprobe Liebestrank BO 2

TANZPROBEN			
Tanz	10.00-11.30	Jean-Marc	Ballettsaal
	11.45-14.15	Sacre	Ballettsaal
	15.30-19.30	neue heimat	Ballettsaal

ORCHESTER	
	s. OH

abwesend	?Dethleffsen?, Dusseljee, ?Erhardt von 10.00 bis 14.00?, Fickenscher, ?Glennon?, ?Harach?, ?Lesaka?, ?Müller?, ?Ringborg?, ?Savelsbergh ab 13.00-20.00?, ?Stachow?, ?Troester?, ?Wieland?, Lis

Example 5. *(continued)*

Solo Rehearsals (*Soloproben*)

The whole cycle of rehearsals begins with solo rehearsals for all ensemble members other than chorus members. These solo rehearsals are coaching sessions for the singer. The study director (*Studienleiter*) assigns each singer enough solo rehearsal time, with a coach or accompanist, to ensure that the role is learned correctly. Rehearsals take place in small rehearsal rooms, usually only large enough for an upright piano, the coach, and the singer. It is the coach's job not only to help singers learn the notes, but to help them learn the correct style and to answer all questions regarding form, diction, language, and emotional expression.

Ensemble Rehearsals (*Ensembleproben*)

When the singers have learned their solo parts adequately, the *Studienleiter* will then assign them to rehearsals with other singers with whom they share duets or ensemble numbers. These *Ensembleproben* are also held in a rehearsal room just large enough to accommodate the singers and a coach or an accompanist, although sometimes they will take place in the *Studien-leiter*'s office or on one of the rehearsal stages. Ensemble rehearsals last until all parties have the ensemble numbers memorized with the correct style, diction, and musical form, including any recitative or dialogue.

First Orchestra Rehearsal (*Sitzprobe*)

When all the solo singers have memorized their roles, and the chorus is completely prepared, the entire ensemble will meet on the large rehearsal stage and sing through the opera. This is often done sitting down, thus the name *Sitzprobe*, which means "sitting rehearsal." The conductor who has been assigned the primary responsibility for the opera will conduct, and the cast is expected to sing with voice and with appropriate expression and drama. In many ways this is the most exciting rehearsal, since it is the first time to hear everything together and to get an idea of what it will be like to perform the role on stage.

Blocking Rehearsals (*Stellproben*)

Following a successful *Sitzprobe*, rehearsals will be held on a large re-hearsal stage to block the opera. These could be held on the main re-hearsal stage (*Probebühne*) or in a large room with an elevated stage area. The size of this rehearsal stage will be close to the actual size of the main stage where the performances will take place.

The stage area will be marked with tape to show the approximate placing of large set pieces, but small items such as chairs, tables, and even door frames are supplied immediately. Platforms are assembled to represent levels, and relatively soon a mock-up of the entire set will be in place. The order of scenes and blocking is entirely up to the stage director, who does not always choose to block the opera chronologically. Blocking rehearsals will have a conductor, an accompanist, a prompter, a directing assistant who keeps track of the blocking, the cast for that scene, and the stage director.

The stage director is totally in charge of these rehearsals. The conductor may be present, or an assistant conductor or even a coach, but they make no comments or suggestions either musically or about the general style.

Sectional Rehearsals (*Stückproben*)

These rehearsals consist of various sections of the opera. They could be on the rehearsal stage or on the main stage. The purpose of these rehearsals is to polish a particular section or act of the opera.

Stage Rehearsals (*Bühnenproben*)

These rehearsals are held on the main stage, with all the components necessary to present the opera—scenery, set, props, prompter, conductor in the pit, and an accompanist on the piano. A large table is set up about halfway back in the audience space (*Zuschauerraum*), and the stage director runs the rehearsals from this position. He or she sits at the table accompanied by the makeup director, the set/lighting designer, the costume designer, and any other personnel needed to contribute to the final rehearsal process. The table will have an amplification system so the stage director can easily talk to the cast.

The stage director and the conductor are responsible for these rehearsals, both finalizing dramatic or musical components.

Lighting Rehearsals (*Lichtproben/Beleuchtungsproben*)

Prior to the final rehearsals there will be a lighting rehearsal, usually an entire day that the stage director uses to add lights and any other special effects to the opera. The stage will have the full set and props. Cast members are expected to be in costume so the effect of lights on the costumes can be duly noted. Sometimes instead of the soloists, extras are used to stand on stage while lights are being adjusted. There will be no actual rehearsing during the lighting process, although action might be walked through to simulate the dramatic flow of a scene or an act.

Final Rehearsals (*Hauptproben*)

Hauptproben are the final rehearsals in the week prior to the dress rehearsal. At this point in the rehearsal process the conductor assumes absolute control of all the remaining rehearsals. If the opera is double cast, there will be additional *Hauptproben* scheduled.

Hauptproben take place on the main stage with the set, props, full costume, and makeup. There is at least one *Hauptprobe* with piano and one with orchestra per cast. All casts, regardless of whether they are the primary cast members (*erste Besetzung*) or second (*zweite*) or third (*dritte*) cast have the right to an orchestra rehearsal prior to performing the opera. Singers are usually required to sing full voice during these rehearsals, depending on what other performances they have at the time.

Photographers will be present during the *Hauptprobe* to take photos for publicity. These rehearsals give them access to the entire seating area as well as the balcony and the sides of the stage.

Dress Rehearsal (*Generalprobe*)

Dress rehearsals are conducted as if they were actual performances. The only difference is that there is usually only a short pause between acts rather than the longer intermission during performances. Everything is handled exactly as if it were a performance—the costumes, makeup, timing, drama, expression. There are no musical corrections or staging changes allowed during these rehearsals, and the conductor is expected to move the opera along without any unnecessary pauses.

If the *Generalprobe* is an "open" dress rehearsal—that is to say an audience is present—the audience will be seeing and hearing the opera exactly as if it were a performance. Sometimes special groups will be in attendance, possibly paying a special price for the privilege. Whether or not the rehearsal is designated as open is up to the stage director, with additional permission from the cast. Photographers will again be present, shooting photos for publicity.

Explanatory Rehearsal (*Verständigungsprobe*)

The explanatory rehearsal is a rehearsal held for the benefit of a guest who is assuming a role for that evening's performance or for a new member of the cast. This rehearsal is held as soon as the guest arrives at the opera house, especially if he or she is performing that night. Most of the other cast members will be more than willing to accommodate this type of last-minute rehearsal. As the guest has already performed the same opera, this rehearsal is mainly to make sure the guest is comfortable with the staging and to check tempi. Since there is no time to learn blocking, the guest mainly reacts to the person with whom he or she is sharing the scene, and the house cast in turn adapts to the actions of the guest.

This type of rehearsal would also be scheduled to accommodate a new cast member added to an opera that is already being performed. In this case, several rehearsals would be scheduled so that the new person has ample time to learn the staging. However, if this new cast member is from the same opera house, he or she will most likely already have seen the opera and be familiar with the staging prior to a *Verständigungsprobe*.

REHEARSAL DEMEANOR (*KORREKT ZU SEIN*)

There is a certain demeanor that is expected of ensemble members during rehearsals. The phrase *korrekt zu sein*, which in German literally means "correct you are," describes this demeanor. In relation to an opera career, this wonderful term also means "knowing how to be professional." To be considered *korrekt zu sein* is both a compliment and an expectation.

An example of *korrekt zu sein* would be standing still and remaining quiet during staging rehearsals while the stage director refines the dramatic motivation or the conductor is discussing musical style.

Other examples include the expectation that the singer will be on time for rehearsals, prepared for all rehearsals, and will sing full voice when that is required. There is no coddling in the opera business, and the rehearsal demeanor of the singer will often be one of the determining factors in whether the singer is retained for subsequent seasons.

Penalty Notice (*Strafzettel*)

Occasionally an ensemble member will fail to observe *korrekt zu sein.* When this happens, opera houses have a method used to reprimand singers called *Strafzettel*, which literally means "penalty notice." These written notices documenting mistakes or misconduct are like getting a traffic violation. Too many and you lose your license—to sing! Singers who miss a rehearsal will be sent a *Strafzettel*. Singers who are late to a rehearsal or disturb the rehearsal in some way will also be sent a *Strafzettel*. Singers who make a significant mistake during a performance, whether musically or with the staging, could also receive a *Strafzettel*. Receiving a *Strafzettel* is a serious reprimand and must be handled carefully and avoided if at all possible. Singers who receive three of these could be dismissed from their contract.

By the time they actually get a contract, most singers already understand how to be professional and will avoid receiving any of these little missives. Even if one is received, a meeting with the *Intendant* can be scheduled to explain the circumstances. Sometimes the fault does not lie with the singer but from incorrect or incomplete instructions, as in the following example.

During a performance of Johann Strauss's *Zigeuner Baron* at the Kassel opera house in the 1980s, the guest soprano, who had rehearsed only briefly in the late afternoon, found herself stuck on an elevated platform at the end of a scene with the curtain closing behind her. There was no way off the platform except to climb down a ladder (accompanied by loud laughter from the audience). Called to the *Intendant*'s office immediately after the performance, she simply explained that the assistant stage director had not told her what to do at the end of this scene. She did not receive a *Strafzettel*.

ONE DAY IN THE LIFE OF THE SINGER

A typical day in the life of an opera singer (using the twenty-four-hour clock) might be the following:

0900   Arrive at the opera house to warm up the voice for rehearsal.
1000   First rehearsal.
1100   Excused from rehearsal for costume fittings.
1130   Break. To the *Kantina* for a coffee or tea (or beer).
1145   Resume rehearsal.
1300   Break for lunch or to go home to rest for evening's performance. (A four-hour rest period is required if a singer has an evening performance.)
1700   Return to the opera house to warm up for evening performance. Sign in to officially register your presence in the opera house.
1730   Report to the makeup department.
1800   Go to dressing room to put on costume and continue warm-up.
1830   Attend last-minute rehearsals, if called for by a conductor for the benefit of someone assuming a role or a last-minute guest.
1930   Performance begins (two-and-a-half-hour opera).
2200   Performance ends. Return to dressing room to change.
2300   Meet fans at the stage entrance and then go out to eat with cast or friends. (Most opera singers eat a very light meal in the midafternoon when singing an evening performance.)

PERFORMANCE TIPS

A whole book could be written about tips to make a performance the best it can be. It would include chapters such as: Stay Healthy—Be Rested—Be Prepared—Be Respectful—Be Considerate—Be Patient—Love Your Fans—and . . . Love Your Profession!

There is another tip that is worth discussing here. It has to do with the singer's partnership with the conductor during a performance.

Reading the Beat

It is important to know the conductor's style and all the little nuances that form the bond of communication between a conductor and a singer. Key to this is learning how to read the conductor's downbeat. The most basic rule would be to *not* anticipate the beat and certainly not to wait for the sound, as one hears sound after it has already traveled some distance. The best rule is to read the conductor's body language and learn what little motion precedes the downbeat. Then singers can time their entrance accordingly. In any case, experience is the only teacher.

When to Look Directly at the Conductor

The initial suggestion would be, never. However, this is not quite true. There are times when singers may need to look at the conductor because they have lost the beat (the singer, not the conductor) or missed a musical entrance. This can be accomplished if the singer looks in the general vicinity of the conductor but does not make eye contact. To do so would draw attention to the conductor, who, although a very important component, is not *in* the opera. Doing so would be similar to breaking character in a theatrical production. The eyes are a very powerful acting tool, and where they look is part of the performance.

If the singer can glance toward the conductor unobtrusively, or coordinate this with the stage action, then it will not be obvious to the audience. What should always be avoided is looking directly at the conductor at the beginning of a vocal selection. Use your peripheral vision.

Most opera houses place video screens around the stage, and sometimes above the stage as well, which makes it possible for singers to "see" the conductor without actually looking directly at him or her. It is important to maintain the aesthetic distance between the audience and singers on stage.

NOTES

1. *Deutches Bühnen Jahrbuch* (Hamburg: Genossenschaft Deutscher Bühnen-Angehöriger im Verlag der Bühenschriften-Bertriebs-Gesellschaft mbH, 2006), 12.
2. *Bayerische Staatsoper Jahresvorschau* 2007–2008, 181.
3. Ibid., 21.

Pearl Yeadon McGinnis in front of the Munich Opera House (*Bayerische Staatsoper*), Munich, Germany. Author's collection.

Wig department of Kassel Opera (*Kassel Staatsoper*), Kassel Germany. Photo courtesy of Dominik Ketz.

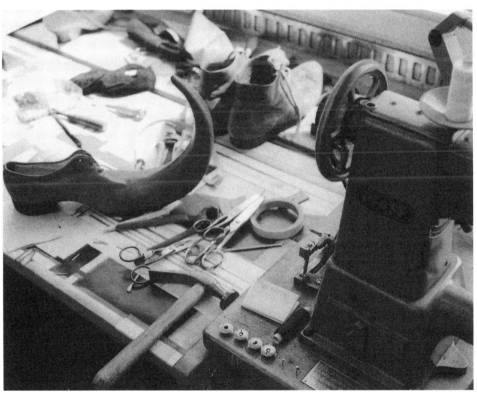

Shoe Shop: Munich Opera (*Bayerische Staatsoper*). Photo courtesy of photographer Mr. Wilfried Hösl.

Pearl's dressing-room preparation of "Manon" for Puccini's *Manon Lescaut* at the Ulmer Theater, Ulm, Germany, 1984. Photo by Herbert Raith. The following two photos are of Pearl performing in this same production.

Act II of *Manon Lescaut.* Photo by Herbert Raith.

Manon's aria: "Solo, perduta, abbandonatta!" from Act IV of *Manon Lescaut*. Photo by Herbert Raith.

10

Maintaining a Career

Once the singer has an ensemble contract (*Normal Vertrag*), fulfilling this contract is the singer's primary responsibility. If a singer is successful, the contract will usually be renewed or a new contract negotiated. However, if the contract is not renewed, the singer must be in a position to quickly secure a new job with another house.

The best way for singers to do this is to take control of all aspects of their career as soon as they have that first contract. Singers who expect agents, directors, or conductors to find work for them will be disappointed. Agents will always arrange auditions and facilitate any contracts resulting from auditions but will not take time to personally manage a singer or plan careers. While an agent may have suggestions about improving the marketability of an individual singer, such as learning a specific role or switching to a new *Fach*, the singer is the person who will make that happen.

To maintain a career a singer must invest in record keeping, publicity, photos, correspondence, maintaining relationships with agents, networking, auditioning, and preparation for "jumping in" (*einspringen*), which will be explained later in this chapter. The result will be new job possibilities. An opera singer could hire a personal manager to take care of many of these details, but this rarely happens until a career is well developed.

RECORD KEEPING

Record keeping must be mentioned first, because efficiently organized records provide documented proof of professional activities. This in turn will facilitate the opera singer's career maintenance and development. Starting with the first engagement, it is the singer's responsibility to document each audition and engagement. Think ahead. It is useful to be able to back up the statement, "I performed in Europe in 2009 . . ." with photos, reviews, and especially names. Keep everything—programs, posters, opera house schedules, brochures—anything that will verify career development.

Programs

Programs provide proof of performances as well as the names of directors, conductors, and house staff. Remember to add the names of conductors and stage directors to all future résumés. Use programs to learn the names of other colleagues in the opera house, matching names with faces, even the support staff such as a makeup lady or the prompter. Keep these programs as important documents. It is surprising how many ways they are useful.

Reviews

Reviews are another important source of names, dates, and especially comments on the performance itself. Any review in a newspaper or magazine greatly adds to the visibility and reputation of the singer.

European reviews usually feature beautiful photos from the production. Keep the original review and translate it, if needed. The correct way to document a review is the following:

> First line: *Name of Newspaper*: reviewer's name; town, country—name of opera house (date of review)
> Second line: "Title of Review"
> Third line: Body of review, followed by (*Name of the Opera*)

Example (translated):

> *Schwäbische Zeitung*: Günter Buhles; Ulm, Germany—Ulmer Theater (11.3.84)
> "Space, Dreams, Beautiful Voices"
> Eva Pearl Yeadon as Manon and Herbert Schaefer as Des Grieux in their luscious big duet managed to fill the empty stage with drama that had the public spellbound. Thanks to the acting ability and vocally brilliant interpretation and power of both actors, this scene, as it is played in a comfortless desert of North America, was the

determining high point beyond any other successes or failures of the production. (*Manon Lescaut*)[1]

Notes and Letters

European fans are marvelous! They are constantly writing delightful little notes of appreciation and sometimes even long letters. They keep track of their favorite singers and regularly write to ask for signed photos. Notes or letters from fans are interesting to keep as mementos and to remind the singer of unusual or special aspects of a particular production.

In Italy, the system of "planting fans" in the audience is still alive and well. Singers pay a small fee to organized groups of attendees called a claque, who then "lead" the applause and generate excitement in the rest of the audience for the singer's performance. The singer also provides claque members with autographed photos.

Posters

European opera houses create beautiful posters of each production. These can be quite large and are displayed in theater advertising spaces, on street corners, and on the sides of buildings and walls around the city. Once all the performances of that particular opera are finished, a poster may be purchased by going to the musicologist (*Dramaturg*) and simply asking for one. Sometimes they will be free. Posters also have all the pertinent information needed for records, as well as those wonderful photos.

Audition Diary

Keep a diary of all auditions. This should include the date, the time of the audition, and the first aria performed, as well as any other arias requested. Also include any comments made by the audition panel. Write down if an agent set up any follow-up house auditions and any other details that relate to that particular audition, such as what you wore or the hotel or pension where you stayed.

Performance Diary

A performance diary can be extremely useful in managing a career. Include details such as which agent was at the performance; mistakes or problems during the performance; any comments from the director, conductor, or colleagues; and any unusual details such as who might have joined the cast as a last-minute guest. Programs can also act as an effective performance diary by organizing them chronologically in a binder along with any added notes pertaining to that performance.

Correspondence Notebook

Set up a folder or three-ring binder and alphabetically place all correspondence from agents, opera houses, and directors. On occasion these materials will need to be found rapidly. Even a few years in Europe can produce an amazing paper trail, so organize it in whatever style is preferred, but be sure to organize.

Keeping a notebook of all correspondence enhances the ability to send publicity materials and photos as a way of maintaining contacts with agents and prospective opera houses. People in the opera world move frequently, so keeping in touch is vital. Opera houses, conductors, and directors will not keep track of what a singer is doing even if they liked what they saw or heard at an initial audition or in a performance. The singer is expected to take the initiative and send updates to them.

PUBLICITY AND PHOTOS

Update publicity materials after every performance. Add information about the performance to your résumé, and include photos. Photos taken during a performance, which show the set, props, ensemble, and of course costumes, illustrate the ability to act a role and can encourage future interest from agents and potential opera houses.

Purchase as many photos from the house photographer as possible, including copies of any head shots the photographer has taken as records for the makeup department. Keep the photos in a binder or notebook. It is useful to put a copy of the opera program with the photos as a quick reference.

Send performance photos and an updated résumé on a regular basis to agents, especially the agent of record for that particular performance or performances. Send the same information to any prospective agents and to opera houses. Even if they throw it away, they will have briefly seen the materials.

RELATIONSHIPS WITH AGENTS

This is one of the most critical elements, not only at the beginning of a career but also in maintaining a career. Improving your relationship with any agent who facilitated a contract is vital. The singer also needs to create new relationships with other agents who can help with future career possibilities.

Acknowledge an agent's expertise. They are not just people who can arrange auditions and contracts. Agents truly understand the opera world and what opera houses expect from singers. They also have vast experience in how best to match singers with possible jobs. Agents are sometimes happy to give advice about possible roles or new career directions, although, as was mentioned previously, they won't personally manage a singer unless they are a manager as well as an agent. If agents feel validated as individuals, not just for what they know or can suggest about the business, they are more likely to remain interested.

Invite the agent responsible for an opera house contract to all performances. Agents will have listings of these, but a personal invitation will go a long way toward getting them to actually attend. Nothing proves the singer's talent to an agent better than being seen on stage in performance.

Opera houses provide the cast with complimentary tickets. Use these for agents, reviewers, or friends. These tickets will be free (*Dienstkarten*) or have only a small fee (*Steuerkarten*) charged to the singer to cover the taxes. If visiting friends in other houses, ask them for complimentary tickets to their performances. Attending as many performances as possible will add to a general knowledge about what operas are in vogue and what roles might be especially interesting to study.

If an agent comes to a performance and doesn't have to leave immediately afterward, invite him or her out for a late dinner or a drink. Agents expect to be fussed over a bit. (Ask for a business receipt.) However, do not use this opportunity to press for promises of future auditions.

The singer's general usefulness to the opera world is of great interest to agents, so keep the primary agent and any potential agencies informed when a new role has been memorized and is ready for performance. The agent might then suggest an audition for that particular role. Also inform your current opera house. They could add this role to your responsibilities. As soon as any new role has been performed, again inform the primary agent, other interested agents, and other opera houses who have this opera in their repertoire.

Be honest about any contacts with other agents. Professional singers in Europe will not necessarily have only one agent, and agents all know this. So if one of them asks about auditions or performances or contracts made through another agency, provide this information. This only reflects well on the singer's talent and desirability.

It is a good idea to visit the primary agent regularly. Personal contact reminds the agent of the singer's confidence, energy, and determination to be a success in the opera world.

Synopsis: Improving Relationships with Agents

- Stay in contact with short letters, e-mails, notes about performances.
- Acknowledge agents' expertise; ask their opinion and advice.
- Send performance head shots and performance photos.
- Send lists of performance dates to all agents.
- Invite primary agent to performances, and invite the agent out afterward.
- Let agents know when you are studying new roles and when the roles are ready to be performed.
- Be honest about all contacts, contracts, and audition offers.

NETWORKING

Networking in any profession is another important element in developing and maintaining a career. Young singers who are used to the cocoon provided by the university or private studio need to develop supporting relationships with colleagues, agents, and opera house personnel. In the process they will build bridges to maintaining their own career.

Networking needs to be pursued in a professional manner. In Germany, a performer who cultivates relationships too aggressively is said to have "elbow technique." This implies that they elbow everyone out of the way to get noticed. Although aggressive behavior might produce significant career advances, this type of networking is not admired.

A more professional approach would be to take a genuine interest in fellow performers. An audition for an agent or for an opera house is a good opportunity to meet people and initiate new relationships.

Visit Colleagues and Rehearsals

If a colleague moves to a new opera house, go visit. Being visible in a new house is one of the best ways of becoming known. *Intendants* and stage directors are always interested in visiting singers, especially if they are new people. Even a casual meeting with an *Intendant* in the *Kantina* can prompt the *Intendant* to think, "I wonder how I can use this singer, and in what role?" This could even lead to an audition offer on the spot, resulting in an ensemble or guest contract with that opera house. This actually happened to the author—one of those fortunate incidents that make this profession so exciting and rewarding.

Also, if possible when visiting a colleague, ask for permission to attend rehearsals. The stage director of each opera is the person to give permission—a good excuse to meet this very important contact. Soak in the music, style, acting, and all the other fascinating details. Attending rehearsals is a way of expanding one's own knowledge about other performers, staging, conducting styles, and all other aspects of performances. Pauses in the rehearsals will provide another opportunity to meet new people. Visiting rehearsals will also give a good indication of what might be expected if a contract is secured in this house.

Be sure to extend invitations to friends to visit you. Reciprocal arrangements are part of the business and lead to some delightful, lifelong friendships.

Also stay in contact with former colleagues who have moved to a different opera house. They will be the first to know if there will be openings in that house for new singers, or if a concert or symphony group is looking for a soloist.

Visit Conductors and Stage Directors

If a conductor or stage director is engaged in the singer's opera house in a *Fest* position, this person undoubtedly also accepts guest contracts in other opera houses or for special projects, such as a staged production of an oratorio or performances during summer opera festivals.

Make sure you establish a relationship with this conductor, as conductors have many opportunities to engage people to perform with them for these events or for symphony concerts, special tours with an orchestra, or even performances on radio and television.

Cultivating a genuine interest in conductors and stage directors adds a personal touch, which can result in significant performance opportunities.

Arrange Coaching Sessions

When visiting another opera house, contact a coach there in advance and ask for some coaching sessions. These might be only one or two sessions and could be to polish a role or begin to learn a new one. It is a good idea to find out something about the coach first, as some specialize in certain styles or languages. Coaching sessions provide ongoing training in languages and style, as well as performance tips, and are another way to be noticed, possibly leading to an unexpected audition. The following is a delightful example of this happening.

A colleague was coaching with Herr Doktor Professor von Nöe at the National Theater in Munich. She was learning the role of Amelia in Verdi's *Un ballo in maschera*. Suddenly the door burst open and a young man came enthusiastically in the room. He said he had heard someone singing the opera and asked if she was going to be performing this role. When she answered that she was only learning the role, he then asked von Nöe (in

Italian) who she was and where she was currently performing. He was obviously pleased with the answers, because he then asked if he could sing through the duets from *Ballo* with her. This was an incredible experience for this young soprano. The chance to sing with a world-class tenor is the type of accidental meeting that could lead to a recommendation for an audition or to sing for an agency, as in this case it did!

Contact Established Singers

Write or telephone an established singer and ask if he or she would coach a specific role. Singers on the international level, having performed their roles several hundred times, know intimately the style and performance expectations of the role. They know when and how to rest the voice while performing, and when to sing out. They also know where the vocally dangerous sections are in the opera and can provide helpful hints and tips to negotiate these areas. Receiving this kind of coaching could be expensive, as a pianist must be hired and a coaching fee paid. But once this is affordable, it is an effective and interesting way to study and improve an opera role and get noticed by the established singer at the same time.

AUDITIONS

To maintain a career, especially between contracts, auditions must be ongoing. There are many opportunities for auditions. These include informative auditions for new opera houses, auditions for specific roles within the singer's own house, or a request to an *Intendant*, conductor, or director to sing through specific roles. Any of these auditions could lead to a new *Festvertrag* or a *Gastvertrag*.

Informative Auditions

Informative auditions can be arranged with opera houses simply by writing and asking for one. This is especially appropriate once several roles have been successfully performed and might be of interest to that particular house.

Include with your request your repertoire, reviews, and sample photos. If invited to audition, travel at least a day early to allow sufficient rest and preparation. Find out who will be accompanying during the audition, and hire this person to rehearse the selections before the audition. This is important! There is nothing worse than worrying about whether the accompanist will match your tempi and levels of expression. Even if just a small part of your attention is concerned about this, it will be noticeable to the audition panel and will detract from your audition. The blend of sound from the singer and the accompanist should be flawless. In fact, the singer should not even be actively aware of the accompanist—just the perfect marriage of sound and expression. Following the audition, contact the primary agent with all the details.

Sometimes an *Intendant* will ask an ensemble member to sing through several arias from an opera planned for the future. This is also an informative audition, and the singer should consider a request such as this a great chance to demonstrate one's talent and potential for future roles.

Auditions for Specific Roles

Since opera house schedules for the coming season or seasons are prepared years in advance, a singer can request to audition for a specific role in a future production. This is a great opportunity to further one's career, and certainly to maintain it.

The ensemble member, in order to be considered, must contact the *Intendant* and ask to be heard singing through the role. This type of audition requires the singer to sing the entire role, accompanied on piano, with the *Intendant*, the conductor assigned the opera, and perhaps other interested parties in attendance. This experience is challenging and fun and is of great value to the singer's development as an artist.

A successful audition could lead to the addition of this role to a singer's contract and also makes the singer "visible" for any future roles of the same type.

Audition for a Conductor

Conductors have significant control over who sings in their productions. As was previously mentioned, when they are the regular conductor in an opera house, they have the right to refuse to conduct an opera if a member of that cast is not up to their expectations. This does happen, although not frequently.

Conductors are vitally interested in who is cast in the various roles for the operas they will be conducting. Any poor or substandard performance by a singer reflects on the conductor, so they stay informed about casting decisions and abilities of ensemble members. They are always interested in hearing new singers, so develop a relationship with the opera house conductors as soon as possible and don't hesitate to let them know if you are interested in a particular role. This could lead to a private audition and result in new singing opportunities.

Prior to casting an opera from the ensemble members, a conductor might request an audition with certain singers in order to match the singer's voice, personality, and development to appropriate roles. A conductor might ask for arias from one opera or several or even request selections from an oratorio he or she might be conducting in future seasons. Any chance to sing for a conductor is important in developing and maintaining a career, so accept all such opportunities.

The Handshake Audition

Remember, contact with anyone in the business can lead to an audition. Sometimes a casual meeting with a conductor or theater director can result in an audition. The secret is being genuinely interested in someone else, inquiring about their career, performances, or life in general. Everyone wants to work with a positive, confident person, so be sure to cultivate this personality as a performer.

GUEST CONTRACTS (*GASTVERTRAG*)

As was mentioned in chapter 7, "Contracts and Casting," once a singer is established as an ensemble member of an opera house, that singer can also accept guest contracts with other opera companies, subject to the approval of the *Betriebsbüro*. However, if the singer is between contracts, auditioning for these guest appearances is extremely important in maintaining a career. Once you have been a guest singer at several opera houses and become known for certain roles, these guest singing opportunities may be even more available or could result in a new *Festvertrag*.

An audition for a guest contract (*Gastvertrag*) may entail singing through an entire opera for the conductor, accompanied on piano by one of the coaches in the house. The conductor will use this opportunity to judge the singer's musicality, style, vocal prowess, and acting capabilities. When accepting this type of audition, be sure to have the role memorized. You will make a more positive impact on the conductor if you sing from memory than if you are holding a score or constantly glancing at a score on a music stand. Having the arias memorized frees you to use your whole body in expressing the emotion of the music. In opera, as in American musical theater, the director and conductor will often choose the singer who can act.

Guest Performance Salary

Salaries for guest appearances depend on the need for the singer's services at the time, as well as on the type of contract offered and the number of performances. Even one performance per month as a guest can provide opera singers with anywhere from half to many times their regular monthly salary. It is no wonder that singers are always eager for the opportunity to accept guest contracts, whether for a single evening or multiple performances.

JUMPING IN (*EINSPRINGEN*)

Einspringen is a talent that can be valuable in maintaining an opera career. *Einspringen* literally means "a jumping" and refers to the ability of a singer to assume a role with little or no musical or stage rehearsals.

Being a singer who is able to *einspringen* is different from being a guest singer who normally is contracted well in advance of any performances. Nor is it the same as being an understudy in the theater who generally is in the cast in some other capacity.

Opera houses do have what are called "cover singers" who are assigned to learn a role as part of their contract. This is generally in anticipation of the singer assuming the role at some later date, but in an emergency the cover singer could be called upon to "jump in." If assigned a role as a cover singer, it is very important to learn the role as soon as possible, just in case.

Generally, though, an opera singer who is able to *einspringen* is not a member of the opera house ensemble but has previously performed the role, or has learned a role on his or her own and has made this known to agents and opera houses.

Often this singer is contacted with very little notice, sometimes only a day before having to perform. In other situations there will be time for rehearsals with the ensemble. Jumping in demands performers who trust their acting instincts, skills, and preparation.

An opera house usually needs someone to assume a role when a singer in the house becomes suddenly ill or incapacitated or for some other reason withdraws and there is no cover singer. There are two main options to solve this emergency:

1. An ensemble member who has learned the role on his or her own can volunteer to *einspringen*.
2. The opera house will contact agents to request a singer to assume the role. This singer is treated as guest soloist, the difference being that a normal guest soloist has been offered a contract long in advance of his or her appearance.

The decision as to whether to use a cover singer to substitute for an indisposed singer or to contract with a singer outside the house to *einspringen* is usually determined by the size of the role to be filled. For small and medium roles, a cover singer is usually adequate. If the role is one of the leads, a guest singer with experience and credentials could be preferred.

There are many situations when an ensemble member could be in a position to jump into a role already being presented in the singer's own house. These include

- The singer is new in the house and because of his or her *Fach* assignment might be expected to take over a specific role at some future date. Someone becomes ill, and that future date becomes a present one.
- The singer was not originally cast in the role but was attending rehearsals in order to indicate interest in assuming the role in the future.
- The singer is attending rehearsals because she is learning the role on her own. Someone drops out, and the singer informs the *Intendant* that she knows the role and asks to be allowed to assume the performances.
- The singer is the third cast (*dritte Besetzung*) and has been watching the rehearsals but because of time constraints has not yet been assigned to any formal rehearsals. One of the other singers becomes suddenly ill, thus creating a need for a substitute.

A singer should be ready to take advantage of any of these opportunities.

Learning a Role in Preparation for *Einspringen*

Several practical steps can be taken to prepare for a chance to jump into a role:

- If the opera is already playing, attend performances and make staging notes.
- If the opera is in rehearsal, ask permission to watch and make staging notes in the opera score.
- Once the staging has been written in the score, practice at home, using chairs, tables, music stands, or anything handy as the other characters.
- Rehearse the opera on your own with an accompanist or a coach from the opera house.
- If possible, ask the conductor of the opera for a chance to sing through the entire role.
- Go on stage before or after the rehearsals or the performances and practice all staging on the actual set.

Lilli Lehmann had some practical suggestions for learning roles.

> When I, for instance, was learning the part of Isolde, I could without weari-
> ness sing the first act alone six times in succession, with expression, action,
> and a full voice. That was my practice with all my roles. After I had rehearsed
> a role . . . in my own room, I would go into the empty theatre and rehearse
> single scenes, as well as the whole opera, for hours at a time. That gave me
> the certainty of being mistress of my resonances down to the last note.[2]

With the proper preparation, it is possible to be ready to jump into a role
even without any formal rehearsals. However, never agree to put on the
costume and step onto the stage without being absolutely sure that the
role can be performed on the same level as the singers who received the
benefit of all those rehearsals.

If an ensemble singer takes over a role, or even a rehearsal, and seems
unsure or unprepared, this will immediately be known all over the opera
community. Even if this was to "save" the performance, the only thing
everyone will remember is that the performance was not at the proper
artistic level. Everyone, including agents, will assume the singer had not
prepared the role properly.

On the other hand, if a role is well prepared, an opportunity to *einspringen* can be a major step to advancing and maintaining a career, as the
following true story illustrates.

During a performance of Verdi's *Il trovatore* at the Kassel Staatsoper
in the early 1980s, a young soprano from the ensemble was sitting in the
wings of the stage, marking her score in preparation for singing the role
sometime in the future. Suddenly the soprano performing the lead role of
Leonora held up her hand and walked off the stage. The curtains quickly
closed, to the great consternation of the audience and all those backstage.
When it was determined that the soprano had lost her voice, the young
soprano in the wings was asked to *einspringen*. She agreed, but asked if
she could sing from the pit and let the hoarse soprano walk through the
rest of the opera, miming to the music. This was agreed upon, and the
young soprano borrowed reading glasses from the string bass player,
took her score, and sang the rest of the opera without even warming
up. The audience roared their approval afterward. The newspaper later
reported, "Leonora dies twice on the opera stage." (Leonora takes poison
at the opera's end to avoid marrying the evil Count di Luna.) The young
soprano took over the role two weeks later.

THE FIFTEEN-YEAR BARRIER

Opera soloists in Europe have the constant worry as to whether their
contract will be renewed. Even for a well-established ensemble member,

contracts are written only for a certain number of years, rarely longer than five at a time, although there is no specific rule about this.

Ensemble members who remain at one opera house during their careers become known to their fans and are recognized for the roles they portray. The opera enthusiast enjoys watching an opera singer's development, from early lyric roles into more mature dramatic character parts. As long as the soloist is continually useful to the opera house and is able to sing a *Fach* that is used every season, that soloist's job is relatively secure. Even during the inevitable changes in *Intendants*, there is a good chance that the soloist can perform as an ensemble member in that opera house for many, many years.

Soloists who remain in one opera house for fifteen years become tenured (*Unkündbar*), a permanent member of that opera house until retirement. As a voice changes due to age and experience, the *Fach* assignment and the roles usually change as well. This natural development throughout a career provides the opera house with mature voices that bring years of experience, and also a constant group of fans, to that opera house.

To be tenured as an opera singer is not as common as it once was in Germany. Singers are often released from their contracts just prior to their fifteen-year anniversary, to avoid keeping them until retirement. This usually happens by July 31 of the fourteenth year. This is done to give the singer an additional year to perform in the house and to have time to find new contracts. It can be argued that this system provides openings for new singers, but it also can be difficult for singers who have made a home in a specific city and then find themselves needing to start over, so to speak.[3] The exception to the above is for singers who are choristers. They are assured of their job until retirement, once they have passed the first probationary year (*Probejahr*).

The best strategy for solo singers may be to move often enough until they find an opera house where they would like to stay. Then they should cultivate fans, learn as many roles as possible, accept as many guest contracts as possible, and hope to be useful enough to the opera house by the fifteen-year barrier that the house will opt to keep them until retirement.

NOTES

1. Günter Buhles, "Space, Dreams, Beautiful Voices," *Schwäbische Zeitung*, November 3, 1984.

2. Lilli Lehmann, *How to Sing*, trans. Richard Aldrich (New York: Macmillan, 1924), 164.

3. Interview with *Intendant* Alexander Senger, founder and artistic director of Operamobile/Kleines Musiktheater, Niedersachsen, Germany, and *Operette Sich Ver Kann* at the Staatsoper, July 3, 2006.

11

Living in Europe

For an American opera singer, life in Europe can be fascinating! Having a positive attitude and a willingness to learn and appreciate the local customs is the key. The right attitude toward your new home will go a long way toward the successful development and maintenance of your career. Keep in mind that the majority of the people you will be working with are "locals," so showing an interest in and appreciation of their culture and customs will be noticed and appreciated.

Some Americans who go to Europe for the first audition trip are intimidated when the customs and foods are strange. They are frustrated by the different languages, don't enjoy the travel, and think that the amount of money offered for beginning contracts is not enough. If you are one of these people, stay home. It takes someone with an adventurous spirit, adaptability, and a true delight in cultural diversity to flourish in Europe.

Life in any of the European countries offers many interesting experiences and life-enhancing possibilities. As with any venture, prepare in advance with as much knowledge as possible about the country and city you will be living in. Many excellent travel guides are available that can familiarize you with all aspects of European life and travel. An excellent series is the DK Eyewitness Travel Guides (see www.dk.com for more information). Not only do these guides have extensive information about every aspect of a city, but they are full of colored pictures of places, palaces, parks—even pictures of the sweet and savory foods of the city. Nothing like being able to see what you're ordering first!

This chapter contains a few suggestions and anecdotes to help make living in Europe and the European opera experience a positive one.

Remember, Europe is a veritable rainbow of possibilities, adventures, and potential professional achievements.

"WHEN IN ROME . . ."

Language

When a contract has been secured in an opera house in Europe and the singer is not fluent in the language of that particular country, what then? Simple! Cultivate personal friends who speak the language. A German agent gave the following advice to a colleague: "What an American soprano needs is a German boyfriend." And he was right. Nothing beats practical day-to-day conversation to absorb all those new words.

Although English has become a universal language in Europe, it is still necessary to learn the native language as soon as possible. A major mistake many Americans make when they move to Europe is to spend too much time with other Americans. If they have only Americans as friends and speak English exclusively when offstage, they can become isolated from the many other colleagues who come from a great variety of countries and speak many languages.

Many Europeans are eager to practice or show off their English. A new American singer in Germany might try hard to speak in German, only to find that the German answers in perfect English. This can be both amusing and frustrating.

French citizens in particular are very proud of their language and culture. Although Americans often study French in school, it is difficult to master the speed and fluidity necessary to sound like a native. Unless one speaks perfect French, with an impeccable accent, attempts to use this language will most often be answered in English.

When in Italy, use every word of Italian you know, even if only a few. It makes Italians truly happy to hear their language used, or misused, in any way. They will smile and show appreciation upon hearing fractured, botched, or clumsily spoken words and phrases. Most likely an Italian will know immediately the American is a singer, as most American singers have learned some Italian from the *Twenty-Four Italian Songs* book and are attempting to speak in some sort of garbled seventeenth-century Italian. This further endears the singer to Italians, so fling Italian words and phrases about with great cheer and abandon.

The Tourist Information Office (*Fremdenverkehrsamt*)

One of the first visits in a new city should be to the tourist information office, the *Fremdenverkehrsamt* in Germany. This office is usually in the main train station or within a block or so of the train station, so it is easy to find.

Offices are usually open from 8 AM until 8 PM, and English is always spoken in some form, usually fluently. Ask these helpful people questions about how to get around; how to buy the appropriate tickets for buses, trains, or subways; and how to find specific addresses. They will smile and provide a city map, or one can be purchased. The information agent will then explain the layout of the city and highlight the easiest routes on the map, describe distances, and even recommend areas in which to live.

APARTMENT HUNTING

The first job has been offered and accepted! The next problem is finding a place to live. This is not as simple as looking for an apartment to rent in the United States, although the procedure is similar.

In Europe, owners of apartments have the right to screen potential renters either by an interview, by mail, or during the prospective renter's visit to the apartment. Owners usually have no trouble attracting renters and are strict about their requirements. Even when making an appointment to view an apartment, expect to be questioned about employment status, nationality, and other details. Often the owner expects a reference from the renter's employer. Since performing artists are valued in Europe, most owners are pleased to rent to them and will choose them over other applicants.

Ask the *Betriebsbüro* director if there is an office within the opera house that helps new employees find housing. Also ask new colleagues if they know of any available apartments. It is much faster to find an apartment with a personal reference of some sort, especially in a city where apartments are scarce.

Check Newspaper Ads

Just as in America, go to the classified ads (*Kleinanzeigen*) of the local paper and then the property section (*Immobilienteil*), which will list apartments for rent. Circle all the appropriate apartments by size, cost, and location. If the descriptions are difficult to read, ask someone at the opera house to help with the meanings and abbreviations. Telephone and make an appointment to see the apartment. English can often be used, but if the owner speaks only German, ask a colleague who is fluent to call for an appointment. Be on time for the appointment. Potential renters who arrive late will be considered unreliable and probably not receive consideration from the owner. There are often too many people looking for apartments.

If the ad simply lists a number, it will be necessary to send a letter to the newspaper with a request to see the apartment. The newspaper will forward the letter to the apartment owner, and the owner will contact the prospective renter. Most newspapers now have websites, and there are even companies that specialize in helping people find apartments.

Some of the abbreviations for ads for apartments in Germany are as follows:

2 ZKB: two rooms with kitchen and full bath
2 ZKBB: two rooms, kitchen, full bath, balcony
EG: ground floor
DG: roof or loft apartment
KM: basic rental price
NK: extra costs
WM: total cost

Monthly Rentals

Another possibility is to find a pension or apartment hotel that rents rooms by the month. There are some excellent residence hotels that only offer these types of rentals, such as the Gästehaus Max Emanuel in Munich. The hotel office at the city train station will have lists of these hotels. The rooms are small, but they have all the amenities of an apartment, including a tiny kitchen and bath. They are comfortable enough to live in until a permanent apartment has been found, and the price is usually less than a regular hotel.

Location

Location is important for several reasons. Whether an apartment is near a bus, streetcar, or subway line is a consideration, especially if you lack a car. Don't rule out the areas around the opera house. It is simply delightful to be able to walk to work, no matter the season.

Europeans use a system different from that used in America for labeling floors in buildings, and initially this can be confusing. The street-level floor in Germany is the *Erdegeschoss* (meaning "ground floor") and will be shown as an "E" on the elevator panel. The next floor, our second floor, is their first floor, and so on.

Size

Americans tend to assume that they need an apartment with at least one separate bedroom, if not two or more. Europeans, on the other hand, think that the apartment size should correspond with the number of people living there. A single person would be assumed to be looking for a studio apartment, a married couple a one-bedroom, and a family with one child, a two-bedroom apartment, and so on. Start small and work up to a larger size is obvious advice.

Furnished or Unfurnished

Another possibility would be to rent a furnished apartment. In Germany these are well kept and clean, as a German owner would rent nothing less. Such an apartment might not be fancy but would have a couch, table and chairs, at least one bed, and would also come with a television set and cable access.

Rent

In a large city, for a particularly desirable apartment, the owner will expect a "yes" or "no" immediately during the first visit. If one waits and calls back later, the apartment will most certainly be gone.

The renter will be expected to pay the basic monthly rent (*Miete* or *Monatsmiete*), plus the extra costs (*Nebenkosten*) for garbage disposal, street- or housecleaning costs, heating, and water. *Warmmiete* is the rent price including any extras. Tenants pay for their own telephone and television. A deposit (*Kaution*) of from one to two months of the basic rental price will need to be paid and is usually deposited in a bank account, where it will earn interest. After moving out the tenant will receive this deposit back, plus any accumulated interest, less any needed repairs to the apartment.

Apartment Etiquette

Europeans have a long tradition of living in close proximity to their neighbors and have developed laws and practices that make apartment living comfortable. Each building or complex will have its own set of house rules. These help regulate all aspects of apartment life—including when a singer can practice—as well as when you can have parties, how and when to take out the garbage, storage of personal items such as bicycles or strollers, and even visits by unexpected guests.

Quiet Time (*Ruhezeit*)

Each country has a specified "quiet time" (*Ruhezeit*) during the day, directed by law. In Germany, these quiet hours are before 8 AM, between noon and 2 PM, and again after 10 PM. During these times workmen cannot use drills, bang on things, or mow lawns, nor can singers practice. Everyone tries to respect these hours. Small businesses will close their doors during these times so the owners and workers can take a break or rest, although the large department stores and most food stores and pharmacies remain open. These are the same hours as in most of the European countries except France, where the afternoon quiet time is from 1 PM to 3 PM.

If you host a special event that could generate an inordinate amount of noise, such as a birthday party, a wise practice is to take a small gift, such as a bottle of wine, to any neighbors who could potentially be bothered by late-night revelry. If the neighbor is not home, leave the bottle and a polite note such as: "Dear Neighbor, my birthday is tonight and I have invited a few friends over. If we are too noisy, please call me at ____," and provide a phone number.

MEDICAL CARE

Finding a physician (*Arzt*) is as important as finding that first apartment. The best way to find a doctor in Europe is by referral. New colleagues, especially Americans who have lived in that city for some time, can suggest names of internists, as primary physicians are called.

Pharmacies (*Apotheken*) in Germany can be identified by a sign with large red *A*. In the rest of the European countries it is a sign with a large green cross.

TRANSPORTATION

Since it is so easy to get around any European city, either on foot or by using public transportation, owning or renting a car is usually not necessary. But if you choose to drive, be aware that driving on the European highways is different from driving in the United States. On the German *Autobahn* there is usually no speed limit, and slower drivers must *always* move right and allow faster cars to pass on the left. This requires drivers to frequently check their rear- and side-view mirrors.

Most other countries, such as Italy and France, have a maximum speed limit, with careful limits for dangerous or problematic areas of road. The average speed is still higher than on most American highways.

Driving in Cities

Aside from the huge problem of where to park, driving in cities is not difficult. Various countries seem to have "personalities" when it comes to city traffic. Paris is famous for its frenetic streams of traffic all trying to negotiate the seemingly impossible circle intersections. Drivers are pulled into the vortex of traffic from one direction and flung out on the far side after frantically flowing around among other similarly stressed drivers. And never forget, in Paris, taxis rule!

Italy is very different. Drivers all seem to be wonderfully friendly and live in a casual "bumper-car" style of driving where they ping from one end of the street to the other, never really running into anyone or each other and managing to stay in a good mood. Remember, in Italy, making eye contact, whether driving or walking, is to yield the right of way!

In German cities, traffic is organized like the trains—efficiently. Not as much fun perhaps, but a driver is more likely to arrive somewhere in one piece and with nerves intact. Pedestrians and bicycles are allowed to share the roads, and pedestrians have the right of way as soon as they step into the crosswalk. Bicyclists do not always respect this right and can come charging through intersections from all directions, a little like courier bikers in New York City.

Be especially careful when parking. If accidentally leaving a scratch or dent, however tiny, do *not* leave a note under the windshield and depart, as this is illegal. Even the tiniest of dents is considered an accident and must be handled the same way. Remain by the car until the other driver or a police officer arrives. Anyone leaving the scene would be charged with a "hit and run," even if the damage is so slight as to be almost invisible. For additional information go to germany.usembassy.gov.

Buses/Streetcars

It can be fun to hop on and off a bus or streetcar, and it's preferable to having to worry about a car. All city buses and streetcars are kept clean, run on time, and are comfortable in varying degrees. Tickets are cheap and available everywhere. Most cities rely on passengers to cancel their own tickets, controlled by the occasional city employee who makes sure riders have a ticket. If not, the city worker will cheerfully issue a ticket of a different sort—a fine of about 30 euros.

Underground Systems (*U-Bahns/S-Bahns*)

Underground systems (*U-Bahns*) and aboveground commuter trains (*S-Bahns*) are smooth, quiet, and fast. Waiting areas are often decorated with beautiful photos of museums or special attractions in the local area. Corridors, tunnels, and platforms are patrolled by guards and watched by cameras.

U-Bahn and *S-Bahn* schedules can be confusing to a newcomer, and it is easy to get on the wrong train. As long as passengers know the end station of the train they want, it is easy to find the correct route to any destination in between. This is because this last station will be shown on the schedule and also be displayed on a small sign at the front of the train. Train platforms are also clearly marked at the entrance, with the names of the train and the direction the train is going, or the end station of that train. With only a few trips around a new city, it is possible to become quickly comfortable with this mode of travel.

Taxis

Taxi drivers worldwide must have a secret competition to see who can drive the fastest. French drivers are voluble, frenetic, and so proud of their cities they gesture with both hands as they talk to point out the tourist spots. Italian drivers seem to love all those close calls with pedestrians. Germans just like to drive fast! "Spass muss sein," they say: "One has to have fun."

Taxis are usually not necessary, unless as a luxury or a way of getting somewhere quickly. Taxis are large, clean, comfortable, and, amazingly enough, safe. But they are also expensive.

Trains

For most Americans, train travel will be the best choice, both for the audition tour and once settled in Europe. Trains in most of Europe are fast, easy to use, comfortable, and relatively inexpensive, and are still the best way to travel any significant distance. The main train station in German-speaking countries is the *Hauptbahnhof*.

In Germany most trains run exactly on time. It is humorous to see a German train pull almost to the station and then hover for a minute or two before it slides into the platform to match the scheduled arrival time. Trains leave the same way—on the second.

An exception would be Italy, where trains try to run on schedule but rarely succeed. What is exciting is a sudden change of track just before the train is to arrive. Passengers hear a garbled "Questa n . . . an . . . o . . . du . . . binario s . . . i" and haven't understood a word. Suddenly everyone runs as fast as possible and finds the correct train just as it slides alongside the platform.

In most other countries, trains also follow specific schedules, come in at the listed track, and depart exactly on time. They will not wait for passengers. So be on time! Also, always check that the individual train car is actually going to the destination city. This will prevent the uncomfortable discovery, after having taken a nap in that comfortable seat, of waking up and finding out that the car is now hooked up to a train traveling to some other part of Europe. The destination of each car is listed on a sign on the outside of the car by the entrance.

Eurail Tickets

The most convenient form of train travel can be a Eurail pass, which will provide travel for a certain number of trips during a specified time. These passes can be purchased through American travel agencies, or on the Internet. Different kinds of Eurail passes are available, and certain restrictions apply, so make sure you get the kind of pass that is best for you.

SHOPPING

Shopping in Europe is still a daily affair for most people, at least for groceries, which are carried home in a small bag (*Tüte*). This is due to the fact that most refrigerators are only about waist high, and freezer space is almost nonexistent.

Locating the local grocery, pharmacy, and small specialty stores is usually as simple as walking around the neighborhood. Large department stores are located in the center of the city, near or around the central squares.

European cities are a plethora of delightful smells emanating from the numerous neighborhood stores and shops. Anyone who is up and about early will smell fresh bread and croissants baking at the local *Bäckerei*.

Something sweet, crunchy, or spicy can be purchased fresh every day. Coffee, candy, meats, and cheeses can all be found in their own individual stores (*Geschäfte*), each with its own personality and aromas. It's a treat just to stand in the doorway of a candy shop (*Konditoreien*) and breathe in a "chocolate high" from French truffle chocolates or Mozart balls (*Mozartkugeln*) from Vienna.

The butcher shop (*Fleischerei/Metzgerei*) carries fresh and processed meat, seafood, and various kinds of sausages (*Würstchen*). Two favorites are the white sausage (*Weisswürst*) and Bratwurst (*Bratwürst*).

A *Kiosk* is a small store specializing in the sale of magazines and newspapers, tickets for travel on public conveyances, and a limited amount of groceries such as milk, coffee, and breads. Other names for this store include a drink hall (*Trinkhalle*) and little stall (*Büdchen*). These are good places for a quick, inexpensive snack.

Store Schedules (*Öffnungszeiten*)

Stores in Germany have specific times they are open (*Öffnungszeiten*), usually 0700 to 1800 hours (7 AM to 6 PM), which have been dictated by law.

Most stores, with the exception of bakeries or cafés and restaurants, are closed on Sunday.

COFFEEHOUSES

Taking time for a coffee and a *Kuchen* (sweet pastry) is a European tradition, which has become fashionable in the United States as well, with the advent of establishments like Starbucks and Panera. European coffeehouses pride themselves on elegant atmospheres, superb coffee, and exquisite pastries.

Customers are allowed to linger in most cafés and coffeehouses. For the price of a simple cup of coffee, customers can enjoy the atmosphere, breathe in the smell of chocolate, soak up the native dialect, or simply enjoy watching other customers. If the coffeehouse is crowded, it is proper to ask to sit with someone if they have a free seat at their table. Even some sort of questioning look or a gesture toward the free chair will be understood. This is often the chance to meet new people and enjoy a wonderful unexpected conversation.

Three Famous Coffeehouses

Demel's, Vienna: This is the quintessential coffeehouse. Ceiling-to-floor mirrors framed by gold trim reflect customers, servers, and an exquisite variety of cakes, candy, and other bakery items. The elegant atmosphere encourages quiet conversation and a sense of timelessness.

Sacher Hotel, Vienna: This is the home of the famous *Sachertorte*, a chocolate cake made on the premises and mailed all over the world. This hotel is right across the street from the Vienna Opera, so all that fabulous chocolate, as well as rich, dark coffee and elegant Viennese atmosphere, is readily available.

Max Rischart's Backhaus, Munich: A bakery and coffeehouse, Rischart's is located on the edge of the Marienplatz, right across from the New Town Hall (*Neues Rathaus*). This neo-Gothic town hall houses the world famous forty-three-bell *Glockenspiel*, along with thirty-two wooden mechanical figures of musicians and knights on horseback who reenact the marriage festivities of Duke Wilhelm V to Renate von Lothringen in 1568. The *Glockenspiel* plays a fifteen-minute carillon three times a day. Rischart's offers some of the most wonderful and tasty varieties of bread and rolls in Europe. Customers who want a sit-down breakfast or lunch can go upstairs to the café overlooking the Marienplatz. For a quick coffee, breakfast on the run, or a *Kuchen*, Rischart's has a *steh* café where the customers stand at small round tables.

EUROPEAN CULTURAL EVENTS AND CUSTOMS

Oktoberfest

The traditional German harvest festival, the famous *Oktoberfest*, also called the *Wiesn* in Munich, is celebrated all over Germany and takes place from mid-September until the first weekend of October. The Munich festival dates back to 1810, when the first *Oktoberfest* was held for one week in mid-October in honor of the marriage of Crown Prince Ludwig to Princess Therese. It quickly became a yearly event and now attracts more than six million visitors every year. Large beer tents the size of school gymnasiums serve traditional German beer, apple-spiced sauerkraut, and roasted chicken and pork, all accompanied by folk bands and endlessly carousing, happy festival visitors. Carousels, roller coasters, and other carnival attractions are also part of this delightful festival. For more information go to www.oktoberfest.de.

Christmas Markets (*Chris Kringle Märkte/Weihnachtsmärkte*)

Another delightful aspect of living in Europe is the opportunity to attend the European outdoor Christmas markets, usually held in the town's square. In Germany this unique winter experience opens the last week in November and runs until Christmas Eve.

The two Christmas markets in Vienna are open from the beginning of Advent until Christmas Eve—one set up at the *Rathaus* downtown and another at the Schönbrunn palace.

In most cities there is some kind of Christmas market where small booths are set up and decorated with garlands of freshly cut pine boughs. Booths sell a variety of specialty gift items such as hand-carved wooden statues and ornaments from Oberammergau, cuckoo clocks from the Black Forest region, hats, gloves, and sweaters, and of course items to eat and drink.

Customers compete for space around the large swinging bratwurst and pork steak sandwich grills. The smell of hot cinnamon-spiced nuts and the pungent odors of hot-spiced wine (*Glühwein*), sausages, pastries, and *Lebkuchen* (a soft gingerbread cookie) are all effective lures to shoppers who congregate at all hours of the day and night to enjoy the season.

Each market features a centrally located Christmas tree, which can be twenty feet tall or more, decorated with thousands of small white electric lights representing white candles. Music is a part of each Christmas market, with performances by instrumental, choral, and folk-dancing ensembles.

There is no way to adequately describe how beautiful, exciting, and charming these various markets are. They simply must be enjoyed in person.

Carnival Season

Karneval, or *Fashing* as it is called in southern Germany, is celebrated prior
to the start of Lent, usually in February. This holiday week is similar to
the New Orleans Mardi Gras celebrations. The highlight is the Rose Monday (*Rosenmontag*) parade. This tradition is based on the old custom of
celebrating the end of winter and the beginning of spring.

Unexpected Customs

Europeans observe many customs that often are unfamiliar to Americans
but add to that special atmosphere that is so pleasing:

- It is normal in Europe to see people of the same sex strolling arm in
  arm or even holding hands.
- In the Mediterranean countries, men are more affectionate and em-
  brace each other enthusiastically when they meet.
- A freshly cut pine tree is placed on the roof of a new building under
  construction.
- The change of seasons in German cities is easily noticed when the hot
  spiced chestnut stands of winter are overnight replaced by the Italian
  ice cream vendors of summer.
- Children's (and sometimes adults') boots or shoes left outside the
  apartment door in northern Germany on December 6 will be filled
  with candy or small trinkets from Saint Nicholas.
- Everyone recycles.

Finale

So there you have it! *The Opera Singer's Career Guide*. It's like an opera subtitled "The Dream Trail" in four acts:

Act 1   Education, Training, and Preparation
Act 2   Auditioning
Act 3   Performing
Act 4   Continued Success!

"The Dream Trail" opera journey will have it all. A cast of thousands—exciting locations—trauma and tribulations—joy and exultation—failures and successes—and above all, love!

> *Ah, to Sing! To soar on wings of thought and light, of joy and melody.*
> *To give only a small part of cloud and air and light back to the world,*
> *Is delight and wonder and love.*

—Pearl Yeadon McGinnis, 2006

Appendix A
Agencies

THE GERMAN STATE AGENCY

The German State Agency, ZBF (Zentrale Bühnen-, Fernseh-, und Film-vermittlung der Bundesanstalt für Arbeit), handles all the performing arts, including singers, coaches, accompanists, beginning conductors, and chorus positions. No fees are charged, either to singers or employers, for contracts obtained through this agency.

Telephone and fax numbers are listed as if dialing the number from within Europe. If dialing from the United States, dial 1, then the country code without the 0 (49 for Germany instead of 049, for example; or 43 for Austria), then the city code (089 for Munich), and then the number.

If writing to an agency from within Europe, add the country prefix before the city. Example: D-80796 München (Munich), or A-1010 Wien (Vienna).

Following is the ZBF contact information for major German cities:

Berlin

Friedrichstrasse 39
10969 Berlin
Tel: (030) 5555996810
Fax: (030) 5555996849/-39
    Opera/Operetta: Wolf-Hildebrand Moser
    Orchestra: Hartmut Wettges, Christoph Czakai
    Musical: Norbert Hunecke
    Conductors/Technical: Katharina Wenzlaff, Petra Rummel

Hamburg

Agentur Hamburg
Gotenstrasse 11
20097 Hamburg
Tel: (040) 28 40 15-99
Fax: (040) 28 40 15-99
    Opera/Operetta: Astrid Stork
    Conducting/Technical: Marina Henning

Köln (Cologne)

Generalagentur Köln
Innere Kanalstrasse 69
59823 Köln
Tel: (0221) 555403-0
Fax: (0221) 55403-555
    Opera/Operetta: Kerstin Holdt, Stefan Poprawka,
        Berenike Jürgens
    Chorus: Martin Geissler
    Dance: Charles Guillaume
    Orchestra: Renate Ulke-Baum
    Conductors/Technical: Sybille Steinfartz

Leipzig

Agentur Leipzig
Georg-Schumann-Strasse 173
04159 Leipzig
Tel: (03341) 5 899 88-0
Fax: (03341) 5 89 88-50

München (Munich)

Agentur München
Leopoldstrasse 19
80802 München 3
Tel: (089) 38 17 07-0
    Opera/Operetta: Christine Strasser
    Conductors/Technical: Thomas Trost

OPERA AGENCIES

Listed is a sampling of opera agencies in a variety of locations in Germany. These agencies do charge a fee, which can vary from agency to agency. Many of the agency websites will ask if you want the page translated—"translate this page?" Click on this and then scroll for the preferred language. Example: "German to English."

Au am Inn

Opern- und Konzertagentur Monika Bundschu
Am Anger 3
83546 Au am Inn
Tel: 08073/7 31
Fax: 08073/26 11
Cell: 0172/7 22 17 38
E-mail: monika.bundschu@arcor.de

Berlin

Konzert-Direktion Hans Adler
Auguste-Viktoria-Strasse 64
14199 Berlin
Tel: 49 (30) 89 59 92-0
Fax: 49 (30) 8 26 35 20
E-mail: info@musikadler.de
Web: www.musikadler.de

Marianne Büttger
Musiktheater und Konzert
Dahlmannstrasse 9
10629 Berlin
Tel: 49 (30) 3 24 85 27
Fax: 49 (30) 3 23 11 93
E-mail: agency@boettger-berlin.de
Web: http://www.boettger-berlin.de

Düsseldorf

Opernagentur Inge Tennigkeit
Musiktheater- und Konzertvermittlung
Kempener Strasse 4
40474 Düsseldorf

Tel: 49 (211) 516 00 60
Fax: 49 (211) 51 60 06 16
E-mail: opera@tennigkeit-ag.de

Hamburg

Günter Ocklenburg
Bühnenvermittlung/Management Oper und Konzert
Neubertstrasse 47
22087 Hamburg
Tel: (040) 25 49 98 17
Web: www.agentur-ocklenburg.de

Hannover

Hannagret Burcker
Musiktheater und Konzert
Fuhselstrasse 2
30419 Hannover
Tel: 49 (511) 2 71 69 10
Fax: 49 (511) 2 71 78 73
E-mail: mail@buekervoice.de
Web: www.buekervoice.de

Lehrte

Artists Management
Hartmut Haase
Aalgrund 8
31275 Lehrte
Tel: 49 (5175) 95 32 32
Fax: 49 (5175) 95 32 33
E-mail: artists@t-online.de
Web: www.artists-haase.de. This website will state if they are taking
auditions or not: "Zur zeit keine vorsingen" means "No auditions at this
time." Many websites list the artists they are currently handling.

Munich

Lore Blümel
Opern- und Konzertagentur
Heglhofstrasse 49
81377 München

Tel: 49 (89) 59 38 64
Fax: 49 (89) 8 59 37 59
E-mail: opkoag-bluemel@t-online.de
Web: www.lore-bluemel.de

James Dietsch
Internationale Künstleragentur
Thierschstrasse 11
80538 München
Tel: (089) 34 08 63-0
Fax: (089) 34 08 63-10
E-mail: JWDietsch@optionline.net

Hilbert Artists Management
Maximilianstrasse 22
80539 München
Tel: (089) 29 07 47-0
Fax: (089) 29 07 47-90
E-mail: agentur@hilbert.de
Web: www.hilbert.de

Karl-Erich Hasse
Musiktheater und Konzert
Martiusstrasse 3
80802 München
Tel: (089) 33 31 62 & 39 41 90
Fax: (089) 34 26 74)
E-mail: info@theateragentur-k-e-hasse.de

Lore-M. Schultz
International Artists Management
Zittelstrasse 8
80796 München
Tel: (089) 308 70 92
Fax: (089) 30870 93
E-mail: artists@lore-m-schultz.com

Stuttgart

Werner Kühnly
Musiktheater und Konzert
Wörthstrasse 31
70563 Stuttgart

Tel: (0711) 7 80 27 64
Fax: (0711) 7 80 44 03
E-mail: agentur-kuehnly@t-online.de

Opera Agents in Vienna, Austria

Künstleragentur Dr. Raab & Dr. Böhm
Opera, Operette und Konzert
Plankengasse 7
1010 Wien
Tel: (0043 -1) 5 12 05 01
Fax: (0043-1) 5 12 77 43
E-mail: office@bartists.at
Web: www.rbartists.at

Künstleragentur Holländer-Calix
Grinzinger Allee 46
A-1190 Wien
Tel: (0043-1) 320 53 17 and 328 47 33
Fax: (0043-1) 328 90 70

AGENTS FOR TOURING THEATER

This category of agent includes those who conduct auditions for operettas, dinner theaters, ensembles, restaurants, and coffeehouses. If one is in between contracts with an opera house and in need of employment, this is a good source of income.

Alexander Senger: Operamobile
Zur Sophienhöhe 3
31832 Springe
Tel: (05041) 91 22 02 and 91 22 03
Fax: (05041) 91 22 04
E-mail: operamobile@t-online.de
Web: www.operamobile.de

Erich Seitter
Bühnen und Konzertvermittlung
Opernring 8
1010 Wien
Tel: (0043-1) 5 13 75 92; (0043-1) 5 12 93 51
Fax: (0043-1) 5 12 93 51
E-mail: office@agentur-seitter.at
Web: www.agentur-seitter.at

This agency website has a good explanation of the audition request procedure and what they require to consider an applicant for an audition. This includes no fax or e-mail applications accepted, and written requests must include the following:

- Current artistic personal record with date of birth (no applicants over age thirty-five)
- Current repertoire list
- Current photo
- Current CD, video, or "audio cartridge"

Selected applicants will receive one written invitation to audition on a set date.

"Opera" Lotte Vladarski
Theateragentur-Opera, Konzert
Döblinger Hauptstrasse 57/18
A-1190 Wien
Tel: (0043-1) 3 68 69 60 and 3 68 69 61
Fax: (0043-1) 3 68 69 62
E-mail: opera.vladarski@utanet.at

Appendix B
European Opera Houses
(Austria, Germany, Switzerland)

For the purposes of this book, only opera houses in Austria, Germany, and Switzerland are listed. A complete listing of all European opera houses can be found by going on the Internet and typing in "list of European opera houses." The Internet also has a good current list that excludes theaters with "opera" in the name but do not actually produce operas. There are also theaters that regularly produce several operas a year but will not be listed as an "opera house." Two examples in Germany are the Aachen Opera, which is produced in the Aachen Municipal Theater, and the Ulm Opera, which is produced in the Ulmer Theater, Ulm. Other good sources are listed in the "References" section following these lists.

Virtually all the opera houses listed have their own website, which will include addresses and names of contact personnel. Most will also give instructions for submitting applications for auditions. An example is

Staatstheater Kassel
Friedrichsplatz 15
34117 Kassel, Germany
Telefon (0561) 10 94 – 0
E-mail: info@staatstheater-kassel.de

Austria

Grosses Festspielhaus, Salzburg
Schonbrunn Schlosstheater, Vienna

Theater an der Wien, Vienna (historic theater associated with Mozart's
   time)
Volksoper Wien (Vienna People's Opera), Vienna
Wiener Kammeroper (Vienna Chamber Opera), Vienna
Wiener Staatsoper (Vienna State Opera), Vienna

Germany

Aachen Opera (Municipal Theater), Aachen
Aalto Theater, Essen
Badisches Staatstheater, Karlsruhe
Bayerische Staatsoper (Bavarian State Opera), Munich
Bayreuth Festspielhaus (Bayreuth Festival Theater), Bayreuth
Bremen Theater, Bremen
Deutsche Oper am Rhein (German Opera of the Rhine), Dusseldorf
Deutsche Oper Berlin (Berlin German Opera), Berlin
Festspielhaus Baden-Baden (Baden-Baden Festival Theater), Baden-
   Baden
Hamburgische Staatsoper (Hamburg State Opera), Hamburg
Komische Oper Berlin, Berlin
Markgrafliches Opernhaus, Bayreuth
Musiktheather im Revier, Gelsenkirchen
Oper Frankfurt (Frankfurt Opera), Frankfurt
Oper Leipzig (Leipzig Opera), Leipzig
Opernhaus Dusseldorf, Dusseldorf
Opernhaus Halle, Halle
Opernhaus Kiel, Kiel
Prinzregententheater, Munich
Semperoper or Sachsische Staatsoper Dresden (Saxon State Opera),
   Dresden
Staatsoper Hannover, Hannover
Staatsoper Unter den Linden (Berlin State Opera), Berlin
Staatstheater am Gartnerplatz, Munich
Staatstheater Kassel, Kassel
Staatstheater Stuttgart, Stuttgart
Theater Duisburg, Duisburg
Theater Lubeck, Lubeck
Ulmer Theater, Ulm

Switzerland

Grand Théâtre de Genève, Geneva
Opéra de Laussanne, Lausanne

Opernhaus Zürich, Zurich
Stadttheater Bern, Bern
Stadttheater Luzern, Lucerne
Theater Basel, Basel
Theater Biel-Solothurn, Solothurn

REFERENCES

The following references can be used to research opera houses other than those listed.

Allison, John, ed. *Great Opera Houses of the World*, supplement to *Opera* magazine. London, 2003.

Beauvert, Thierry. *Opera Houses of the World*. New York: Vendome Press, 1995.

Lynn, Karyl Charna. *Italian Opera Houses and Festivals*. Lanham, Md.: Scarecrow Press, 2005.

———. *Opera: The Guide to Western Europe's Great Houses*. Santa Fe, N.M.: John Muir Publications, 1991.

Plantamura, Carol. *The Opera Lover's Guide to Europe*. New York: Citadel Press, 1996.

Appendix C
Opera Title Abbreviations

Many opera titles are commonly abbreviated, especially by those in the opera field when in conversation. "He's doing *Butterfly* in D.C. and then *Rienzi* in Santa Fe," a singer might say. Or, "I did *Figaro* last month and am rehearsing *Entführung* now." This is similar to the abbreviations used in any profession, such as "We got the perp" (perpetrator, in police talk), or "I'm going TDY next week to Japan" (temporary duty, in military jargon).

Some opera titles became abbreviated because their original titles were very lengthy and people began to refer to them in an abbreviated manner. Good examples are Mozart's *Don Giovanni* and Wagner's *Tannhäuser*, which in their original forms would be *Il dissoluto punito ossia il Don Giovanni* and *Tannhäuser und der Sängerkrieg auf Wartburg*. It's a lot easier to ask "Did you see *Don Giovanni* last night?" It's also easier to advertise a shorter title.

Other titles might be referred to in their most shortened form but would not be advertised as such. For example, *Figaro* would always be advertised as *Le nozze di Figaro*. Also, some smaller regional operas in the United States will advertise the more well known operas such as *Le nozze di Figaro* and *Il barbiere de Siviglia* in English (*The Marriage of Figaro* and *The Barber of Seville*) but still perform the operas in Italian with English subtitles.

Caution must be advised in using some opera abbreviations if there is more than one opera by the same or similar title. For example, there are two *Manon*s and two *Turandot*s: *Manon* (Massenet) and *Manon Lescaut* (Puccini); *Turandot* (Busoni) and *Turandot* (Puccini). And there are four operas that get abbreviated in conversation as *Faust*: Gounod's *Faust*, Berlioz's *La damnation de Faust*, Busoni's *Doktor Faust*, and Schnittke's *Historia von Doktor Fausten.* Faust—a popular guy. To avoid confusion, simply add the composer's name to your abbreviation.

Listed below are examples of opera titles in their original form as well as a common abbreviation. Many of these abbreviations are used in Appendixes D, E, and F.

Composer	Full Title	Abbreviation
Adam	*Le postillon de Lonjumeau*	*Postillon*
Berlioz	*Le damnation de Faust*	*Faust*
Bialas	*Die Geschichte von Aucassin und Nicolette*	*Aucassin und Nicolette*
Bizet	*Les pêcheurs de perles*	*Pêcheurs*
F. Caccini	*La liberazione di Ruggiero dall'isola d'Alcina*	*La liberazione di Ruggiero*
Cavalieri	*Rappresentatione di anima e di corpo*	*Rappresentatione di anima*
Cornelius	*Der Barbier von Bagdad*	*Barbier*
Debussy	*Pelléas et Mélisande*	*Pelléas*
Delius	*A Village Romeo and Juliet*	*Romeo and Juliet*
Donizetti	*Lucia di Lammermoor*	*Lucia*
Flotow	*Martha oder Der Markt zu Richmond*	*Martha*
Gluck	*L'ivrogne corrigé ou Le marriage du diable*	*L'ivrogne corrigé*
	La recontre imprévue ou Les pélerins de la Mecque	*La recontre imprévue*
Handel	*Ottone, re di Germania*	*Ottone*
Henze	*Il re cervo oder Die Irrfahrten der Wahrheit*	*Il re cervo*
Honegger	*Jeanne d'Arc au bûcher*	*Jeanne d'Arc*
Keiser	*Masaniello furioso oder Die napolitanische Fischer-Empörung*	*Masaniello*
Lachenmann	*Das Mädchen mit den Schwefelhölzern*	*Das Mädchen*
Lortzing	*Die Opernprobe oder Die vornehmen Dilettanten*	*Die Opernprobe*
	Der Waffenschmied von Worms	*Der Waffenschmied*
	Der Wildschütz oderDie Stimme der Natur	*Der Wildschütz*

Composer	Full Title	Abbreviation
Matthus	*Die Weise von Liebe und Tod des Cornets Christoph Rilke*	*Die Weise von Liebe und Tod*
Monteverdi	*L'incoronazione di Poppea*	*Poppea*
Mozart	*Il dissoluto punito ossia il Don Giovanni*	*Don Giovanni*
	Die Entführung aus dem Serail	*Die Entführung*
	Le nozze di Figaro	*Figaro*
Nicolai	*Die lustigen Weiber von Windsor*	*Die lustigen Weiber*
Nono	*Al gran sole carico d'amore*	*Al gran sole*
Paisiello	*Il barbiere de Siviglia ovvero La precauzione inutile*	*Il barbiere de Siviglia*
Rossini	*Il barbiere di Siviglia*	*Il barbiere*
Telemann	*Pimpinone oder die ungleiche Heirat*	*Pimpinone*
Verdi	*Un ballo in maschera*	*Un ballo*
Wagner	*Die Meistersinger von Nürnberg*	*Die Meistersinger*
	Rienzi, der lezte der Tribunen	*Rienzi*
	Tannhäuser und der Sängerkrieg auf Wartburg	*Tannhäuser*
Weill	*Aufsteig und Fall der Stadt Mahagonny*	*Mahagonny*
Wolf-Ferrari	*Sly oder die Legende vom wiedererweckten Schläfer*	*Sly*
U. Zimmermann	*Der Schuhu und die fliegende Prinzessin*	*Der Schuhu*

Appendix D
Operatic Roles for Children, Young Lyrics, and Beginners (*Anfängerin*)

The purpose of this appendix is to assemble in one source all the roles that fall in the categories children, young lyric, and beginners (*Anfängerin*). These roles are not recognized as belonging to their own *Fach* categories but would be found in the cast listings of an opera. Many are generic in nature, such as "young boy" or a member of a group such as "three young ladies," and are small or medium parts.

However, the beginner roles are often treated as a *Fach* category, such as *Anfängerin Sopran* or *Anfängerin Tenor*. This designation would be written into a contract for someone accepting his or her first contract in a European opera house and who does not yet have the experience to qualify for one of the more established *Fach* categories.

Information on roles suitable for children, young lyric, and beginners was researched from Rudolf Kloiber, Wulf Konold, and Robert Maschka's *Handbuch der Oper* (2006), with kind permission of Baerenreiter-Verlag, Kassel, www.baerenreiter.com, as well as other sources (see bibliography). Opera titles are formatted with the capitalization style used in the country of origin.

CHILD ROLES

There are many roles suitable for children in operas such as Britten's *A Midsummer Night's Dream* and Janáček's *The Cunning Little Vixen*. Other operas, such as Ravel's *L'enfant et les sortilèges* (*The Enchanted Child*), can be adapted for performance by children. There are also many speaking roles for children, although these are not given in the following lists.

One opera of interest in researching child roles is *Brundibár*, by Hans Krása, which has only children as characters and is written in musical theater style—spoken dialogue with songs. The premiere was in Prague in 1941, but the next time the opera was performed was in the concentration camp at Theresienstadt, where Krása was interred. Shortly after a special June 1944 performance for the International Red Cross's visit to this camp, the opera was banned, and the inmates of Theresienstadt were transferred to Auschwitz, where the composer was put to death in the gas chamber in October 1944. Since 1992 *Brundibár* has been performed more than a hundred times worldwide.

Operas are listed with the most universally used title as listed in the Kloiber *Handbuch der Oper* or *Kobbé's Opera Book*. Operas that were originally titled in a Slavic language are listed in English to avoid transliteration. Roles are listed in English or the given name of the character.

Composer	Opera	Character
Roles for Child (Girl)		
Berg	*Lulu*	A fifteen-year-old
Blow	*Venus and Adonis*	Cupid
Britten	*Albert Herring*	Emmy/Sis
	A Midsummer Night's Dream	Cobweb/Moth/ Mustardseed/ Peaseblossom
	The Turn of the Screw	Flora
Desseau	*Die Verurteilung des Lukullus*	Two children
Egk	*Peer Gynt*	Small gnome or troll
Flotow	*Martha*	Three handmaidens
Fortner	*Bluthochzeit*	Girls
Glass	*Akhnaten*	Bekhetaten/Meretaten/ Maketaten
Gounod	*Mireille*	Andreloun/Clémence
Honegger	*Jeanne d'Arc au bûcher*	Child's voice
Janáček	*The Cunning Little Vixen*	Cricket/frog/fly/ young fox
Kauer	*Das Donauweibchen*	Lilli
Keiser	*Cupido*	Cupid
Kienzl	*Der Evangelimann*	Young child
Krása	*Brundibár*	Pepícek/Aninka/ Brundibár/iceman/ baker/milkman/police/ sparrow/cat

Composer	Opera	Character
Massenet	*Werther*	Gretel/Clara
Mozart	*Apollo und Hyacinth*	Melia
Müller	*Teufelsmühle*	Jeriel
Ravel	*L'enfant et les sortilèges*	An infant
Rihm	*Jakob Lenz*	Two children
Schreker	*Die Gezeichneten*	A child
R. Strauss	*Die ägyptische Helena*	Hermione
Wagner	*Lohengrin*	Two pages
	Tannhäuser	Two pages
Zemlinsky	*Kleider machen Leute*	A cellar boy

Roles for a Child (Boy)

Composer	Opera	Character
Berg	*Wozzeck*	Marien's boy
Boyce	*The Chaplet*	Palaemon
	The Shepherd's Lottery	Thyrsis
Britten	*Albert Herring*	Harry
	Billy Budd	Four sea cadets
	Burning Fiery Furnace	Angel
	Curlew River	Spirit of the boy
	The Little Sweep	Sam
	A Midsummer Night's Dream	Cobweb/Moth/ Mustardseed/ Peaseblossom
	The Turn of the Screw	Miles
Debussy	*Pelléas et Mélisande*	Yniold
Desseau	*Die Verurteilung des Lukullus*	Two children
Falla	*El retablo de Maese Pedro*	Trujamán
Ferrari	*Ciottolino*	Ciottolino
Gluck	*Iphigénie en Tauride*	Artemis
Gounod	*Mireille*	Andreloun
Handel	*Alcina*	Oberto
	Faramondo	Childerico
	Giustino	Fortune
Hara	*Petro Kibe*	Petro (as a child)
Henze	*König Hirsch* (*Il re cervo*)	Two statues
Honegger	*Jeanne d'Arc au bûcher*	Child voice
Janáček	*The Cunning Little Vixen*	Cricket/frog/fly/ young fox
	Osud	Doubek
Kancheli	*Music for the Living*	Young guide
Kienzl	*Der Evangelimann*	A boy
Krása	*Brundibár*	Pepícek/Aninka/ Brundibár/iceman/

Composer	Opera	Character
Krása, *cont.*		baker/milkman/ police/sparrow/ cat
Legeti	*Le Grand Macabre*	Go-Go
Manzoni	*Doktor Faustus*	Nipote
Massenet	*Werther*	Fritz/Max/Hans/ Karl
Menotti	*Amahl and the Night Visitors*	Amahl
Meyerbeer	*Le prophète*	First, second chorister
Mozart	*Apollo und Hyacinth*	Apollo/Hyacinthus/ Zephyrus
	Le nozze di Figaro	Two young maidens
	Die Zauberflöte	Three boys
Penderecki	*Die Teufel von Loudun*	Philippe
Pfitzner	*Palestrina*	Ighino
Pintscher	*Thomas Chatterton*	Master Cheney
Puccini	*Tosca*	Shepherd boy
	Gianni Schicchi	Gherardino (seven years old)
Ravel	*L'enfant et les sortilèges*	An infant
Rihm	*Jakob Lenz*	Two children
Schonthal	*Princess Maleen*	Small child (speaking role)
Schreker	*Die Gezeichneten*	A child
Smith	*The Fairies*	Puck/servant
R. Strauss	*Feuersnot*	A young maiden
	Die Frau ohne Schatten	Six children's voices
Tippett	*King Priam*	Paris
Vaughan Williams	*The Pilgrim's Progress*	Woodcutter's boy
Weill	*Lost in the Stars*	Alex
	Street Scene	Willie
Wagner	*Siegfried*	Forest bird
	Tannhäuser	Four pages
Zemlinsky	*Kleider machen Leute*	Cellar boy

ROLES FOR YOUNG LYRIC SINGERS

As mentioned in chapter 2, young lyric singers in their early twenties should choose short roles for study, with a mind to adding skills without overtaxing a voice that does not yet have the stamina or experience required for longer roles. For example, young sopranos should first select roles from the soubrette *Fach*. If the singer has a flexible voice and developed range, then roles from the lyric coloratura *Fach* would be appropriate. If the student has more acting ability, select from the buffo categories.

Composer	Opera	Character
Soubrette Roles for a Young Soprano		
Donizetti	*L'elisir d'amore*	Gianetta
Haydn	*Lo speziale*	Grilletta
Lortzing	*Der Waffenschmied*	Marie
Mozart	*Le nozze di Figaro*	Barbarina
Lyric Coloratura Roles for a Young Soprano		
Donizetti	*Don Pasquale*	Norina
	L'elisir d'amore	Adina
	La fille du régiment	Marie
Mozart	*Die Entführung aus dem Serail*	Blonde
	Der Schauspieldirektor	Silberklang/Herz
Puccini	*La bohème*	Musetta
Verdi	*Un ballo in maschera*	Oscar
Lyric Roles for a Young Soprano		
Beethoven	*Fidelio*	Marzelline
Humperdinck	*Hänsel und Gretel*	Gretel
Mozart	*Bastien und Bastienne*	Bastienne
	Don Giovanni	Zerlina
	Le nozze di Figaro	Pamina
Smetana	*The Bartered Bride*	Marie
Lyric Roles for a Young Mezzo-Soprano		
Bizet	*Carmen*	Mercédès
Humperdinck	*Hänsel und Gretel*	Hänsel
Mozart	*Bastien und Bastienne*	Bastienne
	Così fan tutte	Dorabella
	Le nozze di Figaro	Cherubino
Puccini	*Madama Butterfly*	Suzuki
Verdi	*Rigoletto*	Maddalena
Lyric Roles for a Young Tenor		
Donizetti	*Don Pasquale*	Ernesto
	L'elisir d'amore	Nemorino

Composer	Opera	Character
Haydn	*La fedeltà premiata*	Lindoro
Mozart	*Così fan tutte*	Ferrando
	La finta semplice	Don Polidoro
Verdi	*Macbeth*	Malcolm
	Otello	Cassio

Buffo Roles for a Young Tenor

Composer	Opera	Character
Beethoven	*Fidelio*	Jaquino
Bizet	*Carmen*	Dancäiro/Remendado
Leoncavallo	*Pagliacci*	Beppo
Mozart	*Le nozze di Figaro*	Basilio/Don Curzio
	Die Zauberflöte	Monostatos
Puccini	*Madama Butterfly*	Goro
	Il tabarro	Tinca
	Turandot	Pang/Pong
R. Strauss	*Ariadne auf Naxos*	Dance master

Lyric Roles for Young Baritone

Composer	Opera	Character
Berlioz	*Béatrice et Bénédict*	Claudio
Bizet	*Les pêcheurs de perles*	Zurga
Donizetti	*Don Pasquale*	Dr. Malatesta
	L'elisir d'amore	Belcore
Mozart	*Così fan tutte*	Guglielmo
	Die Zauberflöte	Papageno
Puccini	*Turandot*	Ping
Rossini	*La Cenerentola*	Dandini
R. Strauss	*Ariadne auf Naxos*	Harlekin

Buffo Roles for Young Bass

Composer	Opera	Character
Berg	*Wozzeck*	Doctor
Donizetti	*Don Pasquale*	Pasquale
Mozart	*Bastien und Bastienne*	Colas
	La finta giardiniera	Nardo
Puccini	*Tosca*	Mesner
Rossini	*Il barbiere di Siviglia*	Bartolo
	L'italiana in Algeri	Mustafa
Verdi	*La forza del destino*	Melitone

BEGINNER ROLES

Beginner (*Anfänger/Anfängerin*) roles can be considered those listed in the Kloiber *Handbuch der Oper* simply by voice designation: soprano, mezzo, alto, tenor, baritone, or bass. As explained earlier, a singer accepting a first contract in a German house might be offered a contract as a beginner. An example would be a stipulation of "tenor" in the contract, or perhaps "tenor" along with one other *Fach* description, such as *Buffo or Charakter*.

Most of the roles in the following list would be either a small role (*kl. P.*) or a medium role (*m. P.*), although a few are large or main roles (*gr. P.*) such as Selysette in *Ariane et Barbe-bleue* (mezzo) and George III in *Eight Songs for a Mad King* (baritone).

Composer	Opera	Character
Beginner Soprano, *Anfänger/Anfängerin Sopran*		
Adam	*Le postillon de Lonjumeau*	Latour
D'Albert	*Die toten Augen*	Shepherd boy/Rebecca/ Esther/Sarah
	Tiefland	Pepa/Antonia/Nuri
Bellini	*Norma*	Klothilde
Berg	*Wozzeck*	Marian's boy
	Lulu	A fifteen-year-old
Berio	*Un re in ascolto*	Nurse
Berlioz	*La damnation de Faust*	Soprano solo
	Le Troyens	Polyxena
Borodin	*Prince Igor*	Wet nurse/ polowezer girl
Britten	*Death in Venice*	Lace seller/ strolling player/ strawberry seller/ paper girl
F. Caccini	*La liberazione di Ruggiero*	A noblewoman/plant/ Oreste/three nymphs
Cavalieri	*Rappresentatione di anima*	Angel in heaven/ guardian angel
Cavalli	*La Calisto*	Echo/Nature/Eternity
Cherubini	*Médée*	Companion of Dircé
Charpentier	*Louise*	Newspaper girl/Elsie/ Madeleine/Camille/ Irma/Arab/bird food vendor
Desseau	*Die Verurteilung des Lukullus*	Three women's voices/ three town criers
Donizetti	*La fille du régiment*	Contessa Craquitorpi
Egk	*Peer Gynt*	Ingrid/three black birds/little troll

Composer	Opera	Character
Einem	*Dantons Tod*	Lady
Falla	*La vida breve*	Four saleswomen
Flotow	*Martha*	Three handmaidens
Fortner	*Bluthochzeit*	Five ladies
Gershwin	*Porgy and Bess*	Clara/Serena
Glass	*Akhnaten*	Bekhetaten/Meretaten/ Maketaten
Gluck	*Armide*	Najade/Koryphäen/ shepherdess/ apparition of Lucindes/apparition of Melisse
	Iphigénie en Tauride	Greek/priestess
	Iphigénie en Aulide	Artemis
	L'ivrogne corrigé	Furie
Goetz	*Der Widerspenstigen Zähmung*	Housekeeper
Goldschmidt	*Der gewaltige Hahnrei*	Cornelie
Gounod	*Mireille*	Voice from heaven/ Clémence
Handel	*Giulio Cesare*	Nirenus
	Rinaldo	Two sirens/ghost
Hara	*Petro Kibe*	Petro (as a child)
Henze	*König Hirsch (Il re cervo)*	Voice of the woods/ voice of the people/ four ladies
Hindemith	*Neues vom Tage*	Chambermaid
Hölszky	*Die Wände*	Chiga
Honegger	*Jeanne d'Arc au bûcher*	Child voice
Humperdinck	*Hänsel und Gretel*	Sandman/boatmen
Janáček	*The Adventures of Mr. Brouček*	Dirne
	The Cunning Little Vixen	Innkeeper/hen/ pullet/Sepp/Franzl
	Jenůfa	Barena/Jano/maid/ jaybird/voice
Kienzl	*Der Evangelimann*	Boy/Frau Huber/ Bowling pin boys
Klebe	*Jacobowsky und der Oberst*	"Easygoing" person/ Hotel and café guests
Korngold	*Die tote Stadt*	Juliette/Lucienne
	Das Wunder der Heliane	Angelic voice
Legeti	*Le Grand Macabre*	Go-Go

Composer	Opera	Character
Lully	*Armide*	Apparition of Lucinde/ apparition of Melisse/ shepherdess/Najade
	Atys	Melpomène/Iris
Massenet	*Don Quichotte*	Italian woman/ voice on the record
	Werther	Kätchen
Meyerbeer	*Le prophète*	Two chorus soloists/ Peasant
Monteverdi	*L'incoronazione di Poppea*	Amor
	L'Orfeo	Euridice/Proserpina/Ninfa/ La Musica
	Il ritorno d'Ulisse in patria	Human Frailty/Fortuna/ Amore/Hera
Mozart	*Ascanio in Alba*	Fauno
	Don Giovanni	Zerlina
	Mitrade, re di Ponto	Sifare
	Le nozze di Figaro	Two maidens
	Il re pastore	Amintas
	Die Zauberflöte	Two young people
Mussorgsky	*Boris Godunov*	A farmer
	Khovanshchina	Susanna
Nielsen	*Saul and David*	Abisaj/young maid
Nono	*Al gran sole carico d'amore*	Four sopranos
Paisiello	*Il barbiere de Siviglia*	Notary
Penderecki	*Die Teufel von Loudun*	Philippe
Pintscher	*Thomas Chatterton*	Nancy/Madame Angel/ four soprano voices
Poulenc	*Dialogues des Carmélites*	Female voice
Prokofiev	*War and Peace*	Peronskaja/Dunjascha
Puccini	*Gianni Schicchi*	Nella
	Madama Butterfly	Kate Pinkerton/aunt/cousin
	Suor Angelica	Genevieve/Osmina/ Dolcina/Cercatrici/ Novitiate
	Il tabarro	Soprano voice/love pair
Purcell	*Dido and Aeneas*	Belinda/wife/spirit/ first sailor/witch
Rameau	*Castor et Pollux*	Two companions of Hebe/ shadow/planet
	Hippolyte et Aricie	Huntress/Ónonc High Priestess of Diane
	Platée	Clarine

Composer	Opera	Character
Ravel	L'enfant et les sortilèges	Owl/bat/shepherdess
Reimann	Melusine	Three ladies
Rihm	Hametmachine	Voice from the coffin
	Jakob Lenz	Two voices
Rimsky-Korsakov	Mayskaya Noch	Hen/raven/stepmother
	Le coq d'or	Golden hen
Saariaho	L'amor de loin	Voice
Schoeck	Penthesilea	Priest
Schönberg	Moses und Aaron	Two naked virgins
Schonthal	Princess Maleen	Spectator
Shostakovich	The Nose	Praskowja Ossipowna/ pretzel seller
Schreker	Der ferne Klang	Young woman/Milli/Mary
	Die Gezeichneten	Young woman/Mother
Schubert	Fierrabras	Maragond/young woman
Smetana	The Bartered Bride	Kathinka
R. Strauss	Die ägyptische Helena	Maidservant/two elves/ Hermione
	Arabella	Woman card dealer
	Capriccio	The Italian singer
	Daphne	Maid
	Elektra	Friend/female overseer/ train bearer/maid
	Feuersnot	Young girl
	Die Frau ohne Schatten	Guardian/voice of the falcon/ two young voices
	Intermezzo	Wife of the notary/girl/lady/ young girl
	Der Rosenkavalier	Three noble orphans/ dressmaker/Marianne
	Salome	Slave
	Schweigsame Frau	Young girl
Tippett	The Midsummer Marriage	Girl
Verdi	Aida	Voice of a priestess
	Don Carlos	Tebaldo/voice from above
	I due Foscari	Pisana
	Ernani	Giovanna
	Macbeth	Lady in waiting
	Nabucco	Anna
	Rigoletto	Countess/page

Composer	Opera	Character
Verdi, *cont.*	*Simon Boccanegra*	Amelia's servant
	Il trovatore	Inez
	I vespri siciliani	Ninetta/maiden
Wagner	*Götterdämmerung*	Norn
	Lohengrin	Two pages
	Parsifal	Page/two flower girls
	Rienzi	Peace maker
	Tannhäuser	Two pages/young shepherd
	Die Walküre	Helmwige/Gerhilde/ Ortlinde
Weber	*Euryanthe*	Bertha
	Oberon	Mermaid
Wolf-Ferrari	*Sly*	Rosalina/lady
Zemlinsky	*Kleider machen Leute*	Cellar boy/innkeeper
U. Zimmermann	*Der Schuhu*	Three sopranos/ seamstress/snail/ spinach plant

Beginner Mezzo-Soprano, *Anfänger/Anfängerin Mezzosopran*

Auber	*La muette de Portici*	Noblewoman
Berg	*Lulu*	Groom/dressing room attendant/ gymnasiast
Berio	*Un re in ascolto*	Countess
Berlioz	*Benvenuto Cellini*	Ascanio
Bialas	*Aucassin und Nicolette*	Cirage
Boito	*Mefistofele*	Pantalis
Borodin	*Prince Igor*	Wet nurse
Britten	*Death in Venice*	Street singer
	A Midsummer Night's Dream	Hermia
	Peter Grimes	Mrs. Sedley
Catalani	*La Wally*	Afra
Cavalieri	*Rappresentatione di anima*	Passion/guardian angel
Cavalli	*La Calisto*	Nature/Eternity/ Diana/ Endimione
Charpentier	*Louise*	Gertrud/milk woman/coal picker/Madelaine
Cimarosa	*Il matrimonia segreto*	Fidalma

Composer	Opera	Character
Cherubini	*Médée*	Companion of Dircé/ Neris/
Delius	*A Village Romeo and Juliet*	Farmer woman/fortune teller/jewelry seller
Desseau	*Die Verurteilung des Lukullus*	Tertullia
Donizetti	*L'elisir d'amore*	Gianetta
	La fille du régiment	Contessa Craquitorpi
	Viva la Mamma	Dorotea Caddini
Dukas	*Ariane et Barbe-bleue*	Selysette
Dvořák	*Der Jakobiner*	Lotinka
	Rusalka	Kitchen child/elf
Egk	*Peer Gynt*	Vogtes's wife
Einem	*Dantons Tod*	Julie
Falla	*La vida breve*	Carmela/saleswoman
Fortner	*Bluthochzeit*	Lady
Gershwin	*Porgy and Bess*	Maria/Lily/Annie/ strawberry woman
Giordano	*Andrea Chénier*	Madelon/comtesse de Coigny
Glass	*Akhnaten*	Ankhesenpaaten/ Neferneferuaten/ Sotopenre
Glinka	*Ruslan und Ludmila*	Naina
Gluck	*Iphigéni en Tauride*	Artemis
	La recontre imprévue	Dardanea
Goldschmidt	*Der gewaltige Hahnrei*	Florence
Gounod	*Mireille*	Andreloun
Handel	*Agrippina*	Giunone
	Giulio Cesare	Nirenus
Hara	*Petro Kibe*	Petro (as a child)
Henze	*Die Bassardien*	Beroe
	The English Cat	Lady Toodle
	König Hirsch (Il re cervo)	Voice of the forest/ voice of the people/ lady/lady in black/ Scolatella III
	Venus und Adonis	Six madrigal singers
Hindemith	*Neues vom Tage*	Chambermaid
Hölszky	*Die Wände*	Habiba/ Mme. Blankensee
Janáček	*Jenůfa*	Maid/Barena

Composer	Opera	Character
	Katya Kabanova	Glascha/Fekluscha
	The Metropoulas Affair	Emilias
Klebe	*Jacobowsky und der Oberst*	Light person/ Madame Bouffier
Korngold	*Die tote Stadt*	Lucienne
Lortzing	*Der Wildschütz*	Nanette
Martinu	*The Greek Passion*	Old woman
Massenet	*Don Quichotte*	Garcias
Meyerbeer	*Le prophète*	Farmer
Monteverdi	*L'incoronazione di Poppea*	Pallas Athene
	L'Orfeo	Messagario/Speranza
	Il ritorno d'Ulisse in patria	Fortuna/Euryclea/Penelope
Mozart	*Ascanio in Alba*	Ascanio
	Bastien und Bastienne	Bastien
	La finta giardinera	Ramiro
	Le nozze di Figaro	Marcellina
	Die Zauberflöte	Boy
Nicolai	*Die lustigen Weiber*	Frau Reich
Offenbach	*Les contes d'Hoffmann*	Niklaus
Penderecki	*Die Teufel von Loudun*	Ninon/Louise/four soprano voices
Poulenc	*Dialogues des Carmélites*	Suor Mathilde
Prokofiev	*The Love for Three Oranges*	Clarisse/Nicoletta/ Smeraldina
	War and Peace	Housemaid/Wassilisa/ Marija Bolkonskaja/ French actress
Puccini	*Madama Butterfly*	Kate Pinkerton/Suzuki/ Cio-Cio San's mother
	Manon Lescaut	Musico
	Suor Angelica	Princepessa/Zelatrice/ nurse/novice/Le Converse/Badessa/ mistress of the novices
	Tosca	Shepherd boy
Purcell	*Dido and Aeneas*	Magician/two witches
Rameau	*Hippolyte et Aricie*	Önone
Ravel	*L'enfant et les sortilèges*	Chinese cup/cat/squirrel
Reimann	*Melusine*	Three ladies
Rihm	*Hamletmaschine*	Voice from the coffin

Composer	Opera	Character
Rimsky-Korsakov	*Mayskaya Noch*	Stepmother
	Das Märchen von Zaren Saltan	Oldest daughter of Barbaricha
Rossini	*L'italiana in Algeri*	Zulima
	Mosè in Egiotto	Amenofi
Schonthal	*Princess Maleen*	Spectator
Schreker	*Der ferne Klang*	A girl/Spanish woman
	Die Gezeichneten	Mother
Schubert	*Fierrabras*	Maragond
Shostakovich	*Lady Macbeth von Mzensk*	Sonjetka
Smetana	*The Bartered Bride*	Kathinka
R. Strauss	*Arabella*	Fortune teller
	Daphne	A maiden
	Elektra	Two maidens
	Feuersnot	Elspeth
	Die Frau ohne Schatten	Four children's voices
	Der Rosenkavalier	Two noble orphans
	Salome	Page
Stravinsky	*The Rake's Progress*	Mother Goose
Sutermeister	*Raskolnikow*	Lene
Thomas	*Mignon*	Friedrich
Tippett	*The Midsummer Marriage*	Maiden
Verdi	*Aida*	Voice of a Priestess
	I due Foscari	Pisana
	Ernani	Giovanna
	La forza del destino	Curra
	Macbeth	Lady in waiting
	Rigoletto	Page/Maddalena
	La traviata	Annina
	I vespri siciliani	Ninetta
Wagner	*Götterdämmerung*	Wellgunde
	Lohengrin	Two noble boys
	Der Meistersinger	Magdalena
	Parsifal	Flower girl
	Das Rheingold	Flosshilde
	Rienzi	Peace maker
	Tannhäuser	Two noble boys
	Die Walküre	Segrune/Rossweisse
Weber	*Oberon*	Mermaid/Fatime
Wolf	*Der Corregidor*	Frasquita

Composer	Opera	Character
Wolf-Ferrari	*I quattro rusteghi*	young maiden
	Sly	lady
Zemlinsky	*Kleider machen Leute*	Mrs. Litumlei/Mrs. Häberlein/cook
U. Zimmermann	*Der Schuhu*	Old neighbor lady/ old snail/old spinach plant

Alto, *Anfänger/Anfängerin Alte*

Auber	*La muette de Portici*	Lady in waiting
Berg	*Lulu*	Groom/dressing room attendant/ Mother
Berlioz	*Benvenuto Cellini*	Ascanio
	Les Troyens	Hekuba
Bialas	*Aucassin und Nicolette*	Cirage
Bizet	*Carmen*	Orange seller
Blacher	*Preussisches Märchen*	Mayor
Boito	*Mefistofele*	Pantalis
Britten	*Death in Venice*	Beggar
	A Midsummer Night's Dream	Hippolyta
F. Caccini	*La liberazione di Ruggiero*	Monster
Cavalieri	*Rappresentatione di anima*	Passion
Cavalli	*La Calisto*	Nature
Charpentier	*Louise*	Gertrud/milk woman/ coal picker
Cherubini	*Médée*	Neris
Delius	*A Village Romeo and Juliet*	Farmer/jewelry saleslady
Desseau	*Die Verurteilung des Lukullus*	Tertullia
Donizetti	*Viva la Mamma*	Dorotea Caddini
Dvořák	*Der Jakobiner*	Lotinka
	Rusalka	Two elves
Egk	*Peer Gynt*	Overseer's wife
Flotow	*Martha*	Three maids
Fortner	*Bluthochzeit*	Three girls
Giordano	*Andrea Chénier*	Old Madelon
Glass	*Akhnaten*	Ankhesenpaaten/ Sotopenre

Composer	Opera	Character
Gluck	*L'ivrogne corrigé*	A fury
Goetz	*Der Widerspenstigen Zähmung*	Witch
Goldschmidt	*Der gewaltige Hahnrei*	Florence
Handel	*Agrippina*	Giunone
Henze	*Die Bassariden*	Beroe
	Elegie für junge Liebende	Carolina
	The English Cat	Lady Toodle
	König Hirsch (Il re cervo)	Lady/lady in black/ Scolatella IV/ voice of the woods/ voice of mankind
	Venus und Adonis	Six madrigal singers
Hindemith	*Cardillac* (1952)	A contralto
Janáček	*Jenůfa*	Aunt
	The Makropoulos Affair	Chambermaid Emilias
Kienzl	*Der Evangelimann*	A ragpicker
Klebe	*Jacobowsky und der Oberst*	Old lady from Arras/ hotel and café guests/ Madame Bouffier
Martinu	*The Greek Passion*	An old woman
Meyerbeer	*Le prophète*	Two peasants
Monteverdi	*Il ritorno d'Ulisse in patria*	Euryclea
Mussorgsky	*Boris Godunov*	Farmer woman
Penderecki	*Die Teufel von Loudun*	Louise/Ninon
Poulenc	*Dialogues des Carmélites*	La Badessa Jeanne
Prokofiev	*War and Peace*	Matrjoscha/Trischka/ Adjutant
Puccini	*Madama Butterfly*	Cio-Cio San's mother
	Suor Angelica	Princepessa/La Badessa
	Tosca	Shepherd boy
Purcell	*Dido and Aeneas*	Witch
Ravel	*L'enfant et les sortilèges*	Mother/Chinese cup/ shepherd
Reimann	*Melusine*	Lady
Rihm	*Jakob Lenz*	Two voices
Rimsky-	*Mayskaya Noch*	Sister of the magistrate
Korsakov	*Das Märchen von Zaren Saltan*	Oldest daughter of Barbaricha
Rossini	*L'italiana in Algeri*	Zulima
Schonthal	*Princess Maleen*	Spectator
Schreker	*Der ferne Klang*	Waitress/Spanish lady

Composer	Opera	Character
Schreker, *cont.*	*Die Gezeichneten*	Martuccia
Shostakovich	*Lady Macbeth von Mzensk*	Sonjetka
R. Strauss	*Die ägyptische Helena*	Elf/omniscient shell
	Die Frau ohne Schatten	Four children's voices/ voices from heaven
	Der Rosenkavalier	Two noble orphans
	Salome	Page
	Die schweigsame Frau	Housekeeper
Stravinsky	*The Rake's Progress*	Mother Goose
Szymanowski	*King Roger*	Nun
Tippett	*The Midsummer Marriage*	Maiden
Verdi	*Rigoletto*	Giovanna
	La traviata	Annina
Wagner	*Der fliegende Holländer*	Mary
	Lohengrin	Two noble boys
	Parsifal	Flower girl/page/ voice from heaven
	Rienzi	Peace maker
	Tannhäuser	Two noble boys
	Die Walküre	Lady
Wolf-Ferrari	*Sly*	Lady
Zemlinsky	*Kleider machen Leute*	Mrs. Litumlei/ Mrs. Häberlein/cook
U. Zimmermann	*Der Schuhu*	Old neighbor lady/old snail/old spinach plant

Tenor, *Anfänger/Anfängerin Tenor*

D'Albert	*Die toten Augen*	Ktesiphar/two Jews
	Tiefland	Nando
Auber	*Frau Diavolo*	Soldier
	La muette de Portici	Lorenzo
Beethoven	*Fidelio*	Prisoner
Bellini	*Norma*	Flavius
	I puritani	Sir Bruno Robertson
Berg	*Wozzeck*	Two apprentices/ fool/soldier
Berio	*Un re in ascolto*	Doctor
Berlioz	*Béatrice und Bénédict*	Notary
	Benvenuto Cellini	Francesco/landlord
	Les Troyens	Hylas/Helenus
Boito	*Mefistofele*	Nereus/Wagner

Composer	Opera	Character
Britten	*Billy Budd*	Red Whiskers/Squeak
	Death in Venice	Street Singer/ glassblower/strolling player/hotel porter
	A Midsummer Night's Dream	Snout
	The Turn of the Screw	Prologue
Busoni	*Doktor Faust*	Beelzebuth/Megäros/ students/lieutenant
F. Caccini	*La liberazione di Ruggiero*	Vistola Fiume/Astolfo/ enchanted plant/ shepherd
Cavalieri	*Rappresentatione di anima*	Worldly Life/Echo/ Passion angel in heaven
Charpentier	*Louise*	Noctambulist/policeman/ student/poet/carrot vendor/green pea vendor/old clothes man/king of fools
Cilea	*Adriana Lecouvreur*	Private tutor
Cornelius	*Der Barbier von Baghdad*	Slaves/armed men
Dallapiccola	*Il Prigioniero*	Priest/inquisitor
Desseau	*Die Verurteilung des Lukullus*	Lasus/cherry tree carrier/ officer/teacher
Dittersdorf	*Doktor und Apotheker*	Gallus
Donizetti	*Don Pasquale*	Notary
Dvořák	*Rusalka*	Hunter
Egk	*Die Zaubergeige*	Flunky/judge
	Peer Gynt	Merchant/overseer/ waiter
Einem	*Dantons Tod*	Young person
	Der Besuch der alten Dame	Alfred's son/peasant/ conductor/voice/ husband no. 4
Eötvös	*Tri Sestri*	Rodé/Fedotik
Falla	*La vida breve*	Voice from the smithy/ voice from the distance/voice of a salesman
Flotow	*Martha*	Tenant/servant
Fortner	*Bluthochzeit*	Two boys
Gershwin	*Porgy and Bess*	Robbins/Peter/Mingo/ Nelson/crab seller

Composer	Opera	Character
Giordano	*Andrea Chénier*	Abbé
Glinka	*A Life for the Tsar*	Messenger
Gluck	*Armide*	Artémidore
	Iphigénie en Tauride	Priest of Thoas/Skythe
Goldschmidt	*Der gewaltige Hahnrei*	The young man from Oskerke
Halévy	*La Juive*	Officer/man from the people
Handel	*Ariodante*	Odoardo
	Rinaldo	Herald
Hara	*Petro Kibe*	Seminarian
Henze	*König Hirsch (Il re cervo)*	Voice of the forest/ voice of the people/ guard/three men
Hindemith	*Cardillac*	Tenor
	Mathis der Maler	The piper
	Neues vom Tage	Headwaiter
Hölszky	*Die Wände*	Man in a brothel/flute player/man who urinated/Srir/ Brahim/Ahmed/ Bachir
Honegger	*Jeanne d'Arc au bûcher*	Writer/voice
Humperdinck	*Königskinder*	Dressmaker
Janáček	*The Adventures of Mr. Brouček*	Streetcar conductor/ traffic minister/ Miroslav
	The Cunning Little Vixen	Pásek
	From the House of the Dead	The drunk convict/ young convict/ Tscherewin/Kedril/ voice/guard
Kienzl	*Der Evangelimann*	Hans
Klebe	*Jacobowsky und der Oberst*	First lieutenant/ wandering Jew/hotel and café guests
Korngold	*Das Wunder der Heliane*	Two judges
Krenek	*Jonny spielt auf*	Hotel director/train employee/police
	Pallas Athene weint	Ktesippos

Composer	Opera	Character
Lully	*Armide*	Artémidore
	Atys	Sleep/Morphé/Phantasy
Marschner	*Der Vampyr*	Richard Scrop
Martinů	*The Greek Passion*	Andoms
Massenet	*Don Quichotte*	Two servants
	Manon	Two guards
	Werther	Brühlmann
Messiaen	*Saint François d'Assise*	Élie
Meyerbeer	*Die Huguenotten*	Bois Rosé/Crossé/ Tavannes
	Le prophète	Soldier/two peasants/ officer
Monteverdi	*L'incoronazione di Poppea*	Nutrice/Liberto /Lucano
	L'Orfeo	Apollo/Echo/shepherd/ Spirito
	Il ritorno d'Ulisse in patria	Zeus/Mercury/ two soldiers
Mozart	*Idomeneo, re di Creta*	High priest of Poseidon
	Die Zauberflöte	Priest
Mussorgsky	*Boris Godunov*	Harbinger of love/ farmer/Boyer Chruschtschow
	Der Jahrmarkt von Sorotshinzy	Two guests
	Khovanshchina	Sharpshooter/Streschnew
Nicolai	*Die lustigen Weiber*	Citizen
Nono	*Al gran sole carico d'amore*	Two tenors
Offenbach	*Les contes d'Hoffmann*	Wilhelm/Nathanael
Orff	*Der Mond*	Village mayor
Paisiello	*Il barbiere di Siviglia*	Giovinetto/Alkalde
Pfitzner	*Palestrina*	Theophilus/chapel singer
Poulenc	*Dialogues des Carmélites*	Two officials
Puccini	*La bohème*	Parpignol/Alcindoro
	La fanciulla del West	Trin/Harry/Joe
	Gianni Schicchi	Ciesca
	Madama Butterfly	Prince Yamadori
	Manon Lescaut	Dancing master/ lamplighter
Purcell	*Dido and Aeneas*	Witch
Ponchielli	*La Gioconda*	Isepo
Prokofiev	*War and Peace*	Dignatory/flunky/ French abbé/orderly

Composer	Opera	Character
Prokofiev, *cont.*		officer/Kaisarow/first field officer/adjutant to the general/ adjutant to Marshal Murat/General Fürst de Tolly/Gérard/ young factory worker/Iwanow/ Platon Karatajew
Rameau	*Castor et Pollux*	High priest of Jupiter/ athlete
	Hippolyte et Aricie	Servant of Amor/ Arcas/Tisiphone
Ravel	*L'enfant et les sortilèges*	Shepherd/clock/ Wedgwood teapot/ old man/frog
Reiman	*Lear*	Bedienter
	Melusine	Two men
Rihm	*Jakob Lenz*	Two voices
Rimsky-Korsakov	*Le coq d'or*	Golden cock/ Bojar
Rossini	*Il barbiere di Siviglia*	Fiorillo
	Guillaume Tell	Fisherman
	Il turco in Italia	Albazar
Saint-Säens	*Samson et Dalila*	Messenger/Philistine
Schillings	*Mona Lisa*	Sisto
Schnittke	*Historia von D. Johann Fausten*	Graf/student
	Leben mit einem Idioten	Young lunatic
Schönberg	*Moses und Aaron*	Young man/ naked youth
Schreker	*Der ferne Klang*	Chorister
	Die Gezeichneten	Senator/citizen/ young man
Schubert	*Fierrabras*	Olgier
Shostakovich	*Lady Macbeth von Mzensk*	Teacher/foreman/ coachman
	The Nose	Grand matron
R. Strauss	*Die ägyptische Helena*	Two servants/elf
	Ariadne auf Naxos	Officer/Brighella
	Capriccio	Monsieur Taupe/ Italian tenor

Composer	Opera	Character
R. Strauss, cont.	*Daphne*	Sheep
	Elektra	Young servant
	Die Frau ohne Schatten	Figure of a youth
	Der Rosenkavalier	Innkeeper/animal handler/ two flunkies/tutor/waiter/ singer
	Salome	Slave/four Jews/Nazarener
Tchaikovsky	*Pique Dame*	Festival organizer
Thomas	*Mignon*	Friedrich/prince
Tippett	*The Midsummer Marriage*	Dancing man
Trojahn	*Was ihr wollt*	Two men/two court ushers
Verdi	*Aida*	Messenger
	Un ballo in maschera	Judge/servant
	Don Carlos	Count of Lerma/ king's herald
	I due Foscari	Soldier/Barbarigo
	Ernani	Don Riccardo
	Luisa Miller	Peasant
	I masnadieri	Roller
	Nabucco	High priest of Baal
	Simon Boccanegra	Commander
	La traviata	Gastone
	Il trovatore	Messenger/Ruiz
	I vespri siciliani	Manfredo/Thibaut/Danieli
Wagner	*Lohengrin*	Two barbaric noblemen
	Die Meistersinger	Bird song/Anger/Eisslinger/ Moser
	Parsifal	Knight of the Holy Grail/ Woman
	Das Rheingold	Happy
	Tannhäuser	Heinrich der Schreiber
	Tristan und Isolde	Melot/shepherd
Weber	*Der Freischütz*	Kilian
Weill		Tobby Higgins
	Mahagonny	
Weinberger	*Švanda Dudák*	Judge/trooper/ Hellish Captain
Wolf-Ferrari	*Le donne curiose*	Asdrubale/Almorò/Alvise
	Sly	Judge/tutor

Composer	Opera	Character
Zemlinsky	*Kleider machen Leute*	Son of the house/ porter/waiter/ apprentice tailor
U. Zimmermann	*Der Schuhu*	Tenor/spinach gardener

Baritone, *Anfänger/Anfängerin Bariton*

Auber	*Fra Diavolo*	Peasant
	La muette de Portici	Fisherman
Berg	*Lulu*	Theaterdirektor
Berlioz	*Benvenuto Cellini*	Bernardino/Pompeo/ officer
	Les Troyens	Mercury
Bialas	*Aucassin und Nicolette*	Anton
Bizet	*Carmen*	Moralés
Blacher	*Preussiches Märchen*	Writer
Boito	*Mefistofele*	Nereus/Wagner
Borodin	*Prince Igor*	Skula
Britten	*Billy Budd*	Bosun/Donald/ Neuling's friend/ sailors/Mr. Redburn
	Death in Venice	Lido boatsman/ ship steward/ travel clerk/ tourist guide
	A Midsummer Night's Dream	Snug
	Peter Grimes	Ned Keene
Busoni	*Doktor Faust*	Lawyer/scholar/ Asmodus
	Turandot	Barak
Cavalieri	*Rappresentatione di anima*	Time/World
Cavalli	*La Calisto*	Sylvanus
Charpentier	*Louise*	Junk man/rag picker/sculptor/ bohemian/painter
Cilea	*Adriana Lecouvreur*	Quinault
Davis	*Eight Songs for a Mad King*	George III

Composer	Opera	Character
Delius	*A Village Romeo and Juliet*	Peasants/bass violin/ carousel man/shooting- gallery man
Desseau	*Die Verurteilung des Lukullus*	Officer
Donizetti	*La fille du régiment*	Hortensio
	Viva la Mamma	Vincenzo Biscroma/ Prospero
Dukas	*Ariane et Barbe-bleue*	Peasant
Dvořák	*Rusalka*	Hunter
Egk	*Peer Gynt*	Two merchants/blacksmith
Einem	*Der Besuch der alten Dame*	Clergyman/doctor/ Hellmesberger/train station master
	Peer Gynt	Old man
	Die Zaubergeige	Two flunkies
Fortner	*Bluthochzeit*	Three guests
Gershwin	*Porgy and Bess*	Jim/Simon Frazier/ grave digger
Giordano	*Andrea Chénier*	Roucer/Fléville/Dumas/ Fouquier-Tinville/ Mathieu
Gluck	*Alceste*	Herald
	Armide	Aronte
	Iphigénie en Aulide	Arkas/Patroklos
	Iphigénie en Tauride	Skythe
Gounod	*Faust*	Wagner
	Mirielle	Ambroise
Halévy	*La Juive*	Albert
Handel	*Agrippina*	Pallante
	Alcina	Melisso
	Deidamia	Nestor
	Gulio Cesare	Achillas
	Rinaldo	Argante
	Tamerlano	Leone
Hara	*Petro Kibe*	Yasaku/Vieillas's voice/Persian
Henze	*Boulevard Solitude*	Francis
	König Hirsch (Il re cervo)	Voice of mankind
Hindemith	*Cardillac (1926)*	The leader
	Mathis der Maler	Truchess von Waldburg
	Neues vom Tage	Guide/hotel director/ manager

Composer	Opera	Character
Hölszky	*Die Wände*	Sir Harold/voice
Humperdinck	*Königskinder*	Two gatekeepers
Janáček	*The Adventures of Mr. Brouček*	Vacek
	From the House of the Dead	Drunken prisoner/ blacksmith/priest/ young prisoner/ Don Juan/two guards
	Jenůfa	Two voices
Klebe	*Jacobowsky und der Oberst*	Salomon/ chauffeur/ Clairon/Brigadier von St. Cyrill/ Franziskus
Korngold	*Das Wunder der Heliane*	Four judges
Krenek	*Jonny spielt auf*	Train employee/ policeman
	Pallas Athene weint	Brasidas
Ligeti	*Le Grand Macabre*	Ruffiak/Schobiak/ Schabernack
Lully	*Atys*	Time/Idas/Fantasie
Marschner	*Der Vampyr*	Robert Creen/ Richard Scrop
Martinů	*The Greek Passion*	Old Man
Massenet	*Don Quichotte*	Servant
	Werther	Man of the swampy meadow
Meyerbeer	*Le prophète*	First officer
Monteverdi	*L'incoronazione di Poppea*	Liberto/Petronio/ Mercury/two soldiers
	L'Orfeo	Apollo
	Il ritorno d'Ulisse in patria	Zeus
Mussorgsky	*Boris Godunov*	Tschernjakowskij
	Der Jahrmarkt von Sorotschinzy	Tschernobog
	Khovanshchina	Warssonofjew/Kuska/ Streschnew
Nono	*Al gran sole carico d'amore*	Two bases
Offenbach	*Les contes d'Hoffmann*	Hermann/Schlémil
Orff	*Die Kluge*	Man
	Der Mond	Farmer
Paisiello	*Il barbiere di Siviglia*	Svegliato

Composer	Opera	Character
Penderecki	*Die Teufel von Loudun*	Prince Henri de Condé/ Bontemps
Pintscher	*Thomas Chatterton*	Richard Smith
Ponchielli	*La Gioconda*	Bootsman/singer/ steersman/church servant
Poulenc	*Dialogues des Carmélites*	Two commissioners/ Jalevinot/Officer Thierry
Prokofiev	*War and Peace*	Old flunky/Gawrila/ Métivier/Matwejew/ Two staff officers/ Marschall Berthier/ General Rajewski/ young factory worker/ French officer
Puccini	*La fanciulla del West*	Sonora/Sid/Handsome/ Happy/Jake Wallace
	Gianni Schicchi	Marco/Amantio di Nicolao
	Madama Butterfly	Yakusidé/registrar/ Bonze/commissioner
	Manon Lescaut	Sergeant
	Turandot	Mandarin
Rameau	*Castor et Pollux*	Athlete
	Hippolyte et Aricie	Jupiter
Ravel	*L'enfant et les sortilèges*	Chair/clock/cat/tree
Reimann	*Melusine*	Bricklayer/ gentleman
Rimsky-Korsakov	*Le coq d'or*	Bojar
	Das Märchen von Zaren Saltan	Messenger/three sailors/fool
Rossini	*Il barbiere di Siviglia*	Fiorillo
Schnittke	*Historia von D. Johann Fausten*	Two counts/two students/Herzog von Bayern/Wineman Schonthal
	Prinzessin Maleen	Spectator
Schreker	*Der ferne Klang*	Policeman
	Die Gezeichneten	Julian Pinelli/Friend/ servant

Composer	Opera	Character
Shostakovich	*Lady Macbeth von Mzensk*	Foreman/mill hand/ administrator/porter/ police/guard/old forced laborer/ghost of Boris/ Timofejewitsch/ police chief/sergeant
	The Nose	Doctor/employee
Smetana	*The Bartered Bride*	Kruschina
R. Strauss	*Arabella*	Count Dominik
	Ariadne auf Naxos	Officer/wig maker
	Daphne	Four sheep
	Elektra	Nurse/old servant
	Die Frau ohne Schatten	Voice of the guard/ one-eyed person
	Intermezzo	Notary/king's counsel
	Die schweigsame Frau	Notary
Sutermeister	*Raskolnikow*	Voices of the priests
Thomas	*Mignon*	Baron
Tippett	*The Midsummer Marriage*	A drunk
Trojahn	*Was ihr wollt*	Two men/two court ushers
Verdi	*Un ballo in maschera*	Judge
	Don Carlos	Monk
	I due Foscari	A servant of the Doge
	Ernani	Jago
	I masnardieri	Roller
	La traviata	Baron Duphal
	I vespri siciliani	Roberto
Wagner	*Die Meistersinger*	Night watchman/Ortel
	Tristan und Isolde	Helmsman
Weber	*Der Freischütz*	Kilian/Ottokar
Weinberger	*Švanda dudák*	Trooper
Wolf-Ferrari	*Sly*	Country court judges/ three servants
Zemlinsky	*Kleider machen Leute*	Innkeeper/coachman/ apprentice tailors

Bass, *Anfänger/Anfängerin Bass*

Adam	*Le postillon de Lonjumeau*	Marquis de Corey/ Alcindor/Bourdon
D'Albert	*Tiefland*	A voice
	Die toten Augen	Two Jews/old Jew

Composer	Opera	Character
Auber	*La muette de Portici*	Selva/Borella/fisherman
Beethoven	*Fidelio*	Prisoner
Berg	*Wozzeck*	Journeyman
Berio	*Un re in ascolto*	Lawyer/singer
Berlioz	*Benvenuto Cellini*	Bernardino/officer
	La damnation de Faust	Brander
	Les Troyens	Two Trojan soldiers/ Mercury/priest
Bizet	*Carmen*	Zuniga
Blacher	*Preussisches Märchen*	Insurance agent/ innkeeper
Britten	*Billy Budd*	Lieutenant Ratcliff
	Death in Venice	Hotel waiter/ship steward/tourist guide/ San Marco priest
	A Midsummer Night's Dream	Snug
Busoni	*Doktor Faust*	Student/Gravis/Levis/ theologian/lawyer
	Turandot	Barak/two doctors/ Tartaglia
F. Caccini	*La liberazione di Ruggiero*	Monster
Cavalieri	*Rappresentatione di anima*	Time/World/souls in hell
Cavalli	*La Calisto*	Jupiter/Pan/Sylvanus
Charpentier	*Louise*	Philosopher
Cilea	*Adriana Lecouvreur*	Quinault
Cornelius	*Der Barbier von Bagdad*	Armed person/muezzin
Dallapiccola	*Il Prigioniero*	Priest
Debussy	*Pelléas et Mélisande*	Doctor/voice of the shepherd
Delius	*A Village Romeo and Juliet*	Bass violin
Dessau	*Die Verurteilung des Lukullus*	Two shadows/judge/ two legionaries
Donizetti	*Don Pasquale*	Notary
	L'elisir d'amore	Soldier
	La fille du régiment	Corporal/Hortensio
	Viva la Mamma	Vincenzo Biscroma/ Orazio
Dukas	*Ariane et Barbe-bleue*	Old peasant/peasant
Egk	*Peer Gynt*	Two merchants/ president/farmer/ old man
	Die Zaubergeige	Two flunkies

Composer	Opera	Character
Einem	*Der Besuch der alten Dame*	Doctor/policeman/ Hellmesberger/train station master/servant/ train conductor/lessee
Flotow	*Martha*	Two servants
Giordano	*Andrea Chénier*	Roucer/Fléville/Fouquier-Tinville/Dumas/ Schmidt/tutor
Glinka	*A Life for the Tsar*	Polish foreman/ Russian foreman
Gluck	*Alceste*	Voice of the oracle
	Armide	Aronte
	Iphigénie en Aulide	Arkas/Patroklos
	Iphigénie en Tauride	Oracle of Thoas
Gounod	*Faust*	Wagner
	Mirielle	Ambroise
Halévy	*La Juive*	Caller/man from the people
Handel	*Agrippina*	Lesbo/Pallante
	Alcina	Melisso
	Deidamia	Nestor
	Gulio Cesare	Achillas
	Rinaldo	Argante
	Tamerlano	Leone
Henze	*Boulevard Solitude*	Son of Lalique
	König Hirsch (Il re cervo)	Guards/voice of the forest/voice of the people
Hindemith	*Mathis der Maler*	Truchess von Waldburg
	Neues vom Tage	Registrar/hotel director/two managers
Hölszky	*Die Wände*	Kadi/Sir Harold
Honegger	*Jeanne d'Arc au bûcher*	Voice/peasant/herald
Humperdinck	*Königskinder*	Innkeeper
Janáček	*From the House of the Dead*	Blacksmith/Greek priest/ prisoner (Don Juan)/ guards
Kienzl	*Der Evangelimann*	Voices of the night watchmen
Klebe	*Jacobowsky und der Oberst*	Salomon/chauffeur/ Clairon/ dice player/ Brigadier von St. Cyrill

Composer	Opera	Character
Korngold	*Das Wunder der Heliane*	Four judges
Krenek	*Jonny spielt auf*	Police
Leoncavallo	*Pagliacci*	Farmer
Ligeti	*Le Grand Macabre*	Ruffiak/Schobiak/ Schabernack
Lortzing	*Die Opernprobe*	Martin/Christoph
	Der Waffenschmied	Blacksmith's apprentice
Lully	*Armide*	Aronte
	Atys	Le Temps Idas/Phobetor
Marschner	*Der Vampyr*	Sir Berkley/Robert Creen/Tom Blunt
Martinů	*The Greek Passion*	Patriarcheas/old man
Massenet	*Manon*	Landlord
	Werther	Brühlmann
Matthus	*Die Weise von Liebe und Tod*	Count Spork
Messiaen	*Saint François d'Assise*	Sylvestre/Rufin
Meyerbeer	*Die Huguenotten*	Guard/three monks
	Le prophète	Four peasants/officer
Monteverdi	*L'incoronazione di Poppea*	Littore
Mozart	*Idomeneo, re di Creta*	Voice of the oracle
Mussorgsky	*Boris Godunov*	Lowitzkij/ Tschernjakowskij/ farmer/foreman
	Der Jahrmarkt von Sorotshinzy	Tschernobog/guest
	Khovanshchina	Warssonofjew/Kuska/ sharpshooters/pastor
Nielsen	*Saul and David*	Guard
Nono	*Al gran sole carico d'amore*	Two basses
Offenbach	*Les contes d'Hoffmann*	Schlémil
Orff	*Die Kluge*	Vagabond
Paisiello	*Il barbiere di Siviglia*	Svegliato/notary
Penderecki	*Die Teufel von Loudun*	Father Ambrose/ Bontemps
Pfitzner	*Palestrina*	Church singer
Pintscher	*Thomas Chatterton*	William Barrett
Ponchielli	*La Gioconda*	Zuane/boatman/ singer/steersman/ church servant
Poulenc	*Dialogues des Carmélites*	Two commissioners

Composer	Opera	Character
Prokofiev	*The Love for Three Oranges*	Herald
	War and Peace	Vallet Bolkonskis/Métivier/Tichon Schtscherbatyn/second staff officer Brilliard/General Bennigsen/General Jermolow/Captain Jacqueau/Marshall Davout
Puccini	*La bohème*	Sergente/Officer/Benoit
	La fanciulla del West	Billy Jackrabbit/Jake Wallace/José Castro/Happy/Larkens
	Gianni Schicchi	Simon/Spinelloccio/Pinellino/Guccio/Betto di Signa
	Madama Butterfly	Yakusidé/official/registrar/Bonze
	Manon Lescaut	Archery servant/innkeeper/sea captain
	Tosca	Jailor/Angelotti
Rameau	*Castor et Pollux*	Jupiter
	Hippolyte et Aricie	Neptune/Hunter/Arcas/Tisiphone/Jupiter
Ravel	*L'enfant et les sortilèges*	Tree
Reimann	*Melusine*	Bricklayer/gentleman
Rihm	*Jakob Lenz*	Two voices
Rimsky-Korsakov	*Le coq d'or*	Bojar
	Das Märchen von Zaren Saltan	Seaman
Rossini	*Il barbiere di Siviglia*	Ambrosio/officer
Saint-Säens	*Samson et Dalila*	Philistine
Schonthal	*Princess Maleen*	Spectator
Schreker	*Der ferne Klang*	Chorister/policeman
	Die Gezeichneten	Senator/Julian Pinelli/slave/Paolo Calvi/Father/citizen/two young people/friend
Schubert	*Fierrabras*	Brutamonte

Composer	Opera	Character
Shostakovich	*Lady Macbeth von Mzensk*	Guard/old forced laborer/ police/sergeant/priest/ ghost of Boris Timofejewitsch
	The Nose	Doctor/employee
Smetana	*The Bartered Bride*	Muff
R. Strauss	*Arabella*	Three players/Graf Lamoral
	Ariadne auf Naxos	Lakai
	Capriccio	Tutor
	Daphne	Sheep
	Elektra	Old servant
	Die Frau ohne Schatten	Three voices of the guards
	Intermezzo	Commercial councillor/ Justizrat
	Der Rosenkavalier	Flunkies/waiters/notary/ police commissioner
	Salome	Two soldiers/Cappadocier
	Die schweigsame Frau	Notary
Stravinsky	*The Rake's Progress*	Caretaker
Sutermeister	*Raskolnikow*	Policeman
Tchaikovsky	*Eugene Onegin*	Foreman
Tippett	*The Midsummer Marriage*	Man
Trojahn	*Enrico*	Giovanni
	Was ihr wollt	Two men/two court ushers
Verdi	*Attilla*	Leo I/Leone
	I due Foscari	Servant of the doge
	Ernani	Jago
	Falstaff	Ford
	Macbeth	Macbeth's servant herald/doctor
	Nabucco	High priest of Baal
	Otello	Herald
	Rigoletto	Servant
	Il trovatore	Old gypsy woman
	I vespri siciliani	Bethune/Count Vandermont/Albiani/ Robert
Wagner	*Lohengrin*	Two barbaric noblemen
	Die Meistersinger	Night watchman/Ortel
	Parsifal	Knight of the Holy Grail
	Rienzi	Colonna/Raimondo
	Tristan und Isolde	A helmsman

Composer	Opera	Character
Wolf-Ferrari	*Le donne curiose*	Lunardo/Mómolo/Mènego/ gondoliere
	Sly	Driver/soldier/three servants/cook
Zemlinsky	*Kleider machen Leute*	Innkeeper/ coachman/ apprentice tailor
U. Zimmermann	*Der Schuhu*	Bass/Duke von Coburg-Gotha/Starost von Holland

Appendix E
Opera Roles by *Fach*

This appendix contains a comprehensive listing of large and medium roles by *the most commonly used Fach* categories but is not all-inclusive. Information was researched from Rudolf Kloiber, Wulf Konold, and Robert Maschka's *Handbuch der Oper* (Bärenreiter-Verlag, 2006) and *The Definitive Kobbé's Opera Book* (G. P. Putnam's Sons, 1987). Operas are listed with the most universally used title as listed in Kloiber or Kobbé's, with capitalization as used in the country of origin. Operas that were originally titled in a Slavic language are listed in English to avoid transliteration. Abbreviations are used for the more lengthy titles.

Roles are as listed in the Kloiber, and those that can be sung by more than one *Fach* category are listed under each applicable *Fach*.

Composer	Opera	Role
Soubrette/Acting Soprano (*Soubrette/Spielsopran*)		
D'Albert	*Die toten Augen*	Arsinoë/Hirtenknabe
Beethovan	*Fidelio*	Marzelline
Berlioz	*Béatrice et Bénédict*	Béatrice
Boieldeau	*La Dame Blanche*	Jenny
Britten	*Albert Herring*	Nancy Waters
Dittersdorf	*Doktor und Apoteker*	Rosalie
Donizetti	*L'elisir d'amore*	Gianetta
	Viva la Mamma	Luigia Boschi
Egk	*Die Zaubergeige*	Gretl
Eötvös	*Tri sestri*	Natascha

Composer	Opera	Role
Fortner	*Bluthochzeit*	Kind
Gluck	*L'ivrogne corrigé*	Colette
	Orfeo ed Euridice	Amor
	La rencontre imprévue	Amina
Handel	*Alcina*	Morgana
	Orlando	Dorinda
	Serse	Atlanta
Haydn	*La fedeltà premiata*	Nerina
	Lo speziale	Grilletta
Henze	*Der junge Lord*	Kammermädchen
	König Hirsch (Il re cervo)	Scolatella II
Hölszky	*Bremer Freiheit*	Luisa Mauer
	Die Wände	Malika
Lortzing	*Die Opernprobe*	Hannchen
	Der Waffenschmeid	Marie
	Der Wildschütz	Gretchen
Mascagni	*Cavalleria rusticana*	Lola
Massenet	*Manon*	Javotte
	Werther	Sophie
Mozart	*Bastien und Bastienne*	Bastienne
	La finta giardiniera	Serpetta
	La finta semplice	Ninetta
	Le nozze di Figaro	Barbarina
	Die Zauberflöte	Papagena
Poulenc	*Dialogues des Carmélites*	Constance
Rameau	*Hippolyte et Aricie*	L'amour
	Platée	Amour
Rossini	*Guillaume Tell*	Gemmy
Schillings	*Mona Lisa*	Dianora
Smetana	*The Two Widows*	Lidka
R. Strauss	*Intermezzo*	Anna
Tchaikovsky	*Pique Dame*	Chloë
Telemann	*Pimpinone*	Vespetta
Wolf-Ferrari	*Le donne curiose*	Rosaura
	I quattro rusteghi	Lucieta

Lyric Coloratura Soprano (*Lyrischer Koloratursopran; Koloratursoubrette*)

Adam	*Le postillon de Lonjumeau*	Madeleine
Adams	*Nixon in China*	Chiang Ch'ing
Auber	*Fra Diavolo*	Zerline
Berio	*Un re in ascolto*	Sopran II

Composer	Opera	Role
Berlioz	*Béatrice et Bénédict*	Hero
Bialas	*Aucassin und Nicolette*	Nicolette
Birtwistle	*Punch and Judy*	Pretty Polly/Hexe
Bizet	*Carmen*	Frasquita
	Le pêcheurs des perles	Leila
Boieldieu	*La dame blanche*	Anna
Britten	*A Midsummer Night's Dream*	Tytania
Catalani	*La Wally*	Walter
Cimarosa	*Il matrimonio segreto*	Carolina
Dittersdorf	*Doktor und Apotheker*	Leonore
Donizetti	*Don Pasquale*	Norina
	L'elisir d'amore	Adina
	La fille du régiment	Marie
	Lucia di Lammermoor	Lucia
	Viva la Mamma	Corilla Sartinecchi
Dvořák	*Der Jakobiner*	Terinka
Flotow	*Alessando Stradella*	Leonore
	Martha	Frau Harriet
Gluck	*Orfeo ed Euridice*	Amor
	La rencontre imprévue	Rezia
Halévy	*La Juive*	Eudoxie
Handel	*Agrippina*	Nerone/Poppea
	Alcina	Alcina
	Ariodante	Dalinda
	Deidamia	Deidamia
	Orlando	Dorinda
	Ottone, re di Germania	Theophano
	Radamisto	Polissena
	Rinaldo	Almirena
	Serse	Romilda
Haydn	*Il mondo della luna*	Flaminia
Henze	*Die Bassariden*	Antonoe/Prosperpina
	Boulevard Solitude	Manon Lescaut
	Elegie für junge Liebende	Hilda Mack
	The English Cat	Minette
	König Hirsch (Il re cervo)	Scolatella
Hölsky	*Die Wände*	Leila
Keiser	*Masaniello*	Mariane
Ligeti	*Le Grand Macabre*	Chef der Gepopo
Massenet	*Manon*	Manon
Meyerbeer	*Les Huguenots*	Urban

Composer	Opera	Role
Mozart	*Ascanio in Alba*	Silvia
	La clemenza di Tito	Servilia
	Così fan tutte	Despina
	Die Entführung aus dem Serail	Blonde
	La finta giardiniera	Sandrina
	La finta semplice	Rosina
	Idomeneo, re di Creta	Ilia
	Lucio Silla	Cecilio/Lucio Cinna
	Le nozze di Figaro	Susanna
	Il re pastore	Elisa
	Der Schauspieldirektor	Mademoiselle Silberklang/ Madame Herz
Offenbach	*Les contes d'Hoffmann*	Olympia
Pfitzner	*Das Christ-Elflein*	Elflein
Poulenc	*Dialogues des Carmélites*	Sister Constance
Puccini	*La bohème*	Musetta
Rameau	*Hippolyte et Aricie*	Aricie
Reimann	*Melusine*	Melusine
Rimsky-Korsakov	*Le coq d'or*	King of Schemacha
Schnittke	*Leben mit einem Idioten*	Frau
Schonthal	*Princess Maleen*	Maleen
Smetana	*The Two Widows*	Karoline
R. Strauss	*Arabella*	Fiaker-Milli/Zdenka
	Ariadne auf Naxos	Zerbinetta/Najade
	Intermezzo	Anna
	Der Rosenkavalier	Sophie
	Die schweigsame Frau	Aminta
Tan Dun	*Marco Polo*	Das Wassner
Thomas	*Mignon*	Philine
Trojahn	*Was ihr wollt*	Viola/Maria
Verdi	*Un ballo in maschera*	Oscar
	Falstaff	Nannetta
	Rigoletto	Gilda
Wagner	*Siegfried*	Waldvogel
Weber	*Abu Hassan*	Fatime
	Der Freischütz	Ännchen
Wolf-Ferrari	*Il segreto di Susanna*	Susanna

Coloratura Soprano (*Koloratursopran*)

Composer	Opera	Role
Dessau	*Die Verurteilung des Lukullus*	Königen
Donizetti	*Lucia di Lammermoor*	Lucia

Composer	Opera	Role
Mozart	*Der Schauspieldirektor*	Herz/Mademoiselle Silberklang

Dramatic Coloratura Soprano (*Dramatischer Koloratursopran*)

Composer	Opera	Role
D'Albert	*Die toten Augen*	Myrtocle
Auber	*La muette de Portici*	Elvira
Bellini	*I puritani*	Elvira
Berg	*Lulu*	Lulu
	Norma	Norma
Berio	*Un re in ascolto*	Protagonisten
Berlioz	*Benvenuto Cellini*	Teresa
Britten	*Albert Herring*	Miss Woodsworth
Cherubini	*Médée*	Dircé
Donizetti	*Anna Bolena*	Anna Bolena
Glinka	*Ruslan und Ljudmila*	Ljudmila
Gounod	*Faust*	Marguerite
Handel	*Agrippina*	Agrippina
	Giulio Cesare	Cleopatra
	Orlando	Angelica
	Rinaldo	Armide
	Rodelinda	Rodelinda
	Tamerlano	Asteria
Hindemith	*Cardillac*	Tochter der Cardillac
Klebe	*Jacobowsky und der Oberst*	Marianne Deloupe
Lortzing	*Undine*	Berthalda
Meyerbeer	*Les Huguenots*	Margarete
Monteverdi	*L'incoronazione di Poppea*	Poppea/Ottavia
	Il ritorno d'Ulisse in patria	Pallas Athene
Mozart	*Ascanio in Alba*	Venus
	La clemenza di Tito	Vitellia
	Così fan tutte	Fiordiligi
	Don Giovanni	Donna Anna/ Donna Elvira
	Die Entführung aus dem Serail	Constanza
	La finta giardiniera	Arminda
	Lucio Silla	Giunia
	Mitridate, re di Ponto	Aspasia
	Le nozze di Figaro	Countess Almaviva
	Die Zauberflöte	Die Königin der Nacht
Nicolai	*Die lustigen Weiber*	Frau Fluth
Puccini	*Manon Lescaut*	Manon

Composer	Opera	Role
Rossini	*Tancredi*	Amenaide
R. Strauss	*Die ägyptische Helena*	Aithra
	Daphne	Daphne
	Die schweigsame Frau	Isotta
Tippett	*The Midsummer Marriage*	Jenifer
Verdi	*Attila*	Odabella
	Ernani	Elvira
	Falstaff	Alice
	Luisa Miller	Luisa
	I masnadieri	Amalia
	Nabucco	Abigail
	La traviata	Violetta
	Il trovatore	Leonora
	I vespri siciliani	Elena
Weber	*Oberon*	Rezia
Wolf-Ferrari	*I quattro rusteghi*	Felice
B. Zimmermann	*Die Soldaten*	Marie

Character Soprano (*Charaktersopran/Zwischenfachstimme*)

Bizet	*Carmen*	Carmen
Britten	*Peter Grimes*	Mrs. Sedley
Debussy	*Pelléas et Mélisande*	Mélisande
Egk	*Peer Gynt*	Die Rothaaige
Fortner	*Bluthochzeit*	Die Bettlerin (der Tod)
Goetz	*Der Widerspenstigen Zähmung*	Katharina
Haydn	*Lo speziale*	Volpino
Humperdinck	*Hänsel und Gretel*	Hexe
	Königskinder	Die Wirtstochter
Menotti	*The Consul*	Maida Sorel
Rameau	*Platée*	La Folie
Reimann	*Melusine*	Madame Laperouse
Rimsky-Korsakov	*Le coq d'or*	Astrologer
	Das Märchen von Zaren Saltan	Tochter des Babarichas
Schillings	*Mona Lisa*	Ginevra
Shostakovich	*Lady Macbeth von Mzensk*	Aksinja
R. Strauss	*Feuersnot*	Margaret
Wolf-Ferrari	*Le donne curiose*	Colombina

Lyric Soprano (*Lyricher Sopran*)

Adams	*Nixon in China*	Pat Nixon
D'Albert	*Tiefland*	Nuri

Composer	Opera	Role
Auber	*Fra Diavolo*	Zerline
Beethoven	*Fidelio*	Marzelline
Berio	*Un re in ascolto*	Sopran I
Berlioz	*Les Troyens*	Askanius
Bizet	*Carmen*	Micaëla/Frasquita
Boito	*Mefistofele*	Helena
Britten	*Albert Herring*	Miss Wordsworth
	A Midsummer Night's Dream	Helena/Tytania
	Peter Grimes	First niece/ second niece
	The Turn of the Screw	Governess
F. Caccini	*La liberazione di Ruggiero*	Alcina
Cavalli	*La Calisto*	La Calisto
Cilea	*Adriana Lecouvreur*	Jouvenot
Cimarosa	*Il matrimonio segreto*	Lisetta
Cornelius	*Der Barbier von Bagdad*	Margiana
Delius	*A Village Romeo and Juliet*	Vrenchen
Donizetti	*Viva la Mamma*	Luigia Boschi
Dvořák	*Der Jakobiner*	Terinka
Egk	*Der Revisor*	Maja
Einem	*Dantons Tod*	Lucile
Eötvös	*Tri sestri*	Irina
Gershwin	*Porgy and Bess*	Bess
Glass	*Akhnaten*	Teje
Glinka	*Ruslan und Ljudmila*	Gorislawa
Gluck	*Armide*	Sidonie
	Le cadi dupé	Zelmire
	Orfeo ed Euridice	Euridice
Goetz	*Der Widerspenstigen Zähmung*	Bianca
Goldschmidt	*Der gewaltige Hahnrei*	Stella
Gounod	*Faust*	Siebel
Handel	*Acis and Galatea*	Galatea
	Alcina	Morgana/Alcina/ Ruggiero
	Ariodante	Ginevra
	Deidamia	Deidamia/Achilles/ (Pirrha) Sextus/ Pompeus/Cleopatra
	Orlando	Angelica
	Ottone, re di Germania	Gismonda
	Poro, re dell'Indie	Cleofide
	Radamisto	Radamisto/Fraarte
	Tamerlano	Asteria

Composer	Opera	Role
Hara	*Petro Kibe*	Ursula Osato/ Mansho Konishi
Haydn	*La fedeltà premiata*	Nerina
Hindemith	*Mathis der Maler*	Regina
Humperdinck	*Hänsel und Gretel*	Gretel
Janáček	*Jenůfa*	Karolka
Keiser	*Masaniello*	Aloysia
Lachenmann	*Das Mädchen*	Solo sopran
Leoncavallo	*Pagliacci*	Nedda
Ligeti	*Le Grand Macabre*	Clitoria
Lortzing	*Die Opernprobe*	Luise
	Undine	Undine
	Zar und Zimmermann	Marie
Lully	*Armide*	Phénice
	Atys	Sangaride
Massenet	*Werther*	Sophie
Matthus	*Die Weise von Liebe und Tod*	Gedankenstimme der Gräfin
Messiaen	*Saint Françios d'Assise*	Engel
Monteverdi	*L'incoronazione di Poppea*	Drusilla
Mozart	*Bastien und Bastienne*	Bastienne
	La clemenza di Tito	Servilia
	Così fan tutte	Despina
	Don Giovanni	Zerlina
	Le nozze di Figaro	Susanna/Cherubino
	Il re pastore	Tamiris
	Die Zauberflöte	Pamina
Mussorgsky	*Boris Godunov*	Xenia
	Der Jahrmarkt von Sorotshinzy	Parassja
Nicolai	*Die lustigen Weiber*	Anna
Orff	*Catulli Carmina*	Soprano
Paisiello	*Il barbiere di Siviglia*	Rosina
Pergolesi	*La serva padrona*	Serpina
Pfitzner	*Der arme Heinrich*	Agnes
	Das Christ-Elflein	Christkinchen
	Palestrina	Ighino
Puccini	*La bohème*	Mimi
	Gianni Schicchi	Lauretta
	Manon Lescaut	Musico
	Suor Angelica	Angelica/Genoveva
	Turandot	Liù

Composer	Opera	Role
Purcell	*Dido and Aeneas*	Dido
Rameau	*Castor et Pollux*	Venus/Télaire
Rimsky-Korsakov	*Das Märchen von Zaren Saltan*	Prinzessin Swanhild
Rossini	*Guillaume Tell*	Gemmy
	Mosè in Egitto	Elcia
Saariaho	*L'amour de loin*	Clémence
Schönberg	*Moses und Aron*	Ein jungen Mädchen
	Von Heute auf Morgen	Die Freundin
Schubert	*Fierrabras*	Emma/Florinda
Smetana	*The Bartered Bride*	Marie
R. Strauss	*Arabella*	Zdenka
	Ariadne auf Naxos	Echo/Najade
	Der Rosenkavalier	Sophie
Stravinsky	*The Rake's Progress*	Anne
Telemann	*Pimpinone*	Vespetta
Tippett	*The Midsummer Marriage*	Bella
Trojahn	*Enrico*	Frida
Ullman	*Der Kaiser von Atlantis*	Bubikopf
Verdi	*Falstaff*	Nannetta
Wagner	*Das Rheingold*	Wellgunde
	Tannhäuser	Hirt
Weber	*Der Freischütz*	Ännchen
	Oberon	Fatime
Weill	*Mahagonny*	Jenny
U. Zimmermann	*Der Schuhu*	Die Prinzessin
	Die weisse Rose	Sophie Scholl

Young Dramatic Soprano/Acting Soprano (*Jugendlich-dramatischer Sopran/Spinto Sopran*)

Composer	Opera	Role
Bartók	*Duke Bluebeard's Castle*	Judith
Bellini	*Norma*	Norma
Berg	*Wozzeck*	Marie
Berlioz	*Benvenuto Cellini*	Teresa
	La damnation de Faust	Marguerite
Bizet	*Carmen*	Micaëla
Boito	*Mefistofele*	Margarete/Helena
Britten	*Albert Herring*	Lady Billows
	Peter Grimes	Two nieces/Ellen Orford
	The Turn of the Screw	Miss Jessel
Busoni	*Arlecchino*	Colombina

Composer	Opera	Role
Busoni,	Doktor Faust	Herzogin von Parma
cont.	Turandot	Turandot
Catalini	La Wally	Wally
Cavalli	La Calisto	Calisto
Charpentier	Louise	Louise
Cherubin	Médée	Dircé
Cilea	Adriana Lecouvreur	Adriana Lecouvreur
Debussy	Pelléas et Mélisande	Mélisande
Delius	A Village Romeo and Juliet	Vrenchen
Dukas	Ariane et Barbe-bleue	Bride
Dvořák	Der Jakobiner	Julia
	Rusalka	Rusalka
Egk	Peer Gynt	Solveig
	Die Zaubergeige	Nenabella
Falla	La vida breve	Salud
Fortner	Bluthochzeit	Braut
Gershwin	Porgy and Bess	Bess
Giordano	Andrea Chénier	Maddalena
		von Coigny
Glinka	A Life for the Tsar	Antonida
	Ruslan und Ljudmila	Gorislawa
Gluck	Armide	Armide
	Iphegénie en Tauride	Iphegénie
Gounod	Faust	Marguerite
	Mireille	Mireille
Halévy	La Juive	Rachel
Handel	Radamisto	Tigrane
	Serse	Romilda
Henze	Elgie für junge Liebende	Elisabeth Zimmer
	The English Cat	Miss Crisp
	Der junge Lord	Luise
	König Hirsch (Il re cervo)	Costanza
	Venus und Adonis	Prima donna
Hindemith	Cardillac (1926)	Dame/Tochter
	Cardillac (1952)	Tochter/erste Sängerin
	Mathis der Maler	Ursula
	Neues vom Tage	Laura
	Sancta Susanna	Susanna
Honegger	Jeanne d'Arc au bûcher	Margarete
Humperdinck	Königskinder	Gänsemagd
Janáček	The Adventures of Mr. Brouček	Amálka

Composer	Opera	Role
Janáček, cont.	*Jenůfa*	Jenůfa
	Katya Kabanoa	Katja
Kienzl	*Der Evangelimann*	Martha
Klebe	*Jacobowsky und der Oberst*	Marianne Deloupe
Korngold	*Das Wunder der Heliane*	Heliane
Krenek	*Jonny spielt auf*	Anita
	Pallas Athene weint	Timaea
Leoncavallo	*Pagliacci*	Nedda
Lortzing	*Undine*	Bertalda
Lully	*Armide*	Armide
	Atys	Cybele
Marschner	*Hans Heiling*	Anna
	Der Vampyr	Malwina/Janthe
Martinů	*The Greek Passion*	Katerina
Matthus	*Die Weise von Liebe und Tod*	Gräfin
Menotti	*The Consul*	Magda Sorel
Meyerbeer	*Les Huguenots*	Valentine
	Le prophète	Bertha
Monteverdi	*L'incorinatione di Poppea*	Drusilla
	Il ritorno d'Ulisse in patria	Pallas Athene
Mozart	*Ascanio in Alba*	Venus
	Così fan tutte	Fiordiligi
	Don Giovanni	Donna Elvira/ Donna Anna
	La finta giardiniera	Arminda
	Le nozze di Figaro	Countess Almiviva
	Die Zauberflöte	Pamina/Dame 1/Dame 2
Mussorgsky	*Boris Godunov*	Xenia
	Khovanshchina	Emma
Nono	*Intolleranza 1960*	Gefährtin
Offenbach	*Les contes d'Hoffmann*	Giulietta/Antonia
Orff	*Antigonae*	Ismene
	Die Kluge	Des Bauern Tochter
Pfitzner	*Das Christ Elflein*	Das Elflein
Ponchielli	*La Gioconda*	Gioconda
Poulenc	*Dialogues des Carmélites*	Madame Lidoine
	La voix humaine	Ein junge Frau
Prokofiev	*War and Peace*	Natascha
Puccini	*La bohème*	Mimi
	La fanciulla del West	Minnie
	Madama Butterfly	Cio-Cio San

Composer	Opera	Role
Puccini, *cont.*	*Manon Lescaut*	Manon
	Suor Angelica	Angelica
	Il tabarro	Giorgetta
	Tosca	Tosca
Rameau	*Hippolyte et Aricie*	Phèdra
Reimann	*Lear*	Regan/Cordelia
Rihm	*Hamletmachine*	Ophelia

Rimsky-
  Korsakov
	*Das Märchen von
	  Zaren Saltan*
		Zatin Militrissa

Rossini	*Guillaume Tell*	Mathilde
Schönberg	*Von Heute auf Morgen*	Die Frau
Schreker	*Der ferne Klang*	Grete
	Die Gezeichneten	Carlotta Nardi
Schubert	*Fierrabras*	Emma/Florinda
Smetana	*The Bartered Bride*	Marie
	The Two Widows	Agnes
R. Strauss	*Die ägyptische Helena*	Menelas
	Arabella	Zdenka/Arabella
	Ariadne auf Naxos	Ariadne/Komponist/Echo
	Capriccio	Gräfini/Clarion
	Daphne	Daphne
	Elektra	Chrysothemis
	Feuersnot	Diemut
	Die Frau ohne Schatten	Kaiserin
	Intermezzo	Christine
	Der Rosenkavalier	Feldmarchallin
	Salome	Salome
	Die schweigsame Frau	Isotta
Stravinsky	*The Rake's Progress*	Anne
Szymanowski	*King Roger*	Roxana
Tchaikovsky	*Eugene Onegin*	Tatiana
	Pique Dame	Lisa
Thomas	*Mignon*	Mignon
Tippett	*The Midsummer Marriage*	Jennifer
Trojahn	*Enrico*	Marchesa Matilde Spina
	Was ihr wollt	Olivia
Verdi	*Aida*	Aida
	Atilla	Odabella
	Un ballo in maschera	Amalia
	Don Carlos	Elisabeth
	I due Foscari	Lucrezia Contarini

Composer	Opera	Role
Verdi, *cont.*	*Falstaff*	Alice
	La forza del destino	Leonore
	Luisa Miller	Luisa
	I masnadieri	Amalia
	Nabucco	Fenena
	Otello	Desdemona
	Simon Boccanegra	Maria
	Il trovatore	Leonora
	I vespri siciliani	Elena
Wagner	*Der fliegende Holländer*	Senta
	Götterdämmerung	Gutrune
	Lohengrin	Elsa
	Die Meistersinger	Eva
	Das Rheingold	Freia
	Rienzi	Irene
	Tannhäuser	Elisabeth
	Die Walküre	Sieglinde
Weber	*Euryanthe*	Euryanthe
	Der Freischütz	Agathe
Weill	*Mahagonny*	Jenny
Wolf	*Der Corregidor*	Frasquita
Wolf-Ferrari	*Le donne curiose*	Eleonora
	I quattro rusteghi	Marina
	Il segreto di Susanna	Susanna
	Sly	Dolly
Zemlinsky	*Eine florentinische Tragödie*	Bianca
	Kleider machen Leute	Nettchen
U. Zimmermann	*Der Schuhe*	Die Prinzessin

Dramatic Soprano (*Dramatischer Sopran*)

D'Albert	*Tiefland*	Marta
	Die toten Augen	Myrtocle
Beethoven	*Fidelio*	Leonore
Berg	*Lulu*	Gräfin Geschwitz
	Wozzeck	Marie
Berio	*Un re in ascolto*	Protagonist
Berlioz	*Les Troyens*	Dido
Borodin	*Prince Igor*	Jaroslawna
Britten	*Albert Herring*	Lady Billows
	Peter Grimes	Ellen Orford
	The Turn of the Screw	Miss Jessel

Composer	Opera	Role
Cherubini	*Médée*	Médée
Dallapiccola	*Il Prigioniero*	The mother
Dukas	*Ariane et Barbe-bleue*	Ariane
Dvořák	*Rusalka*	Die fremde Fürstin
Gluck	*Alceste*	Alceste
	Iphigénie en Tauride	Iphigénie
Hindemith	*Cardillac* (1956)	Erste Sängerin der Oper
	Mathis der Maler	Ursula
Hölszky	*Die Wånde*	Die Mutter
Janáček	*Jenůfa*	Küsterin
	The Makropoulos Affair	Emilia Marty
Korngold	*Die tote Stadt*	Marietta
Mascagni	*Cavalleria rusticana*	Santuzza
Meyerbeer	*Les Huguenots*	Valentine
Monteverdi	*L'incoronazione di Poppea*	Ottavia
Mozart	*Don Giovanni*	Donna Anna
	Idomeneo, re di Creta	Electra
Mussorgsky	*Boris Godunov*	Marina
Orff	*Antigonae*	Antigonae
Penderecki	*Die Teufel von Loudun*	Jeanne
Pfitzner	*Der arme Heinrich*	Hilde
Prokofiev	*The Love for Three Oranges*	Fata Morgana
Puccini	*La fanciulla del West*	Minnie
	Suor Angelica	Angelica
	Tosca	Tosca
	Turandot	Turandot
Reimann	*Lear*	Goneril
Rihm	*Die Eroberung von Mexico*	Montezuma
	Hamletmaschine	Ophelia
Schillings	*Mona Lisa*	Mona Lisa
Schoeck	*Penthesilea*	Prothoe
Schönberg	*Erwartung*	Frau
Shostakovich	*Lady Macbeth von Mzensk*	Katerina Ismailowa
Smetana	*Dalibor*	Milada
R. Strauss	*Die ägyptische Helena*	Helena
	Arabella	Arabella
	Ariadne auf Naxos	Ariadne
	Capriccio	Gräfin
	Electra	Electra
	Die Frau ohne Schatten	Färberin/Kaiserin/ Amme/Weib

Composer	Opera	Role
R. Strauss, cont.	*Intermezzo*	Christine
	Der Rosenkavalier	Feldmarschallin
	Salome	Salome
Tan Dun	*Marco Polo*	Schatten II
Verdi	*Aida*	Aida
	Un ballo in Maschera	Amelia
	Don Carlos	Elisabeth
	La forza del destino	Leonora
	Macbeth	Lady Macbeth
Wagner	*Der fliegende Holländer*	Senta
	Götterdämmerung	Brünnhilde/Gutrune
	Lohengrin	Ortrud
	Parsifal	Kundry
	Siegfried	Brünnhilde
	Tannhäuser	Venus
	Tristan und Isolde	Isolde
	Die Walküre	Brünnhilde/Sieglinde
Weber	*Euryanthe*	Eglantine
	Oberon	Rezia
Wolf	*Der Corregidor*	Mercedes

High Dramatic Soprano (*Hochdramatischer Sopran*)

Composer	Opera	Role
D'Albert	*Tiefland*	Marta
Gluck	*Alceste*	Alceste
R. Strauss	*Elektra*	Elektra
	Die Frau ohne Schatten	Amme
Wagner	*Der fliegende Holländer*	Senta
	Götterdämmerung	Brünnhilde
	Lohengrin	Ortrud
	Parsifal	Kundry
	Siegfried	Brünnhilde
	Tannhäuser	Venus
	Tristan und Isolde	Isolde
	Die Walküre	Brünnhilde

Coloratura Mezzo-Soprano (*Koloratur-Mezzosopran*)

Composer	Opera	Role
Donizetti	*Anna Bolena*	Jane Seymour
Handel	*Rinaldo*	Rinaldo
Rossini	*Il barbiere di Siviglia*	Rosina
	La Cenerentola	Angelina
	L'italiana in Algeri	Isabella
	Tancredi	Tancredi

Composer	Opera	Role

Dramatic Coloratura (*Dramatischer Koloratur-sopran*)

Composer	Opera	Role
Handel	*Agrippina*	Agrippina
	Rinaldo	Armide
	Tamerlano	Andronico

Lyric Mezzo-Soprano (*Lyrischer Mezzosopran*)

Composer	Opera	Role
Berio	*Un re in ascolto*	Mezzo soprano
Berlioz	*La damnation de Faust*	Marguerite
Birtwistle	*Punch and Judy*	Judy/fortune teller
Bizet	*Carmen*	Mercédès
Britten	*Albert Herring*	Nancy Waters
	A Midsummer Night's Dream	Hermia
Cilea	*Adriana Lecouvreur*	Madamoiselle Dangeville
Cimarosa	*Il matrimonio segreto*	Fidalma
Eötvös	*Tri sestri*	Mascha
Gershwin	*Porgy and Bess*	Serena
Handel	*Alcina*	Ruggiero
	Ariodante	Ariodante
	Giulio Cesare	Cesare/Tolomeo
	Orlando	Orlando/Medoro
	Ottone, re di Germania	Ottone
	Poro, re dell'Indie	Poro
	Rinaldo	Goffredo
	Tamerlano	Tamerlano
Haydn	*La fedeltà premiata*	Amaranta
	Il mondo della luna	Ernesto/Clarice
Humperdinck	*Hänsel und Gretel*	Hänsel
Ligeti	*Le Grand Macabre*	Spermando
Massenet	*Werther*	Charlotte
Matthus	*Die Weise von Liebe und Tod*	Rilke
Monteverdi	*L'incoronazione di Poppea*	Ottone
	Il ritorno d'Ulisse in Patria	Telemaco
Mozart	*Bastien und Bastienne*	Bastien
	La clemenza di Tito	Sextus/Annius
	Così fan tutte	Dorabella
	Don Giovanni	Zerlina
	Idomeneo, re di Creta	Idamante
	Lucio Cilla	Celia
	Le nozze di Figaro	Cherubino
Nicolai	*Die lustigen Weiber*	Frau Reich
Offenbach	*Les contes d'Hoffmann*	Niklaus

Composer	Opera	Role
Pfitzner	*Palestrina*	Silla
Prokofiev	*War and Peace*	Sonja
Puccini	*Madama Butterfly*	Suzuki
Purcell	*Dido and Aeneas*	Dido
R. Strauss	*Ariadne auf Naxos*	Dryade
	Der Rosenkavalier	Annina/Octavian
	Die schweigsame Frau	Carlotta
Thomas	*Mignon*	Mignon
Ullman	*Der Kaiser von Atlantis*	Trommler
Verdi	*Falstaff*	Meg Page
	Luisa Miller	Laura
	Rigoletto	Maddalena
	La traviata	Flora Bervoix
Wagner	*Götterdämmerung*	Wellgunde
	Die Meistersinger	Magdalena
	Das Rheingold	Flosshilde
Weber	*Oberon*	Puck
Wolf-Ferrari	*Le donne curiose*	Beatrice

Dramatic Mezzo-Soprano (*Dramatischer Mezzosopran*)

Composer	Opera	Role
Bartók	*Herzog Blaubarts Burg*	Judith
Bellini	*Norma*	Adalgisa
	I puritani	Henrietta
Berg	*Lulu*	Gräfin Geschwitz
	Wozzeck	Marie
Berio	*Un re in ascolto*	Mezzo
Berlioz	*Les Troyens*	Kassandra/Dido
Bizet	*Carmen*	Carmen
Borodin	*Prince Igor*	Kontschakowna
Britten	*Albert Herring*	Mrs. Herring
	The Turn of the Screw	Mrs. Grose
Cilea	*Adriana Lecouvreur*	Furstin von Bouillon
Dukas	*Ariane et Barbe-bleue*	Ariane
Dvořák	*Rusalka*	Die fremde Fürstin/Hexe
Einem	*Der Besuch der alten Dame*	Claire Zachanassian
Fortner	*Bluthochzeit*	Mutter
Gershwin	*Porgy and Bess*	Serena
Gluck	*Armide*	Der Hass
	Iphigénie en Aulide	Klytämnestra
Handel	*Agrippina*	Agrippina
Henze	*Die Bassariden*	Agaue/Venus

Composer	Opera	Role
Hölszky	*Bremer Freiheit*	Geesche
Humperdinck	*Hänsel und Gretel*	Mutter
Janáček	*Katya Kabanova*	Kabanicha
Marschner	*Hans Heiling*	Königin der Erdgeister
Menotti	*The Consul*	Secretary
Meyerbeer	*Die Heugenotten*	Valentine
	Le prophète	Fidés
Monteverdi	*L'incoronazione di Poppea*	Ottavia
Mozart	*La clemenza di Tito*	Sextus
Mussorgsky	*Der Jahrmarkt von Sorotshinzy*	Chiwrja
	Khovanshchina	Marfa
Nono	*Intolleranza 1960*	Frau
Pintscher	*Thomas Chatterton*	Sarah Chatterton
Ponchielli	*La Gioconda*	Laura
Poulenc	*Dialogues des Carmélites*	Marie
Prokofiev	*War and Peace*	Achrossimowa
Puccini	*Gianni Schicchi*	Zita
Rossini	*Guillaume Tell*	Hedwige
Saariaho	*L'amour de loin*	Pilger
Saint-Saëns	*Samson et Dalila*	Dalila
Schoeck	*Penthesilea*	Penthesilea/Meroe
Schrecker	*Die Gezeichneten*	Carlotta Nardi
Schönberg	*Erwartung*	Die Frau
R. Strauss	*Arabella*	Adelaide
	Ariadne auf Naxos	Komponist
	Capriccio	Clairon
	Elektra	Klytämnestra Salome
	Die Frau ohne Schatten	Amme
	Der Rosenkavalier	Octavian
	Salome	Herodias
Stravinsky	*The Rake's Progress*	Baba
Tchaikovsky	*Pique Dame*	Gräfin
Tippett	*The Midsummer Marriage*	She-Ancient
Verdi	*Aida*	Amneris
	Don Carlos	Eboli
	La forza del destino	Preziosilla
	Luisa Miller	Amalia
	Macbeth	Lady Macbeth
	Nabucco	Fenena
	Otello	Emilia
	Il trovatore	Azucena

Composer	Opera	Role
Wagner	*Götterdammerung*	Waltraute
	Lohengrin	Ortrud
	Parsifal	Kundry
	Das Rheingold	Fricka
	Rienzi	Adriano
	Siegfried	Brünnhilde
	Tristan und Isolde	Brangäne
	Die Walküre	Fricka
Weber	*Euryanthe*	Eglantine
Weill	*Mahagonny*	Leokadja
B. Zimmermann	*Die Soldaten*	Charlotte/ Stolzius's Mutter

Character Alto (*Spielalt*)

Composer	Opera	Role
Auber	*Fra Diavolo*	Pamela
Berlioz	*Béatrice et Bénédict*	Ursula
	Les Troyens	Anna
Britten	*Albert Herring*	Florence Pike
Cimarosa	*Il matrimonio segreto*	Fidalma
Dittersdorf	*Doktor und Apotheker*	Claudia
Donizetti	*Lucia di Lammermoor*	Alisa
Egk	*Der Revisor*	Anna
Falla	*La vida breve*	Grossmutter
Flotow	*Martha*	Nancy
Fortner	*Bluthochzeit*	Magd/Frau Leonardos
Giordano	*Andrea Chénier*	Bersi
Gluck	*Le cadi dupé*	Fatime
	L'ivrogne corrigé	Mathurine
	La recontre imprévue	Balkis
Gounod	*Faust*	Marthe
	Mireille	Taven
Handel	*Agrippina*	Narciso
Haydn	*Il mondo della luna*	Lisetta
Henze	*The English Cat*	Babette
Lortzing	*Der Waffenschmeid*	Irmentraut
Marschner	*Hans Heiling*	Gertrud
Mascagni	*Cavalleria rusticana*	Lola
Mozart	*La finta semplice*	Donna Giacinta
	Le nozze di Figaro	Marcellina
Nicolai	*Die lustigen Weiber*	Frau Reich
Offenbach	*Les contes d'Hoffmann*	Niklaus

Composer	Opera	Role
Puccini	*Madama Butterfly*	Suzuki
	Il tabarro	Frugola
Reimann	*Melusine*	Madame Laperouse
Rimsky-Korsakov	*Mayskaya Noch*	Hanna
	Das Märchen von Zaren Saltan	Muhme Babaricha
Schonthal	*Princess Maleen*	Kammerjungfer
Smetana	*The Bartered Bride*	Agnes
R. Strauss	*Arabella*	Adelaide
	Ariadne auf Naxos	Dryade
	Feuersnot	Ursula
	Die schweigsame Frau	Carlotta
Verdi	*Falstaff*	Meg Page
	Otello	Emelia
	La traviata	Flora Bervoix
Wagner	*Die Meistersinger*	Magdalena
Weber	*Oberon*	Puck
Wolf-Ferrari	*I quattro rusteghi*	Margherita

Lyric Alto (*Lyrischer Alt*)

Composer	Opera	Role
Cornelius	*Der Barbier von Bagdad*	Bostana
Eötvös	*Tri sestri*	Olga
Glass	*Akhnaten*	Nofretete
Glinka	*A Life for the Tsar*	Wanja
	Ruslan und Ljudmila	Ratmir
Gluck	*Orfeo ed Euridice*	Orfeo
Handel	*Agrippina*	Ottone
	Alcina	Bradamante
	Orlando	Orlando
	Poro, re dell'Indie	Erissena/Gandarte
	Radamisto	Zenobia
	Tamerlano	Irene/Tamerlano
Haydn	*La fedeltà premiata*	Celia
Kienzl	*Der Evangelimann*	Maidalena
Lortzing	*Der Wildschütz*	Gräfin
Mozart	*Mitradate, re de Ponto*	Farnace
Puccini	*Gianni Schicchi*	Ciesca
Rossini	*Tancredi*	Isaura
Verdi	*Falstaff*	Mrs. Quickly
Wagner	*Der fliegende Holländer*	Mary
	Götterdämmerung	Flosshilde

Composer	Opera	Role
Dramatic Alto (*Dramatischer Alt*)		
D'Albert	*Die toten Augen*	Maria von Magdala
Bizet	*Carmen*	Carmen
Borodin	*Prince Igor*	Kontschakowna
Britten	*Albert Herring*	Florence Pike / Mrs. Herring
	Peter Grimes	Tantjen
Charpentier	*Louise*	Louise's mother
Cherubini	*Médée*	Neris
Debussy	*Pelléas et Mélisande*	Genoveva
Dvořák	*Rusalka*	Hexe
Egk	*Peer Gynt*	Aase
Fortner	*Bluthochzeit*	Schwiegermutter / Leonardos
Handel	*Ariodante*	Polinesso
	Giulio Cesare	Cornelia
	Serse	Amastris
Hindemith	*Sancta Susanna*	Klementia
Hölszky	*Die Wände*	Ommou
Humperdinck	*Königskinder*	Hexe
Janáček	*Jenůfa*	Alte Buryja
Mascagni	*Cavalleria rusticana*	Lucia
Menotti	*The Consul*	Mother
Meyerbeer	*Le prophète*	Fidès
Poulenc	*Dialogues des Carmélites*	Madame de Croissy
Puccini	*Gianni Schicchi*	Zita
Reimann	*Melusine*	Pythia
Schnittke	*Historia von D. Johann Fausten*	Mephostophila
R. Strauss	*Daphne*	Gae
	Salome	Herodias
Tippett	*The Midsummer Marriage*	Sosostris
Verdi	*Aida*	Amneris
	Un ballo in maschera	Ulrica
	Falstaff	Mrs. Quickley
	Luisa Miller	Amalia
	Il trovatore	Azucena
Wagner	*Die Walküre*	Waltraute
Low Alto (*Tiefer Alt*)		
Debussy	*Pelléas et Mélisande*	Genoveva
Handel	*Ariodante*	Polinesso
	Deidamia	Odysses

Composer	Opera	Role
Kienzl	*Der Evangelimann*	Magdalena
Mozart	*Die Zauberflöte*	Dame 3
Rihm	*Die Eroberung von Mexico*	Solistin aus dem Orchester
R. Strauss	*Daphne*	Gaea
	Feuersnot	Wigeli
Wagner	*Siegfried*	Erda
	Die Walküre	Waltraute
Weill	*Mahagonny*	Leokadja

Countertenor (*Contratenor*)

Composer	Opera	Role
Britten	*Death in Venice*	Voice of Apollo
	A Midsummer Night's Dream	Oberon
Cavalli	*La Calisto*	Endimone
Eötovös	*Tri sestri*	Irina/Mascha/Olga/ Natascha
Glass	*Akhnaten*	Akhnaten
Gluck	*Orfeo ed Euridice*	Orpheo
Handel	*Agrippina*	Ottone/Narciso
	Ariodante	Ariodante
	Deidamia	Odysseus
	Giulio Cesare	Cesare/Ptolemy/ Sextus/Nirenus
	Orlando	Orlando
	Ottone, re di Germania	Ottone/Adalberto
	Poro, re dell'Indie	Poro/Gandarte
	Rinaldo	Rinaldo/Goffredo/ Eustazio
	Rodelinda	Bertaridus/Unulf
Haydn	*Il mondo della luna*	Ernesto
Keiser	*Masaniello*	Duca d'Arcos
Ligeti	*Le Grand Macabre*	Go-Go
Lully	*Atys*	Atys
Monteverdi	*L'incoronazione di Poppea*	Nerone/Ottone
Mozart	*Ascanio in Alba*	Ascanio
	Mitridate, re di Ponto	Farnace
Purcell	*Dido and Aeneas*	Spirit/magician
Ravel	*L'enfant et les sortilèges*	Old man
Reimann	*Lear*	Edgar
Schnittke	*Historia von D. Johann Fausten*	Mephostophiles
	Leben mit einem Idioten	Junger Irrer

Composer	Opera	Role
Countertenor (*Haute-Contre*)		
Eötvös	*Tri sestri*	Olga
Gluck	*Armide*	Renaud/Danish knight
	Iphigénie en Aulide	Achilles
	Orfeo ed Euridice	Orphée
Lully	*Armide*	Renaud/Danish knight
	Atys	Atys/le sommeil/Morphée
Rameau	*Castor et Pollux*	Amor/Castor
	Hippolyte et Aricie	Hippolyte
	Platée	Thespis/Platée/Mercure
Ravel	*L'enfant et les sortilèges*	Le petit vieillard
Buffo Tenor (*Tenorbuffo/Spieltenor*)		
Adam	*Le postillon de Lonjumeau*	Marquis de Corcy
Auber	*Fra Diavolo*	Beppo
Beethoven	*Fidelio*	Jaquino
Berg	*Lulu*	Prinz/Kammerdiener/ Marquis
	Wozzeck	Andres/Hauptmann
Birtwistle	*Punch and Judy*	Lawyer
Bizet	*Carmen*	Dancaïro/Remendado
Boieldieu	*La dame blanche*	Dikson
Britten	*Albert Herring*	Mr. Upfold
	A Midsummer Night's Dream	Flute
	Peter Grimes	Boles
Busoni	*Turandot*	Truffaldino
Cilea	*Adriana Lecouvreur*	Poisson
Cimarosa	*Il matrimonio segreto*	Paolino
Cornelius	*Der Barbier von Bagdad*	Mustapha
Dittersdorf	*Doktor und Apotheker*	Sichel
Einem	*Danons Tod*	De Séchelles
Flotow	*Alessando Stradella*	Barbarino
Gershwin	*Porgy and Bess*	Sporting Life
Gluck	*Le cadi dupé*	Omega
	L'ivrogne corrigé	Zipperlein
	La rencontre imprévue	Osmin
Haydn	*La fedeltà premiata*	Fileno
	Il mondo della luna	Cecco
	Lo speziale	Sempronio/Megone
Humperdinck	*Königskinder*	Besenbinder

Composer	Opera	Role
Keiser	*Masaniello*	Bassian
Leoncavallo	*Pagliacci*	Beppo
Lortzing	*Undine*	Veit
	Der Waffenschmeid	Georg
Monteverdi	*L'incoronazione di Poppea*	Arnalta
Mozart	*Die Entführung aus dem Serail*	Pedrillo
	La finta giardiniera	Don Anchise
	La finta semplice	Fracasso
	Le nozze di Figaro	Basilio/Don Curzio
	Der Schauspieldirektor	Herr Vogelsang
	Die Zauberflöte	Monostatos
Mussorgsky	*Boris Godunov*	Missail
Nicolai	*Die lustigen Weiber*	Spärlich
Offenbach	*Les contes d'Hoffmann*	Andreas/Cochenille/ Pitichinaccio/Franz
Pfitzner	*Das Christ-Elflein*	Frieder/Jochen
Puccini	*La fanciulla del West*	Nick
	Madama Butterfly	Goro
	Manon Lescaut	Edmond
	Il tabarro	Tinca
	Tosca	Spoletta
	Turandot	Pang/Pong
Purcell	*Dido and Aeneas*	Aeneas
Smetana	*The Bartered Bride*	Wenzel
R. Strauss	*Ariadne auf Naxos*	Tanzmeister/Scaramuccio
	Feuersnot	Tulbeck/Aspeck
	Intermezzo	Kapellmeister
	Der Rosenkavalier	Valzacchi
Thomas	*Mignon*	Friedrich/Laertes
Trojahn	*Enrico*	Bertoldo
Ullman	*Der Kaiser von Atlantis*	Harlekin
Verdi	*Falstaff*	Bardolph
	La forza del destino	Trabuco
	Rigoletto	Borsa
Wagner	*Die fliegende Holländer*	Steuermann
	Die Meistersinger	David
	Das Rheingold	Mime
	Siegfried	Mime
Weber	*Abu Hassan*	Hassan
	Oberon	Sherasmin
Weill	*Mahagonny*	Fatty
Wolf	*Der Corregidor*	Pedro

Composer	Opera	Role
Zender	*Don Quijote de la Mancha*	Barbier I/Lektor I/ Häscher I/Teufel/ Don Pedro

Lyric Tenor (*Lyrischer Tenor*)

Adam	*Le postillon de Lonjumeau*	Chapelou
D'Albert	*Die toten Augen*	Der Hirt
Auber	*Fra Diavolo*	Lorenzo/Fra Diavolo
	La muette de Portici	Alfonso/Masaniello
Bellini	*I puritani*	Lord Arthur Talbot
Berg	*Lulu*	Mahler/Neger
	Wozzeck	Andres
Berio	*Un re in ascolto*	Regisseur
Berlioz	*Béatrice et Bénédict*	Bénédict
Bialas	*Aucassin und Nicolette*	Anton I
Bizet	*Les pêcheurs des perles*	Nadir
Boieldieu	*La dame blanche*	George Brown
Borodin	*Prince Igor*	Wladamir Igorewitsch
Britten	*Albert Herring*	Albert Herring
	A Midsummer Night's Dream	Lysander/Flute
	Peter Grimes	Pastor Adams
	The Turn of the Screw	Quint/Prolog
Busoni	*Arlecchino*	Leandro
	Doktor Faust	Herzog von Parma
Cilea	*Adriana Lecouvreur*	Abbé von Chazenil/Poisson
Cimarosa	*Il matrimonio segreto*	Paolino
Cornelius	*Der Barbier von Bagdad*	Nurredin
Dallapiccola	*Il Prigionero*	Kerkerminister
Debussy	*Pelléas et Mélisande*	Pelléas
Delius	*A Village Romeo and Juliet*	Sali
Dittersdorf	*Doktor und Apotheker*	Gotthold
Donizetti	*Anna Bolena*	Percy
	Don Pasquale	Ernesto
	L'elisir d'amore	Nemorino
	La fille du régiment	Tonio
	Lucia di Lammermoor	Edgardo/Arturo
	Viva la mamma	Guglielmo
Dvořák	*Der Jakobiner*	Jiri
Egk	*Der Revisor*	Chlestakow
Einem	*Dantons Tod*	Desmoulins
Flotow	*Alessando Stradella*	Alessando Stradella
	Martha	Lyonel

Composer	Opera	Role
Fortner	*Bluthochzeit*	Mond
Gershwin	*Porgy and Bess*	Sporting Life
Glass	*Akhnaten*	Amuns
Glinka	*A Life for the Tsar*	Bogdan Sobinin
Gluck	*Le cadi dupé*	Nuradin
	La recontre imprévue	Ali
Goetz	*Der Widerspenstigen Zähmung*	Lucentio
Gounod	*Faust*	Faust
	Mireille	Vincent
Handel	*Acis and Galatea*	Acis/Damon
	Alcina	Oronte
	Ariodante	Lurcanio
	Poro, re dell'Indie	Alessandro
	Radamisto	Tiridate
	Rodelinda	Grimwald
	Tamerlano	Bajazet
Haydn	*La fedeltà premiata*	Fileno/Lindoro
	Il mondo della luna	Ecclitico
Henze	*Die Bassariden*	Dionysos
	Boulevard Solitude	Armand des Grieux
	Elegie für junge Liebende	Toni Reischmann
Hindemith	*Cardillac*	Geselle
Hölszky	*Bremer Freiheit*	Rumpf
	Die Wände	Said
Janáček	*Katya Kabanova*	Boris
	The Makropoulos Affair	Janek
Keiser	*Masaniello*	Don Velasco/ Don Pedro
Lortzing	*Die Opernprobe*	The young baron
	Der Wildschütz	Baron
	Zar und Zimmermann	Chateauneuf/Iwanow
Martinů	*The Greek Passion*	Michelis/Yannakos
Massenet	*Manon*	Des Grieux
Messiaen	*Saint François d'Assise*	Massée
Meyerbeer	*Le prophète*	Jonas
Monteverdi	*L'Orfeo*	Orfeo
	Il ritorno d'Ulisse in patria	Telemaco/Ulisse
Mozart	*Ascanio in Alba*	Aceste
	Cosí fan tutte	Ferrando
	Don Giovanni	Ottavio
	Die Entführung aus dem Serail	Belmonte

Composer	Opera	Role
Mozart, cont.	*La finta giardiniera*	Belfiore
	La finta semplice	Don Polidoro
	Idomeneo, re di Creta	Idamante/Idomeneo/ Arbace
	Lucio Silla	Silla
	Le nozze di Figaro	Basilio
	Il re pastore	Alexander/Agenor
	Der Schauspieldirektor	Vogelsang
	Die Zauberflöte	Tamino
Nicolai	*Die lustigen Weiber*	Fenton
Paisiello	*Il barbiere di Siviglia*	Almaviva
Pfitzner	*Palestrina*	Abdisu/bishop of Budoja
Pinscher	*Thomas Chatterton*	Peter Smith
Poulenc	*Dialogues des Carmélites*	Father confessor
Puccini	*La bohème*	Rodolfo
	La fanciulla del West	Nick
	Gianni Schicchi	Rinuccio/Gherardo
	Madama Butterfly	Pinkerton
	Manon Lescaut	Edmond
	Turandot	Altoum
Ravel	*L'heure espagnole*	Gonzalvo
Rossini	*Il barbiere di Siviglia*	Graf
	La Cenerentola	Ramiro
	Guillaume Tell	Arnold
	L'italiana in Algeri	Lindoro
	Il turco in Italia	Don Narciso
Schillings	*Mona Lisa*	Arrigo
Schnittke	*Historia von D. Johann Fausten*	Der Alte
	Leben mit einem Idioten	Wowa
Schonthal	*Princess Maleen*	Der Prinz
Schubert	*Fierrabras*	Eginhard
Smetana	*The Two Widows*	Ladislav
R. Strauss	*Die ägyptische Helena*	Da-ud
	Arabella	Matteo/Graf Elemer
	Ariadne auf Naxos	Tanzmeister
	Daphne	Leukippos
	Intermezzo	Lummer
	Salome	Narraboth
	Die schweigsame Frau	Henry
Tchaikovsky	*Eugene Onegin*	Lenski
Thomas	*Mignon*	Wilhelm Meister

Composer	Opera	Role
Tippett	*The Midsummer Marriage*	Jack
Trojahn	*Enrico*	Carlo di Nolli
	Was ihr wollt	Orsino
Verdi	*Falstaff*	Fenton
	Macbeth	Malcolm
	I masnadieri	Karl/Hermann
	Nabucco	Ismael
	Otello	Cassio
	Rigoletto	Duke of Mantua
	La traviata	Alfredo
Wagner	*Der fliegende Holländer*	Steuermann
	Rienzi	Baroncelli
	Tannhäuser	Walther
Weber	*Abu Hassan*	Hassan
	Oberon	Oberon
Weill	*Mahagonny*	Fatty/Jack
Wolf	*Der Corregidor*	Pedro
Wolf-Ferrari	*Le donne curiose*	Florindo/Leandro
	I quattro rusteghi	Filipeto
Zender	*Don Quijote de la Mancha*	Cardenio/Löwenwärter/ Soldaten/Höfling I/ Küster/Lektor IV
B. Zimmermann	*Die Soldaten*	Desportes
U. Zimmermann	*Der Schuhu*	Tenor/Oberster/ Gelehrter/ Krieger
	Die weisse Rose	Hans Scholl

Young Dramatic Tenor (Spinto) (*Jugendlicher Heldentenor*)

D'Albert	*Tiefland*	Pedro
	Die toten Augen	Galba/Der Hirt
Auber	*Le muette de Portici*	Masaniello
Beethoven	*Fidelio*	Florestan
Bellini	*Norma*	Pollione
Berg	*Lulu*	Alwa
	Wozzeck	Tambourmajor
Berlioz	*Benvenuto Cellini*	Benvenuto Cellini
	La damnation de Faust	Faust
	Les Troyens	Jopas
Bioto	*Mefistofele*	Faust
Bizet	*Carmen*	Don José
Borodin	*Prince Igor*	Vladimir

Composer	Opera	Role
Britten	*Billy Budd*	Edward Fairfax Vere
	Peter Grimes	Peter Grimes
Busoni	*Doktor Faust*	Mephistopheles
	Turandot	Calaf
Charpentier	*Louise*	Julien
Cherubini	*Médée*	Jason
Cilea	*Adriana Lecouvreur*	Moritz
Dessau	*Die Verurteilung des Lukullus*	Lukullus
Donizetti	*Anna Bolena*	Percy
	Lucia di Lammermoor	Arturo
Dvořák	*Rusalka*	Prinz
Falla	*La vida breve*	Paco
Giordano	*Andrea Chénier*	Andrea Chénier
Glinka	*A Life for the Tsar*	Bogdan Sobinin
Gluck	*Alceste*	Admetos
	Iphigénie en Tauride	Pylades
Gounod	*Faust*	Faust
Halévy	*La Juive*	Éléazar
Handel	*Tamerlano*	Bajazet
Hara	*Petro Kibe*	Ferreira
Henze	*Die Bassariden*	Dionysos
	König Hirsch (Il re cervo)	König
	Venus und Adonis	Clemente
Hindemith	*Cardillac (1952)*	Junger Kavalier
	Cardillac (1926)	Offizier/Kavalier
	Mathis der Maler	Hans Schwalb
Humperdinck	*Königskinder*	Königssohn
Janáček	*Jenůfa*	Laca
	Katya Kabanova	Tichon
	The Makropoulos Affair	Albert Gregor
Kienzl	*Der Evangelimann*	Matthias
Klebe	*Jacobowsky und der Oberst*	Oberst Stjerbinsky
Korngold	*Das Wunder der Heliane*	Der Fremde
Krenek	*Jonny spielt auf*	Max
Leoncavallo	*Pagliacci*	Canio
Lortzing	*Undine*	Hugo
Marschner	*Hans Heiling*	Konrad
	Der Vampyr	Edgar Aubry
Martinů	*The Greek Passion*	Maniolos
Mascagni	*Cavalleria rusticana*	Turridu
Messiaen	*Saint François d'Assise*	Der Aussätzige

Composer	Opera	Role
Meyerbeer	*Les Huguenots*	Raoul
	Le prophète	Jean de Leyde
Mozart	*La clemenza di Tito*	Titus
	Idomeneo, re di Creta	Idomeneo
	Mitridate, re di Ponto	Mithridates
	Die Zauberflöte	Tamino
Mussorgsky	*Boris Godunov*	Grigori
	Der Jahrmarkt von Sorotshinzy	Gritzko
	Khovanshchina	Andrej
Nielsen	*Saul and David*	Jonathan/David
Nono	*Intolleranza 1960*	Emigrant
Offenbach	*Les contes d'Hoffmann*	Hoffmann
Orff	*Antigonae*	Hämon
Pfitzner	*Palestrina*	Palestrina
Ponchielli	*La Gioconda*	Enzo Grimaldo
Prokofiev	*The Love for Three Oranges*	Prince
Puccini	*La bohème*	Rudolfo
	La fanciulla del West	Johnson
	Manon Lescaut	Des Grieux
	Il tabarro	Luigi
	Tosca	Cavaradossi
	Turandot	Calaf
Riemann	*Lear*	Edmund
Rimsky-Korsakov	*Mayskaya Noch*	Lewko
	Das Märchen von Zaren Saltan	Prince Gwidon
Saint-Saëns	*Samson et Dalila*	Samson
Schillings	*Mona Lisa*	Giovanni
Schoeck	*Penthesilea*	Diomedes
Schönberg	*Moses und Aaron*	Aaron
Schreker	*Der ferne Klang*	Fritz
	Die Gezeichneten	Alviano Salvago
Schubert	*Fierrabras*	Fierrabras
Shostakovich	*Lady Macbeth von Mzensk*	Sergei
Smetana	*The Bartered Bride*	Hans
	Dalibor	Dalibor
R. Strauss	*Arabella*	Matteo/Graf Elemer
	Ariadne auf Naxos	Bacchus
	Capriccio	Flamand
	Daphne	Apollo
	Die Frau ohne Schatten	Kaiser

Composer	Opera	Role
R. Strauss, cont.	*Helena*	Menelas
	Intermezzo	Baron
	Der Rosenkavalier	Ein Sänger
	Salome	Narraboth
Sutermeister	*Raskolnikow*	Raskolnikow
Tan Dun	*Marco Polo*	Polo
Tippett	*The Midsummer Marriage*	Mark
Verdi	*Aida*	Radamès
	Attila	Foresto
	Un ballo in maschera	Richard
	Don Carlos	Carlos
	I due Foscari	Jacopo Foscari
	Ernani	Ernani
	La forza del destino	Alvaro
	Luisa Miller	Rudolf
	Macbeth	Macduff
	I masnadieri	Karl
	Nabucco	Ismael
	Rigoletto	Duke of Mantua
	Simon Boccanegra	Adorno
	La traviata	Alfredo
	Il trovatore	Manrico
	I vespri siciliani	Arrigo
Wagner	*Die fliegende Holländer*	Erik
	Lohengrin	Lohengrin
	Die Meistersinger	Stolzing
	Parsifal	Parsifal
	Das Rheingold	Loge
	Tannhäuser	Walther
	Die Walküre	Siegmund
Weber	*Euryanthe*	Adolar
	Der Freischütz	Max
	Oberon	Hüon/Oberon
Weill	*Mahagonny*	Jim Mahoney
Wolf-Ferrari	*Sly*	Sly
Zemlinsky	*Eine florentinische Tragödie*	Guido Bardi
	Kleider machen Leute	Wenzel Strapinski
B. Zimmermann	*Die Soldaten*	Desportes

Dramatic Tenor (*Heldentenor*)

D'Albert	*Tiefland*	Pedro
Beethoven	*Fidelio*	Floristan

258 Appendix E

Composer	Opera	Role
Berg	*Lulu*	Dr. Schön/ Chefredakteur/Jack
	Wozzeck	Tambourmajor
Berlioz	*Les Troyens*	Aeneas
Britten	*Peter Grimes*	Peter Grimes
Debussy	*Pelléas et Mélisande*	Goland
Egk	*Peer Gynt*	Der Alte
Einem	*Der Besuch der alten Dame*	Bürgermeister
Halévy	*La Juive*	Éléazar
Hindemith	*Mathis der Maler*	Albrecht
Hölszky	*Bremer Freiheit*	Gottfried
Korngold	*Die tote Stadt*	Paul
Meyerbeer	*Le prophète*	Jean de Leyde
Mussorgsky	*Boris Godunov*	Schujskij
Pfitzner	*Der arme Heinrich*	Heinrich
Saint-Saëns	*Samson et Dalila*	Samson
Schönberg	*Moses und Aaron*	Aaron
R. Strauss	*Ariadne auf Naxos*	Baccus
	Salome	Herodes
Verdi	*Aida*	Radames
	Otello	Otello
Wagner	*Götterdämmerung*	Siegfried
	Die Meistersinger	Stolzing
	Parsifal	Parsifal
	Rienzi	Rienzi
	Siegfried	Siegfried
	Tannhäuser	Tannhäuser
	Tristan und Isolde	Tristan
	Die Walküre	Siegmund

Character Tenor (*Charaktertenor*)

Composer	Opera	Role
Adam	*Le postillon de Lonjumeau*	Marquis de Corcy
Adams	*Nixon in China*	Mao Tse-tung
Berg	*Wozzeck*	Hauptmann
Bizet	*Carmen*	Remendado
Britten	*Albert Herring*	Mr. Upfold
	Billy Budd	Edward Fairfax Vere
	Death in Venice	Hotel porter/Gustav
	Peter Grimes	Boles
	The Turn of the Screw	Quint
Dittersdorf	*Doktor und Apotheker*	Sturmwald

Composer	Opera	Role
Donizetti	*Anna Bolena*	Sir Hervey
Gershwin	*Porgy and Bess*	Sporting Life
Henze	*The English Cat*	Lord Puff
Hölszky	*Bremer Freiheit*	Zimmermann
Humperdinck	*Hänsel und Gretel*	Hexe
Korngold	*Das Wunder der Heliane*	Der Schwertichter
Massenet	*Manon*	Guillot
Meyerbeer	*Le prophète*	Jonas
Mozart	*La finta giardiniera*	Don Anchise
	Lucio Silla	Aufidio
Offenbach	*Les contes d'Hoffmann*	Spalazani
Pfitzner	*Palestrina*	Novagerio
Prokofiev	*War and Peace*	Anatol Kuragin
Puccini	*La fanciulla del West*	Nick
	Gianni Schicchi	Gherardo
	Madama Butterfly	Goro
	Il tabarro	Tinca
	Turandot	Altoum/Pang/Pong
Rameau	*Platée*	Momus
Rossini	*Guillaume Tell*	Rudolph
Schnittke	*Historia von D. Johann Fausten*	Erzähler
Smetana	*The Bartered Bride*	Wenzel
R. Strauss	*Ariadne auf Naxos*	Tanzmeister/ Scaramuccio
	Feuersnot	Von Gundelfingen
	Helena	Da-ud
	Intermezzo	Kapellmeister
	Der Rosenkavalier	Valzacchi
	Salome	Herodes
Trojahn	*Was ihr wollt*	Aguecheek
Verdi	*Attila*	Uldino
	Falstaff	Dr. Cajus
	La forza del destino	Trabuco
	I masnadieri	Hermann
	Otello	Rodrigo
	Rigoletto	Borsa
	Simon Boccanegra	Albiani
Wagner	*Der fliegende Holländer*	Steuermann
	Das Rheingold	Loge/Mime
	Siegfried	Mime
Weill	*Mahagonny*	Jim Mahoney

Composer	Opera	Role
Wolf	*Der Corregidor*	Der Corregidor
Wolf-Ferrari	*I quattro rusteghi*	Riccardo
Zender	*Don Quijote de la Mancha*	Sancho Panza
U. Zimmermann	*Der Schuhu*	Tenor/Oberster/
		Gelehrter/Krieger
	Die weisse Rose	Hans Scholl

Lyric Baritone (*Lyricher Bariton*)

Composer	Opera	Role
Adams	*Nixon in China*	Chou En-lai
Auber	*Fra Diavolo*	Lord Kookburn
Berg	*Lulu*	Ein Journalist
Berlioz	*Béatrice et Bénédict*	Claudio
	Benvenuto Cellini	Fieramosca
	Les Troyens	Choröbus
Bialas	*Aucassin und Nicolette*	Aucassin
Birtwistle	*Punch and Judy*	Punch
Bizet	*Les pêcheurs de perles*	Zurga
Britten	*Albert Herring*	Mr. Gedge
	Billy Budd	Billy Budd
	A Midsummer Night's Dream	Demetrius
Busoni	*Arlecchino*	Abbate Cospicuo
	Doktor Faust	Des Mädchens Bruder
Cavalli	*La Calisto*	Merkur
Debussy	*Pelléas et Mélisande*	Pelléas
Donizetti	*Don Pasquale*	Dr. Malatesta
	L'elisir d'amore	Belcore
	Viva la Mamma	Stefano
Dvořák	*Der Jakobiner*	Bohus
Eötvös	*Tri sestri*	Tusenbach/Andrej
Gershwin	*Porgy and Bess*	Porgy
Glass	*Akhnaten*	Haremhab
Gounod	*Faust*	Valentin
Handel	*Deidamia*	Phönix
Haydn	*La fedeltà premiata*	Perruchetto
	Il mondo della luna	Ernesto
Henze	*Boulevard Solitude*	Lescaut
Humperdinck	*Königskinder*	Spielmann
Krenek	*Jonny spielt auf*	Jonny
Lortzing	*Die Opernprobe*	Johann
	Der Waffenschmeid	Liebenau
Martinů	*The Greek Passion*	Kostandis

Composer	Opera	Role
Massenet	*Werther*	Albert
Monteverdi	*L'Orfeo*	Orfeo
	Il ritorno d'Ulisse in patria	Ulisse
Mozart	*Così fan tutte*	Guglielmo
	La finta giardiniera	Roberto (Nardo)
	La finta semplice	Don Cassandro
	Le nozze di Figaro	Count Almaviva
	Die Zauberflöte	Papageno
Nicolai	*Die lustigen Weiber*	Fluth
Paisiello	*Il barbiere di Siviglia*	Figaro
Pfitzner	*Das Christ-Elflein*	Gumpach
Prokofiev	*War and Peace*	Dennisow
Puccini	*La bohème*	Schaunard
	Madama Butterfly	Sharpless
	Turandot	Ping
Purcell	*Dido and Aeneas*	Aeneas
Reimann	*Melusine*	Graf von Lusignan
Rossini	*Il barbiere di Siviglia*	Figaro
	La Cenerentola	Dandini
R. Strauss	*Ariadne auf Naxos*	Harlekin
	Die schweigsame Frau	Barbier
Trojahn	*Was ihr wollt*	Sebastiano
Verdi	*Un ballo in maschera*	Silvano
	Rigoletto	Ceprano
Wagner	*Rienzi*	Cecco del Vecchio
Weber	*Oberon*	Scherasmin
Weill	*Mahagonny*	Bill
Wolf-Ferrari	*Le donne curiose*	Lelio
B. Zimmermann	*Die Soldaten*	Stolzius
U. Zimmermann	*Der Schuhu*	Der Schuhu

Cavalier Baritone (*Kavalierbariton*)

Composer	Opera	Role
Adams	*Nixon in China*	Richard Nixon
Auber	*La muette de Portici*	Pietro
Beethoven	*Fidelio*	Don Fernando
Bellini	*I puritani*	Sir Richard Forth
Berlioz	*Benvenuto Cellini*	Fieramosca
Bialas	*Aucassin und Nicolette*	Aucassin
Birtwistle	*Punch and Judy*	Choregos
Bizet	*Carmen*	Escamillo
	Les pêcheurs de perles	Zurga

Composer	Opera	Role
Cimarosa	*Il matrimonio segreto*	Robinsone
Donizetti	*Anna Bolena*	Lord Rochefort
	L'elisir d'amore	Belcore
	Lucia di Lammermoor	Ashton
	Viva la Mamma	Stefano
Dvořák	*Der Jakobiner*	Bohus
Eötvös	*Tri sestri*	Werschinin
Fortner	*Bluthochzeit*	Leonardo
Gluck	*Armide*	Ubalde
Goetz	*Der Widerspenstigen Zähmung*	Petruchio
Gounod	*Faust*	Valentin
	Mireille	Ourrias
Handel	*Deidamia*	Phönix
Henze	*The English Cat*	Tom
Korngold	*Die tote Stadt*	Frank
Krenek	*Jonny spielt auf*	Daniello
Lortzing	*Undine*	Kühleborn
	Der Wildschütz	Graf
	Zar und Zimmermann	Zar
Massenet	*Manon*	Brétigny/Lescaut
Meyerbeer	*Les Huguenots*	Nevers
Monteverdi	*Il ritorno d'Ulisse in patria*	Ulisse
Mozart	*Così fan tutte*	Guglielmo
	Don Giovanni	Don Giovanni
	Le nozze di Figaro	Count Almaviva
	Die Zauberflöte	Sprecher
Mussorgsky	*Khovanshchina*	Schaklowity
Pfitzner	*Palestrina*	Graf Luna
Pintscher	*Thomas Chatterton*	Thomas Chatterton
Prokofiev	*War and Peace*	Dennisow
Puccini	*La bohème*	Marcel
	Madama Butterfly	Sharpless
	Manon Lescaut	Lescaut
	Tosca	Scarpia
Ravel	*L'heure espagnole*	Ramiro
Schreker	*Die Gezeichneten*	Count Tamare
Schubert	*Fierrabras*	Roland
R. Strauss	*Arabella*	Mandryka
	Capriccio	The Count/Olivier
	Intermezzo	Storch
Tchaikovsky	*Eugene Onegin*	Onegin

Composer	Opera	Role
Trojahn	*Enrico*	Enrico
Ullman	*Der Kaiser von Atlantis*	Overall
Verdi	*Attila*	Ezio
	Un ballo in maschera	René
	Don Carlos	Posa
	Ernani	Don Carlos
	Falstaff	Ford
	La forza del destino	Don Carlos di Vargas
	I masnadieri	Franz
	La traviata	Germont
	Il trovatore	Count di Luna
	I vespri siciliani	Guido de Montfort
Wagner	*Tannhäuser*	Wolfram
Wolf-Ferrari	*Il segreto di Susanna*	Gil
	Sly	Count von Westmoreland
Zemlinsky	*Kleider machen Leute*	Melchior Böhm
B. Zimmermann	*Die Soldaten*	Stolzius

Dramatic Baritone (*Heldenbariton*)

Composer	Opera	Role
D'Albert	*Tiefland*	Sebastiano
Bartók	*Herzog Blaubarts Burg*	Herzog Blaubart
Beethoven	*Fidelio*	Don Pizarro
Bellini	*I puritani*	Sir Richard Forth
Berg	*Lulu*	Dr. Schön/Jack
	Wozzeck	Wozzeck
Berlioz	*La damnation de Faust*	Méphistophélès
Borodin	*Prince Igor*	Igor
Britten	*Death in Venice*	Traveler/elderly fop/ old gondolier/ hotel porter/barber/ leading player/ voice of Dionysus
	Peter Grimes	Balstrode
Busoni	*Arlecchino*	Ser Matteo del Sarto
	Doktor Faust	Doktor Faust
Charpentier	*Louise*	Louisens Vater
Cherubini	*Médée*	Kreon
Cilea	*Adriana Lecouvreur*	Michonnet
Dallapiccola	*Il Prigioniero*	Der Gefangener
Debussy	*Pelléas et Mélisande*	Golaud
Delius	*A Village Romeo and Juliet*	Manz/Marti

Composer	Opera	Role
Donizetti	*Viva la Mamma*	Agatha
Egk	*Peer Gynt*	Peer Gynt
Einem	*Der Besuch der alten Dame*	Alfred III
	Dantons Tod	Danton
Gershwin	*Porgy and Bess*	Porgy
Giordano	*Andrea Chénier*	Gérard
Glinka	*Ruslan und Ljudmila*	Ruslan
Gluck	*Alceste*	Oberpriester
	Armide	Hidraot
	Iphigénie en Aulide	Agamemnon
	Iphigénie en Tauride	Orest/Thoas
Gounod	*Faust*	Mephistopheles
Hara	*Petro Kibe*	Petro Kibe
Henze	*Die Bassariden*	Pentheus
	Elegie für junge Liebende	Gregor Mittenhofer
	König Hirsch (Il re cervo)	Statthalter
Hindemith	*Cardillac*	Cardillac
	Mathis der Maler	Mathis
Janáček	*The Makropoulos Affair*	Jaroslaw Prus
Klebe	*Jacobowky und der Oberst*	Jacobowky
Korngold	*Das Wunder der Heliane*	Der Herrscher
Leoncavallo	*Pagliacci*	Tonio
Ligeti	*Le Grand Macabre*	Nekrotzar
Marschner	*Hans Heiling*	Heiling
	Der Vampyr	Lord Ruthven
Mascagni	*Cavalleria rusticana*	Alfio
Messiaen	*Saint François d'Assise*	François
Meyerbeer	*Les Huguenots*	Nevers
	Le prophète	Oberthal
Mozart	*Don Giovanni*	Don Giovanni
	Die Zauberflöte	Sprecher
Mussorgsky	*Boris Godunov*	Boris Godunov
Nielsen	*Saul and David*	Saul
Offenbach	*Les contes d'Hoffmann*	Lindorf/Coppelius/ Dapertutto/Mirakel
Orff	*Die Kluge*	König
Penderecki	*Die Teufel von Loudun*	Grandier
Pfitzner	*Der arme Heinrich*	Dietrich
	Palestrina	Borromeo
Ponicelli	*La Gioconda*	Barnaba
Puccini	*La fanciula del West*	Jack Rance
	Gianni Schicchi	Gianni Schicchi

Composer	Opera	Role
Puccini, cont.	*Il tabarro*	Michele
	Tosca	Scarpia
Reimann	*Lear*	König Lear
Rossini	*Guillaume Tell*	Tell
Saint-Saëns	*Samson et Dalila*	Oberpriester
Schillings	*Mona Lisa*	Francesco
Schoeck	*Penthesilea*	Achilles
Schönberg	*Die glückliche Hand*	Mann
	Von Heute auf Morgen	Der Mann
Schreker	*Der ferne Klang*	Dr. Vigelius
	Die Gezeichneten	Antoniotto Adorno
Schubert	*Fierrabras*	Roland
Shostakovich	*Lady Macbeth von Mzensk*	Boris Ismailov
R. Strauss	*Die ägyptische Helena*	Altair
	Arabella	Mandryka
	Ariadne auf Naxos	Musiklehrer
	Elektra	Orest
	Feuersnot	Kunrad
	Die Frau ohne Schatten	Barak
	Intermezzo	Storch
	Der Rosenkavalier	Faninal
	Salome	Jochanaan
	Die schweigsame Frau	Merosus
Stravinsky	*The Rake's Progress*	Nick Shadow
Tchaikovsky	*Pique Dame*	Tomsky
Tippett	*The Midsummer Marriage*	King Fisher
Trojahn	*Enrico*	Belcredi
	Was ihr wollt	Sir Toby
Verdi	*Aida*	Amonasro
	Attila	Enzio
	Don Carlos	Phillip II/Posa/ grand inquisitor
	I due Foscari	Francesco Foscari
	Ernani	Don Carlos
	Falstaff	Falstaff
	La forza del destino	Don Carlos
	Luisa Miller	Miller
	Macbeth	Macbeth
	Nabucco	Nebukadnezar
	Otello	Iago
	Rigoletto	Rigoletto
	La traviata	Germont

Composer	Opera	Role
Verdi, *cont.*	*Il trovatore*	Count di Luna
	Simon Boccanegra	Simon
	I vespri siciliani	Guido de Montfort
Wagner	*Der fliegende Holländer*	Holländer
	Götterdämmerung	Gunther
	Lohengrin	Telramund/Heerrufer
	Die Meistersinger	Sachs
	Parsifal	Amfortas/Klingsor
	Das Rheingold	Wotan
	Rienzi	Orsini
	Siegfried	Wanderer
	Tristan und Isolde	Kurwenal
	Die Walküre	Wotan
Weber	*Euryanthe*	Lysiart
Zemlinsky	*Eine florentinische Tragödie*	Simone
U. Zimmermann	*Der Schuhu*	Bass/Schneider/König von Tripolis

Acting Baritone (*Spiel Bariton*)

Gluck	*L'ivrogne corrigé*	Cléon
Puccini	*Turandot*	Ping
R. Strauss	*Ariadne auf Naxos*	Harlekin
Weber	*Oberon*	Scherasmin

Character Baritone (*Charakterbariton*)

Adams	*Nixon in China*	Henry Kissinger
D'Albert	*Tiefland*	Setastiano/Moruccio
	Die toten Augen	Arcesius/Der Schnitter
Auber	*La muette de Portici*	Pietro
Bartók	*Herzog Blaubarts Burg*	Herzog Blaubart
Beethoven	*Fidelio*	Don Pizarro
Berg	*Lulu*	Schigolch
	Wozzeck	Wozzeck
Berlioz	*Béatrice et Bénédict*	Leonato
	La damnation de Faust	Méphistophélès
	Les Troyens	Pantheus
Bizet	*Carmen*	Escamillo
Borodin	*Albert Herring*	Mr. Gedge
	Prince Igor	Igor/Wladamir Jaroslawitch
Britten	*Peter Grimes*	Swallow/Balstrode

Composer	Opera	Role
Cilea	*Adriana Lecouvreur*	Michonnet
Debussy	*Pelléas et Mélisande*	Golaud
Delius	*A Village Romeo and Juliet*	Black violin
Dittersdorf	*Doktor und Apotheker*	Doktor Krautmann
Donizetti	*Don Pasquale*	Don Pasquale
Dvořák	*Der Jakobiner*	Adolf
Gershwin	*Porgy and Bess*	Crown
Gluck	*Alceste*	Hercule
	Le cadi dupé	Omar
	La recontre imprévue	Meister Überschwang
Hölszky	*Bremer Freiheit*	Miltenberger
Humperdinck	*Hänsel und Gretel*	Besenbinder
Janáček	*Jenůfa*	Altgesell
Kienzl	*Der Evangelimann*	Johannes
Lully	*Atys*	Celenus
Meyerbeer	*Les Huguenots*	Saint-Bris
	Le prophète	Mathisen/Oberthal
Mozart	*Le nozze di Figaro*	Figaro
	Die Zauberflöte	Sprecher
Pfitzner	*Palestrina*	Morone/Avosmediano Ercole Severolus
Puccini	*La bohème*	Schaunard
	La fanciulla del West	Jack Rance
	Gianni Schicchi	Gianni Schicchi
	Manon Lescaut	Lescaut
	Il tabarro	Michele
	Tosca	Scarpia
	Turandot	Ping
Rihm	*Die Eroberung von Mexico*	Cortez
Schnittke	*Historia von D. Johann Fausten*	Faustus
Schönberg	*Moses und Aaron*	Ephraimit
	Von Heute auf Morgen	Der Mann
Schrecker	*Die Gezeichneten*	Antoniotto Adorno
R. Strauss	*Ariadne auf Naxos*	Musiklehrer
	Capriccio	Olivier
	Feuersnot	Hämerleiin
	Der Rosenkavalier	Faninal
	Die Schweigsame Frau	Morbio
Stravinsky	*The Rake's Progress*	Nick Shadow
Trojahn	*Enrico*	Dottore
	Was ihr wollt	Malvolio/Narr

Composer	Opera	Role
Verdi	*Rigoletto*	Rigoletto
	Simon Boccanegra	Paolo
Wagner	*Die Meistersinger*	Beckmesser
	Parsifal	Klingsor
	Das Rheingold	Alberich
	Rienzi	Paolo Orsini/Cecco del Vecchio
	Siegfried	Alberich
Weill	*Mahagonny*	Bill/Joe
Wolf	*Der Corregidor*	Tio Lucas
Wolf-Ferrari	*I quattro rusteghi*	Maurizio
U. Zimmermann	*Der Schuhu*	Der Schuhu

Bass Buffo (*Spielbass*)

Composer	Opera	Role
Auber	*Fra Diavolo*	Giacomo/ Lord Kookburn
Berg	*Wozzeck*	Doktor
Berlioz	*Béatrice et Bénédict*	Somarone
Bialas	*Aucassin und Nicolette*	Graf von Bauclaire
Bizet	*Carmen*	Dancaïro
Boieldieu	*La dame blanche*	Mac Irton
Britten	*Albert Herring*	Mr. Budd
	A Midsummer Night's Dream	Quince
Cimarosa	*Il matrimonio segreto*	Geronimo
Dittersdorf	*Doktor und Apotheker*	Stössel
Donizetti	*Don Pasquale*	Pasquale
	L'elisir d'amore	Dulcamara
	La fille du régiment	Sulpiz
Dvořák	*Der Jakobiner*	Filip
Einem	*Dantons Tod*	Simon
Eötvös	*Tri sestri*	Kulygin
Flotow	*Alessando Stradella*	Malvolino
	Martha	Lord Tristan
Gluck	*Le cadi dupé*	Kadi
	L'ivrogne corrigé	Lucas
Goetz	*Der Widerspenstigen Zähmung*	Hortensio/Grumio
Handel	*Acis and Galatea*	Polypheme
Haydn	*La fedeltà premiata*	Melibeo
	Il mondo della luna	Buonafede
Humperdinck	*Königskinder*	Holzhacker

Composer	Opera	Role
Lortzing	*Die Opernprobe*	Graf
	Undine	Hans
	Der Waffenschmeid	Adelhof
	Der Wildschütz	Baculus
Mozart	*Bastien und Bastienne*	Colas
	Così fan tutte	Don Alfonso
	Don Giovanni	Leporello
	La finta giardiniera	Roberto (Nardo)
	La finta semplice	Simone
	Le nozze di Figaro	Figaro
Mussorsky	*Boris Godunov*	Warlaam
Orff	*Die Kluge*	Bauer
Paisiello	*Il barbiere di Siviglia*	Bartolo
Pergolesi	*La serva padrona*	Uberto
Puccini	*Il tabarro*	Talpa
	Tosca	Mesner
Ravel	*L'heure espagnole*	Don Inigo Comez
Rimsky-Korsakov	*Le coq d'or*	King Dodon
Rossini	*Il barbiere di Siviglia*	Doctor Bartolo
	La Cenerentola	Don Magnifico
	L'italiana in Algeri	Mustafa
	Il turco in Italia	Don Geronio
Schnittke	*Leben mit einem Idioten*	Wärter
R. Strauss	*Arabella*	Graf Waldner
	Ariadne auf Naxos	Truffaldin
	Capriccio	La Roche
	Feuersnot	Kofel
	Die schweigsame Frau	Vanuzzi/Farfallo/Barbier
Telemann	*Enrico*	Ordulfo
	Pimpinone	Pimpinone
Ullman	*Der Kaiser von Atlantis*	Der Lautsprecher
Verdi	*Un ballo in maschera*	Tom
	Falstaff	Pistol
	La forza del destino	Melitone
	Luisa Miller	Miller
Wagner	*Götterdämmerung*	Gunther/Alberich
	Die Meistersinger	Beckmesser/Kothner
	Siegfried	Alberich
Wolf	*Der Corregidor*	Tonuelo

Composer	Opera	Role
Wolf-Ferrari	*Le donne curiose*	Arlecchino
U. Zimmermann	*Der Schuhu*	Kaiser von Mesopotamien

Heavy Bass Buffo (*Schwerer Spielbass/Bassbuffo*)

Composer	Opera	Role
Adam	*Le postillon de Lonjumeau*	Bijou
Berg	*Lulu*	Tierbändiger/Rodrigo
Berlioz	*Benvenuto Cellini*	Giacomo Balducci
Birtwistle	*Punch and Judy*	Arzt
Busoni	*Arlecchino*	Dottore Bombasto
	Turandot	Pantalone
Catalani	*La Wally*	Der Wirtshaus besucher
Cornelius	*Der Barbier von Bagdad*	Abul Hassan
Donizetti	*Viva la Mamma*	Mamma Agata
Dvořák	*Der Jakobiner*	Filip
Egk	*Der Revisor*	Stadthauptmann
Flotow	*Martha*	Plumkett
Glinka	*Ruslan und Ljudmila*	Farlaf
Gounod	*Faust*	Mephistopheles
Handel	*Acis and Galatea*	Polypheme
	Serse	Elviro
Lortzing	*Der Waffenschmeid*	Stadinger
	Zar und Zimmermann	van Bett
Meyerbeer	*Les Huguenots*	Marcel
Mozart	*Die Entführung aus dem Serail*	Osmin
Mussorsky	*Der Jahrmarkt von Sorotshinzy*	Tscherewik
Nicolai	*Die lustigen Weiber*	Falstaff
Pfitzner	*Das Christ-Elflein*	Knecht Ruprecht
Puccini	*La bohème*	Colline
	Gianni Schicchi	Gianni Schicchi
Rossini	*Il barbiere di Siviglia*	Basilio
Smetana	*The Bartered Bride*	Kezal
R. Strauss	*Der Rosenkavalier*	Ochs
	Die schweigsame Frau	Morbio/Vanuzzi/ Farfallo
Trojahn	*Was ihr wollt*	Antonio
Ullman	*Der Kaiser von Atlantis*	Der Tod
Wagner	*Der fliegende Holländer*	Daland
Weber	*Der Freischütz*	Caspar
Wolf	*Der Corregidor*	Repela

Composer	Opera	Role
Wolf-Ferrari	*Le donne curiose*	Ottavio
	I quattro rusteghi	Lunardo

Character Bass/Bass Baritone (*Charakterbass/Bassbariton*)

Composer	Opera	Role
D'Albert	*Tiefland*	Moruccio
Auber	*Fra Diavolo*	Matteo
Berg	*Lulu*	Theaterdirektor/ Bankier/Tierbändiger/ Rodrigo/Schilgolch
Berio	*Un re in ascolto*	Prospero
Berlioz	*Béatrice et Bénédict*	Leonato
	Les Troyens	Pantheus/Narbal/ Priamus
Bizet	*Carmen*	Zuniga
Boieldieu	*La dame blanche*	Gaveston
Boito	*Mefistofele*	Mefistofele
Borodini	*Prince Igor*	Wladimir Jaroslawitch
Britten	*Albert Herring*	Mr. Budd
	Billy Budd	Mr. Flint
	Death in Venice	Traveler/elderly fop/ old gondolier/ hotel manager/ barber/leading player/ voice of Dionysus
	A Midsummer Night's Dream	Bottom
	Peter Grimes	Hobson/Swallow
Busoni	*Turandot*	Tartaglia
Cilea	*Adriana Lecouvreur*	Quinault
Delius	*A Village Romeo and Juliet*	Marti
Dittersdorf	*Doktor und Apotheker*	Doktor Krautmann
Donizetti	*Don Pasquale*	Don Pasquale
	Viva la Mamma	Vincenzo/Orazio
Egk	*Die Zaubergeige*	Bürgermeister
Einem	*Dantons Tod*	St.-Just
Flotow	*Alessando Stradella*	Bassi
Goetz	*Der Widerspenstigen Zähmung*	Baptista
Goldschmidt	*Der gewaltige Hahnrei*	Petrus
Handel	*Serse*	Ariodate
Hara	*Petro Kibe*	Martino Hara/Inoue Chikugonokami

Composer	Opera	Role
Keiser	*Masaniello*	Masaniello
Korngold	*Das Wunder der Heliane*	Der Pförtner
Lortzing	*Undine*	Tobias
Lully	*Armide*	Hidraot/Ubalde
Martinů	*The Greek Passion*	Priester Grigoris
Meyerbeer	*Les Huguenots*	Saint-Bris
	Le prophète	Mathisen/Oberthal
Mozart	*Così fan tutte*	Don Alfonso
	Don Giovanni	Masetto
	Le nozze di Figaro	Figaro
Mussorgsky	*Boris Godunov*	Rangoni
Puccini	*La fanciulla del West*	Ashby
	Manon	Geronte
	Il tabarro	Talpa
	Turandot	Timu
Rameau	*Hippolyte et Aricie*	Pluton
Rossini	*La Cenerentola*	Alidoro
	Guillaume Tell	Walter Fürst
	Mosè in Egitto	Faraone
Schrecker	*Der ferne Klang*	Dr. Vigelius
	Die Gezeichneten	Lodoveco Nardi
Schubert	*Fierrabras*	Boland
R. Strauss	*Capriccio*	La Roche
	Feuersnot	Gilgenstock
	Die Frau ohne Schatten	Einarmige
	Der Rosenkavalier	Ochs
	Die schweigsame Frau	Morbio/Vanuzzi/Farfallo
Tan Dun	*Marco Polo*	Schatten III
Verdi	*Aida*	Der König
	Un ballo in maschera	Samuel
	Don Carlos	Inquisitor/monk
	Ernani	Don Ruy Gomez de Silva
	Falstaff	Pistol
	Luisa Miller	Wurm/Walter
	Otello	Montano
	Rigoletto	Monterone
	Il trovatore	Ferrando
	Simon Boccanegra	Albiani/Pietro
Wagner	*Götterdämmerung*	Alberich
	Lohengrin	Heerrufer des Königs
	Die Meistersinger	Kothner/Konrad Nachtigal

Composer	Opera	Role
Wagner, *cont.*	*Das Rheingold*	Donner/Alberich
	Siegfried	Alberich
	Tannhäuser	Biterolf/Reinmar
	Die Walküre	Hunding
Weber	*Der Freischütz*	Kuno
Weill	*Mahagonny*	Dreieinigkeitsmoses/Joe
Wolf	*Der Corregidor*	Alkalde
Wolf-Ferrari	*I quattro rusteghi*	Simon
B. Zimmermann	*Die Soldaten*	Wesener
U. Zimmermann	*Der Schuhu*	Keiser von Mesopotamien

Serious Bass (*Seriöser Bass/Swartzer Bass*)

Adam	*Le postillon de Lonjumeau*	Bijou
D'Albert	*Tiefland*	Tommaso
Beethoven	*Fidelio*	Rocco
Bellini	*Norma*	Orovisto
	I puritani	Lord Walter Walton/ Sir George
Berg	*Lulu*	Tierbändiger/Rodrigo
Berlioz	*Béatrice et Bénédict*	Don Pedro
	Benvenuto Cellini	Pope Clement VII/ Cardinal Salviati
	Les Troyens	Schatten
Bialas	*Aucassin und Nicolette*	Anton
Bizet	*Carmen*	Zuniga
	Les pêcheurs de perles	Nourabad
Boito	*Mefistofele*	Mefistofele
Borodin	*Prince Igor*	Kontschak
Britten	*Billy Budd*	John Claggart
	A Midsummer Night's Dream	Theseus
Busoni	*Doktor Faust*	Wagner
	Turandot	Altoum
Catalani	*La Wally*	Strominger
Cilea	*Adriana Lecouvreur*	Fürst von Bouillon
Cornelius	*Der Barbier von Bagdad*	Abu Hassan
Debussy	*Pelléas et Mélisande*	Arkel
Dessau	*Die Verurteilung des Lukullus*	König
Donizetti	*Anna Bolena*	Henry VIII
	Lucia di Lammermoor	Raimondo
Dvořák	*Rusalka*	Wassermann

Composer	Opera	Role
Eötvös	*Tri sestri*	Soljony
Glass	*Akhnaten*	Ajeh
Glinka	*A Life for the Tsar*	Iwan Sussanin
Gounod	*Faust*	Mephistopheles
Handel	*Agrippina*	Claudio
	Ariodante	King of Scotland
	Deidamia	Lycomedes
	Orlando	Zoroastro
	Radamisto	Farasmane
	Serse	Ariodates
Halévy	*La Juive*	Gian Francesco
Hara	*Petro Kibe*	Romano Kibe
Henze	*Die Bassariden*	Kadmos
	The English Cat	Arnold
Hindemith	*Cardillac* (1926)	Goldhändler
	Cardillac (1952)	Offizier
	Mathis der Maler	Lorenz von Pommersfelden
Hölszky	*Bremer Freiheit*	Pater Markus
Kaiser	*Masaniello*	Don Antonio
Massenet	*Manon*	Graf des Grieux
Messiaen	*Saint François d'Assise*	Bernard
Meyerbeer	*Les Huguenots*	Marcel
Monteverdi	*L'incoronazione di Poppea*	Seneca
	Il ritorno d'Ulisse in patria	Nettuno
Mozart	*La clemenza di Tito*	Publius
	Don Giovanni	Commendatore
	Die Entführung aus dem Serail	Osmin
	Le nozze di Figaro	Bartolo
	Die Zauberflöte	Sarastro
Mussorgsky	*Boris Godunov*	Pimen
	Khovanshchina	Fürst Iwan Chowanskij/Dosifej
Nielsen	*Saul and David*	Samuel
Offenbach	*Les contes d'Hoffmann*	Crespel
Orff	*Antigonae*	Kreon
Pfitzner	*Der arme Heinrich*	Arzt
	Palestrina	Papst/Madruscht/ Kardinal
Ponchielli	*La Gioconda*	Alvise Badoero

Composer	Opera	Role
Prokofiev	*The Love for Three Oranges*	King of Clubs
	War and Peace	Kutusow
Puccini	*La bohème*	Colline
	La fanciulla del West	Ashby
	Manon Lescaut	Geronte
	Turandot	Timur
Rameau	*Platée*	Jupiter
Rimsky-Korsakov	*Das Märchen von Zaren Saltan*	Zar Saltan
	Mayskaya Noch	Dorfschulze
Rossini	*La Cenerentola*	Alidoro
	Guillaume Tell	Gesler
	Mosè in Egitto	Mosè
Schönberg	*Moses und Aaron*	A priest
Schreker	*Die Geziechneten*	Lodovico Nardi
Schubert	*Fierrabras*	König Karl
R. Strauss	*Arabella*	Graf Waldner
	Daphne	Peneios
	Electra	Orest
	Feuersnot	Sentlinger
	Intermezzo	Kammersänger
	Die schweigsame Frau	Morosus
Stravinsky	*The Rake's Progress*	Trulove
Tan Dun	*Marco Polo*	Kublai Khan
Thomas	*Mignon*	Lothario
Tippett	*The Midsummer Marriage*	He-Ancient
Tchaikovsky	*Eugene Onegin*	Prince Gremin
Verdi	*Aida*	Ramphis/König
	Attila	Attila
	Un ballo in maschera	Samuel
	Don Carlos	Philip II/ grand inquisitor
	I due Foscari	Jacopo Loredano
	Ernani	Don Ruy Gomez de Silva
	La forza del destino	Guardian
	Luisa Miller	Count/Walter
	Macbeth	Banquo
	I masnadieri	Maximilian
	Nabucco	Zacharias
	Otello	Lodovico

Composer	Opera	Role
Verdi, *cont.*	*Rigoletto*	Sparafucile
	Simon Boccanegra	Fiesco
	La traviata	Dottor Grenvil
	Il trovatore	Ferrando/Guardiano
	I vespri siciliani	Giovanni
Wagner	*Götterdämmerung*	Hagen
	Lohengrin	König Heinrich
	Die Meistersinger	Pogner
	Parsifal	Gurnemanz
	Das Rheingold	Fasolt/Fafner
	Tannhäuser	Hermann
	Tristan und Isolde	Marke
	Die Walküre	Hunding
Weber	*Euryanthe*	Ludwig VI
	Der Freischütz	Caspar
Wolf-Ferrari	*I quattro rusteghi*	Cancian
Zemlinsky	*Kleider machen Leute*	Amstrat
U. Zimmermann	*Der Schuhu*	Bass/Schneider/ König von Tripolis

Appendix F
Suggested Audition Arias

This appendix lists a selection of suggested audition arias for the established *Fach* categories as listed in Kloiber's *Handbuch der Oper* (Bärenreiter-Verlag, 2006).

This listing does not include the categories for child/young lyric/ beginners, as most of these roles do not have solo arias that could be used for audition purposes. Singers auditioning for those roles are advised to select a simple and comfortable aria from the established *Fach* categories that most closely match their vocal characteristics.

Some audition arias are listed in more than one *Fach* category, as they are suitable for both. An asterisk (*) indicates those arias that are highly recommended.

Opera titles are as listed in Kloiber's *Handbuch der Oper* or *Kobbé's Opera Book*. Abbreviations are used for the more lengthy opera titles.

Composer	Opera	Role	Aria
Soubrette/Acting Soprano (*Soubrette/Spielsopran***)**			
Beethoven	*Fidelio*	Marzelline	* "O wär ich schon mit dir vereint"
Haydn	*Lo speziale*	Grilletta	"A fatti tuoi bader tu puoi"
Mozart	*Le nozze di Figaro*	Barbarina	"L'ho perduta, me meschina" "Deh vieni, non tarder"

Composer	Opera	Role	Aria
Poulenc	*Dialogues des Carmélites*	Constance	"Salve Regina"

Lyric Coloratura Soprano (*Koloratursoubrette*)

Composer	Opera	Role	Aria
Donizetti	*La fille du régiment*	Marie	* "Chacun le sait"
	Linda di Chamounix	Linda	* "O luce di quest' anima"
Mozart	*Die Entführung*	Blonde	"Durch Zärtlichkeit und Schmeicheln"
	Idomeneo	Ilia	* "Padre germani, addio! Se il padre perdei"
	Le nozze di Figaro	Susanna	"Deh vieni non tardar"
Puccini	*La bohème*	Musetta	* "Quando m'en vo"
Verdi	*Un ballo in maschera*	Oscar	* "Volta la terrea!"
	Rigoletto	Gilda	* "Caro nome"

Dramatic Coloratura Soprano (*Dramatischer Koloraturasopran*)

Composer	Opera	Role	Aria
Gounod	*Faust*	Marguerite	* "Ah! Je ris de me voir" (The Jewel Song)
Monteverdi	*Poppea*	Poppea	"Speranza, tu mi vai il cor accarezzando"
Mozart	*Die Entfuhrüng*	Constanze	"Ach, ich liebte, war so glücklich"
	Le nozze di Figaro	Countess Almaviva	"Porgi amor"
Puccini	*Madama Butterfly*	Cio-Cio San	* "Un bel di"
	Manon Lescaut	Manon	* "Sola, perduta, abbandonata"
			"In quelle trine morbide"
Verdi	*Attila*	Odabella	"Allor che i forti corrano"
	Ernani	Elvira	* "Ernani, involami"
	Luisa Miller	Luisa	* "Lo vidi e'l primo palpito"
	Nabucco	Abigail	* "Anch'io dischioso un giorno"
	La traviata	Violetta	* "Sempre libra"

Composer	Opera	Role	Aria
Verdi, *cont.*			"Estrano, e strano"
			"Ah fors'è lui"
	Il trovatore	Leonora	* "Tacea la notte placida"
	I vespri siciliani	Elena	"Mercè, dilette amiche"
Weber	*Oberon*	Rezia	"Ozean du Ungeheuer"

Character Soprano (*Charaktersopran/Zwischenfachstimme*)

Bizet	*Carmen*	Carmen	* "En vain, pour éviter"
			* "Près des remparts de Séville" (Seguidilla)
			"L'amour est un oiseau rebelle" (Habanera)
Debussy	*Pelléas et Mélisande*	Mélisande	"Mes longs cheveux"
Monteverdi	*Poppea*	Nerone	"Hor che Seneca è morto, cantiam" (aria at the end of this duet)

Lyric Soprano (*Lyrischer Sopran*)

Bizet	*Carmen*	Micaëla	* "Je dis que rein ne m'épouvante"
Leoncavallo	*Pagliacci*	Nedda	"Stridono lassù"
Mozart	*Don Giovanni*	Zerlina	* "Batti, batti"
	Die Zauberflöte	Pamina	* "Ach, ich fühl's"
Puccini	*La bohème*	Mimi	* "Si, mi chiamano Mimì"
			"Donde leita"
		Musetta	"Quando m'en vo soletta"
	Gianni Schicchi	Lauretta	* "O mio babbino caro"
	Turandot	Liù	"Signore, ascolta"
			"Tu che de gel sei cinta"

Young Dramatic Soprano (*Spinto Sopran/Jugendlich-dramatischer Sopran*)

Bellini	*Norma*	Norma	* "Casta Diva, che inargenti"
Catalini	*La Wally*	Wally	* "Ebben? Ne andrò lontana"
Dvořák	*Rusalka*	Rusalka	* "Song to the Moon"

Composer	Opera	Role	Aria
Giordano	*Andrea Chénier*	Maddelena	* "La mamma morta"
Gounod	*Faust*	Marguerite	* "Ah! Je ris de me voir" (The Jewel Song)
Mozart	*Così fan tutte*	Fiordiligi	* "Come scoglio"
	Don Giovanni	Donna Anna	* "Non mi dir"
	Le nozze di Figaro	Countess Almaviva	* "Dove sono"
	Die Zauberflöte	Pamina	"Ach, ich fühl's"
Offenbach	*Les contes d'Hoffmann*	Antonia	* "Elle a fui, la tourterelle"
Puccini	*La bohème*	Mimi	"Si, mi chiamano Mimì"
	La fanciulla del West	Minnie	* "Oh, se sapeste"
	Madama Butterfly	Cio-Cio San	* "Un bel di"
	Manon Lescaut	Manon	* "In quelle trine morbide"
	Tosca	Tosca	* "Vissi d'arte"
R. Strauss	*Ariadne auf Naxos*	Ariadne	"Es gibt ein Reich"
Verdi	*Aida*	Aida	* "Ritorna vincitor!"
	Atilla	Odabella	"Allor che i forti corrono"
			"Oh! Nel fuggente nuvolo"
	Un ballo in maschera	Amelia	"Morrò, ma prima in grazia"
	Don Carlos	Elisabetta	* "Tu che le vanità conosce"
	La forza del destino	Leonora	"Pace, pace, mio Dio"
	Luisa Miller	Luisa	* "Lo vidi, e'l primo palpito"
	Otello	Desdemona	* "Salce, sulce"
	Simon Boccanegra	Maria	"Come in quest'ora bruna"
	Il trovatore	Leonora	* "Tacea la notte placida"
	I vespri siciliani	Elena	"Mercè, dilette amiche"
Wagner	*Der fliegende Holländer*	Senta	* "Traft ihr das Schiff?"

Composer	Opera	Role	Aria
Wagner, cont.	*Götterdämmerung*	Gutrune	"War dus sein Horn?"
	Die Meistersinger	Eva	"O Sachs! Mein Freund"
	Tannhäuser	Elisabeth	* "Dich' theure Halle"
	Die Walküre	Sieglinde	* "Der Männer Sippe"
Weber	*Der Freischütz*	Agathe	* "Wie nahte mir der Schlümmer"
			"Leise, leise, fromme Weise"

Dramatic Soprano (*Dramatischer Sopran*)

Composer	Opera	Role	Aria
Beethoven	*Fidelio*	Leonore	* "Abscheulicher! Wo eilst du hin?"
Mozart	*Idomeneo*	Electra	"Tutto nel cor vi sento"
Puccini	*Tosca*	Tosca	* "Vissi d'arte"
	Turandot	Turandot	* "In questa reggia"
R. Strauss	*Ariadne auf Naxos*	Ariadne	"Es gibt ein Reich"
	Die Frau ohne Schatten	Färberin	"Barak, mein Mann"
Verdi	*Aida*	Aida	* "Ritorna vincitor!"
			"O cieli azzuri"
	Un ballo in maschera	Amelia	* "Morrò, ma prima in grazia"
	Macbeth	Lady Macbeth	* "Vieni! T'affretta! Accendere"
			"La luce langue"
			"Una macchia, é qui tuttora!"
Wagner	*Der fliegende Holländer*	Senta	"Traft ihr das Schiff?"
	Götterdämmerung	Brünnhilde	"Starke, Scheite schrichten mir dort"
			"Fliegt heim, ihr Raben"
	Tristan und Isolde	Isolde	* "Mild und leise" (Liebestod)
	Die Walküre	Brünnhilde	* "Hojotoho! Heiaha"

High Dramatic Soprano (*Hochdramatischer Sopran*)

Composer	Opera	Role	Aria
Wagner	*Götterdämmerung*	Brünnhilde	"Starke, Scheite schrichten mir dort"

Composer	Opera	Role	Aria
Wagner, *cont.*			"Fliegt heim, ihr Raben"
	Tristan und Isolde	Isolde	* "Mild und leise"
	Die Walküre	Brünnhilde	* "Hojotoho Heiaha"

Coloratura Mezzo-Soprano (*Koloratur-Mezzosopran*)

Composer	Opera	Role	Aria
Gounod	*Roméo et Juliette*	Stephano	"Que fais-tu, blanche tourterelle?"
Handel	*Rinaldo*	Rinaldo	"Cara sposa, amante cara"
Meyerbeer	*Die Hugenotten*	Urbain	"Nobles seigneurs, salut!"
Rossini	*Il barbiere di Siviglia*	Rosina	* "Una voce poco fa"
	La Cenerentola	Cenerentola	* "Non più mesta"
	L'italiana in Algeri	Isabella	* "Cruda sorte!"
	Semiramide	Arsaces	"In sì barbara sciagura"

Lyric Mezzo-Soprano (*Lyrischer Mezzosopran/Spielalt*)

Composer	Opera	Role	Aria
Gounod	*Faust*	Siebel	"Faites-lui mes âveux"
Massanet	*Werther*	Charlotte	* "Va! laisse couler mes larmes"
Monteverdi	*Poppea*	Arnalta	"Oblivion soave"
Mozart	*Così fan tutte*	Dorabella	"Smanie implacabili"
	La clemenza di Tito	Sextus	"Parto, parto"
			"Non più di fiori"
	Don Giovanni	Zerlina	"Batti, batti"
	Le nozze di Figaro	Cherubino	* "Non so più cosa son, cosa faccio"
			"Voi, che sapete"
Thomas	*Mignon*	Mignon	"Connais-tu le pays"
Wagner	*Ariodante*	Ariodante	"Scherza infida"

Dramatic Mezzo-Soprano (*Dramatischer Mezzosopran*)

Composer	Opera	Role	Aria
Bizet	*Carmen*	Carmen	* "En vain, pour èviter"
			* "Près des remparts de Séville" (Seguidilla)

Composer	Opera	Role	Aria
Bizet, *cont.*			"L'amour est un oiseau rebelle" (Habanera)
Meyerbeer	*Der Prophet*	Fides	"Ah, mon fils!"
Mozart	*La clemenza di Tito*	Sextus	* "Parto, parto"
		Vitellia	"Non piu di fiori" (aria only)
Ponchielli	*La Gioconda*	Gioconda	* "Suicidio"
Saint-Saëns	*Samson et Dalila*	Dalila	* "Mon coeur s'ouvre à ta voix"
			"Printemps qui commence"
			"Amour! Viens aider ma faiblesse!"
Tchaikovsky	*Pique Dame*	Pauline	Pauline's Aria
Verdi	*Don Carlos*	Eboli	* "O don fatale"
	Il trovatore	Azucena	* "Stride la vampa!"
Wagner	*Götterdämmerung*	Waltraute	* "Höre mit Sinn"
	Lohengrin	Ortrud	* "Entweihte Gütter"
	Die Walküre	Fricka	"Wo in Bergen du dich birgst"

Lyric Alto (*Lyrischer Alt*)

Gluck	*Orfeo ed Euridice*	Orfeo	"Che farò senza Euridice"
Handel	*Alcina*	Bradamante	"È gelosia"
			"Vorrei vendicarmi"
	Tamerlano	Irene	"Dal crudel che m'ha tradita"
			* "Crudel più non son io"
Verdi	*Falstaff*	Mrs. Quickly	"Reverenza"

Dramatic Alto (*Dramatischer Alt*)

Bizet	*Carmen*	Carmen	* "En vain, pour éviter"

Composer	Opera	Role	Aria
Bizet, *cont.*			* "Près des remparts de Séville" (Seguidilla)
			"L'amour est un oiseau rebelle" (Habanera)
Handel	*Giulio Cesare*	Cornelia	"Priva son d'ogni conforto"
Menotti	*The Consul*	The Mother	"Lullaby"
Tchaikovsky	*Pique Dame*	Pauline	Pauline's Aria
Verdi	*Un ballo in maschera*	Ulrica	"Re dell' abisso affrettati"
	Il trovatore	Azucena	* "Stride la vampa!"
			"Condotta ell'era in ceppi"

Low Alto (*Tiefer Alt Kontra-Alt*)

Composer	Opera	Role	Aria
Debussy	*Pelléas*	Geneviève	"Voici ce qu'il écrit à son frère Pelléas"
Verdi	*Un ballo in maschera*	Ulrica	"Re dell'abisso, affrettati"
Weill	*Mahagonny*	Leokadja Begbick	"Sie soll sein wie ein Netz"

Countertenor (*Contratenor*)

Composer	Opera	Role	Aria
Britten	*A Midsummer Night's Dream*	Oberon	"I know a bank"
Cavalli	*La Calisto*	Endimone	"Erme e solinghi cime"
Gluck	*Orfeo ed Euridice*	Orfeo	* "Che farò senza Euridice"
Handel	*Giulio Cesare*	Cesare	"Va tacito e nascosto"
			"Al lamp dell'armi"
		Sesto	"Svegliatevi nel core"
	Orlando	Orlando	"Ah! Stigie larve"
	Ottone	Adalberto	"Tu puoi straziarmi"

Composer	Opera	Role	Aria
Handel, cont.		Ottone	"Ritorna, o dolce amore"
			"Dell'onda ai fiori moti"
	Rinaldo	Eustazio	* "Scorta Rea"
		Goffredo	"Sorge nel petto"
		Rinaldo	* "Cara sposa"
	Rodelinda	Bertarido	"Con rauco mormorio"
			"Dove sei? Amato bene!"
	Serse	Arsamene	"Non so se sia la speme"
	Tamerlano	Andronico	"Bella Asteria"
		Tamerlano	"Dammi pace"
Haydn	*Il mondo della luna*	Ernesto	"Begli occhi vezzosi"
Reimann	*Lear*	Edgar	"Habe ich mein Leben"

Countertenor (*Haute-Contre*)

Composer	Opera	Role	Aria
Gluck	*Orfeo ed Euridice*	Orfeo	* "Che farò senza Euridice"
Lully	*Armide*	Renaud	"Plus j'observe ces lieux"
	Atys	Atys	"Je vous aime"
Rameau	*Castor et Pollux*	Castor	"Sejours de l'éternelle paix"
	Platée	Platée	"Que ce sejour"
			"Quittez, nymphes, quittez"
		Thespis	"Charmant Bacchus"

Buffo Tenor (*Tenorbuffo/Spieltenor*)

Composer	Opera	Role	Aria
Berg	*Lulu*	Prinz	"Würden Sie es für möglich"
Leoncavallo	*Pagliacci*	Beppe	* "O, Colombina"
Monteverdi	*Poppea*	Arnalta	* "Oblivion soave"
Mozart	*Die Entführung*	Pedrillo	* "Frisch zum kampfe"
			"Im Mohrenland"
	La finta giardiniera	Don Anchise	"Dentro il mio petto"

Composer	Opera	Role	Aria
Mozart *cont.*	*La finta semplice*	Fracasso	"Guarda la donna in viso"
	Le nozze di Figaro	Basilio	"In quegli anni"
	Die Zauberflöte	Monostatos	"Alles fühlt der Liebe"
Offenbach	*Les contes d'Hoffmann*	Franz	"Jour et nuits je me mets"
Wagner	*Die Meistersinger*	David	"Am Jordan Sankt Johannes"
Weber	*Abu Hassan*	Hassan	"Ich gebe Gastereien"

Lyric Tenor (*Lyrischer Tenor*)

Composer	Opera	Role	Aria
Adam	*Postillon*	St. Phar	"À la noblesse"
Auber	*Fra Diavolo*	Lorenzo	"Pour toujours"
		Marquis	"Agnes la jouvencelle"
	La muette de Portici	Masaniello	* "Du pauvre seul ami"
Berg	*Lulu*	Mahler	"Ich möchte tauschen"
	Wozzeck	Andres	"Die schöne Jägerei"
Berlioz	*Béatrice et Bénédict*	Bénédict	"Ah! Je vais l'aimer"
Bizet	*Les pêcheurs de perles*	Nadir	"De savanes et des forêts"
			* "Je crois entendre encore"
Boieldieu	*La dame blanche*	George Brown	"Viens, gentile dame"
Borodin	*Prince Igor*	Vladamir	"Ah! Wo bist du?"
Britten	*Albert Herring*	Albert Herring	"Albert the good!"
Cornelius	*Der Barbier*	Nurredin	"Vor deinem Fenster"
Debussy	*Pelléas et Mélisande*	Pelléas	"Ah! Je respire enfin!"
			"Oh! Qu'est-ce-que c'est?"
Delius	*Romeo and Juliet*	Sali	"What will you do?"

Composer	Opera	Role	Aria
Donizetti	*Anna Bolena*	Percy	"Nel veder la tua constanza"
	Don Pasquale	Ernesto	*"Com'è gentil"
	L'elisir d'amore	Nemorino	* "Quanto è bella"
			* "Una furtive lagrima"
	La fille du régiment	Tonio	"Ah! mes amis"
	Lucia di Lammermoor	Edgardo	"Fra poca a me ricovero"
	Viva la Mamma	Guglielmo	"Ah! Tu mi vuoi?"
Flotow	*Alessandro Stradella*	Stradella	"Serenade"
	Martha	Lyonel	* "Ach, so fromm"
Gershwin	*Porgy and Bess*	Sporting Life	"It ain't necessarily so"
Gounod	*Faust*	Faust	* "Salut! demeure chaste et pure"
	Mireille	Vincent	"Agnes du paradis"
Handel	*Acis and Galatea*	Acis	"Love sounds th'alarm"
		Damon	"Love in her eyes"
	Alcina	Oronte	"Un momento di contento"
	Radamisto	Tiridate	"Abzo al volo"
	Rodelinda	Grimoaldo	"Tra sospetti"
	Tamerlano	Bajazet	"Figlia mia, non pianger"
Haydn	*Il mondo della luna*	Ecclitico	"Un poco di dinarao"
Henze	*Die Bassariden*	Dionysus	"Dionysus' aria"
Massanet	*Manon*	Des Grieux	* "Ah fuyez, douce image!"
			* "En ferment les yeux"
Monteverdi	*L'Orfeo*	Orfeo	"Possente spirto"
			"Rosa del ciel"
			"Vi ritorni"
Mozart	*Così fan tutte*	Ferrando	"Ah! Lo veggio"
			* "Un aura amorosa"
	Don Giovanni	Ottavio	"Dalla sua pace"
			"Il mio tesoro"

Composer	Opera	Role	Aria
Mozart, *cont.*	*Die Entführung*	Belmonte	"Ich baue ganz" "O wie ängstlich"
	La finta giardiniera	Belfiore	"Che beltà" "Care pupille"
	Idomeneo	Arbace	"Se cola ne fati"
		Idomeneo	"Fuor del mar" "Vedrommi intorno"
	Le nozze di Figaro	Basilio	"In quegli anni"
	Die Zauberflöte	Tamino	* "Dies Bildniss"
Nicolai	*Die lustigen Weiber*	Fenton	"Horch, die Lerch"
Puccini	*La bohème*	Rodolfo	"Che gelida manina"
	Gianni Schicchi	Rinuccio	"Fienze è come un albero fiorito"
	Madama Butterfly	Pinkerton	"Amore o grillo" * "Addio, fiorito asil"
Rossini	*Il barbiere di Siviglia*	Almaviva	"Ecco ridente in cielo" "Cessa di più resistere"
	La Cenerentola	Ramiro	"Si, ritrovarla io guiro"
	Guillaume Tell	Arnold	"Asile héréditaire"
	L'italiana in Algeri	Lindoro	"Ah come un cor di giubilo"
	Il turco in Italia	Don Narciso	"Tu seconda il mio disegno"
R. Strauss	*Der Rosenkavalier*	Italian singer	"Di rigori"
Tchaikovsky	*Eugene Onegin*	Lenski	* "Kuda vy udalilis?"
Thomas	*Mignon*	Wilhelm Meister	"Oui, je veux par le monde"
Verdi	*Falstaff*	Fenton	"Dal labbro il canto"
	Macbeth	Macduff	"Ah, la paterno mano"
	I masnadieri	Carlo	"Di ladroni attorniato"
	Rigoletto	Duke of Mantua	* "La donna è mobile"

Composer	Opera	Role	Aria
Verdi, *cont.*			"Parmi veder le lagrime"
			* "Questa o quella"
	La traviata	Alfredo	"De miei bollenti spiriti"
Wagner	*Der fliegende Holländer*	Steuermann	"Mit Gewitter und Sturm"
Weber	*Oberon*	Oberon	"Schreckensschwur!"

Young Dramatic Tenor (*Spinto/Jugendlicher Heldentenor*)

Composer	Opera	Role	Aria
Beethoven	*Fidelio*	Florestan	"In des Lebens Frühlingstagen"
Bellini	*Norma*	Pollione	"Me protegge, me difende"
			"Va, crudele"
Berlioz	*Le damnation de Faust*	Faust	"Merci, doux crépuscule"
			"Nature immense"
	Les Troyens	Iopas	"O blonde Cérès"
Bizet	*Carmen*	Don José	"La fleur que tu m'avais jetée" (The Flower Song)
Boito	*Mephistofele*	Faust	"Giunto sul passo"
Borodin	*Prince Igor*	Vladimir	"Ah! Wo bist du?"
Britten	*Billy Budd*	Vere	"I am an old man"
			"We committed his body"
	Peter Grimes	Peter Grimes	"In dreams I've built myself"
			"Picture what that day"
Cilea	*Adriana Lecouvreur*	Maurizio	"La dolcissima effigie"
			"L'anima ho stanca"
Donizetti	*Anna Bolena*	Percy	"Nel veder nel tuo constanza"
Dvořák	*Rusalka*	Prince	"A week you've followed"
Giordano	*Andrea Chénier*	Andrea Chénier	* "Come un bel di"
			"Un di all'azzuro spazio"

Composer	Opera	Role	Aria
Gluck	*Alceste*	Admetos	"Misero! E che farò"
	Iphigénie in Tauris	Pylades	"Ah, mon ami"
Gounod	*Faust*	Faust	"Salut! Demeure chaste e pure"
	Roméo et Juliette	Roméo	* "Ah! Lève-toi, soleil"
Halévy	*La juive*	Éléazar	"Rachel quand du Seigneur"
Hindemith	*Cardillac* (original)	Kavalier	"Wagschalen diese Welt!"
Leoncavallo	*Pagliacci*	Canio	"Vesti la giubba"
Marschner	*Der Vampyr*	Edgar Aubry	"Frühlingsmorgen"
Mascagni	*Cavalleria rusticana*	Turridu	"O Lola, bianca come fior"
			"Mamma, quel vino"
Meyerbeer	*Die Hugenotten*	Raoul	"Plus banche"
Mozart	*La clemenza di Tito*	Tito	"Del più sublime soglio"
	Idomeneo	Idomeneo	"Vedrommi intorno"
	Die Zauberflöte	Tamino	* "Dies Bildniss"
Nielsen	*Saul und David*	David	"Saul's fortress"
		Jonathan	"Look upward, Michal"
Offenbach	*Les contes d'Hoffmann*	Hoffmann	"Ah, vivre deux!"
Ponchielli	*La Gioconda*	Enzo	* "Cielo e mar"
Prokofiev	*The Love for Three Oranges*	Prince	Laughing aria
Puccini	*La bohème*	Rodolfo	"Che gelida manina"
	La fanciulla del West	Johnson	* "Ch'ella mi creda"
	Manon Lescaut	Des Grieux	"Donna no vidi mai"
			"Tra voi, belle"
	Il tabarro	Luigi	"Hai ben ragione"
	Tosca	Cavaradossi	"E lucevan le stele"
			* "Recondita armonia"

Composer	Opera	Role	Aria
Puccini, cont.	*Turandot*	Calaf	"Nessun dorma" "Non piangere, Liù"
Saint-Saëns	*Samson et Dalila*	Samson	"Arrêtez, o mes frères"
Schubert	*Fierrabras*	Fierrabras	"In tiefbewegter Brust"
Smetana	*The Bartered Bride*	Jenik	"Soon now, my dearest"
R. Strauss	*Ariadne auf Naxos*	Bacchus	"Circe, Circe"
	Die Frau ohne Schatten	Kaiser	"Wenn das Herz aus Kristall"
	Der Rosenkavalier	Italian singer	* "Di rigori"
	Salome	Narraboth	"Ah! Du willst nicht"
Verdi	*Aida*	Radames	"Celeste Aida"
	Attila	Foresto	"Che non avrebbe"
	Un ballo in maschera	Ricardo	"Ma se m'è forza"
	Don Carlos	Carlos	"Io la vida"
	I due Foscari	Jacopo Foscari	"Dal più remoto esiglio"
	Ernani	Ernani	"Come ruggiada al cespite"
	La forza del destino	Alvaro	"O, tu che in seno"
	Luisa Miller	Rodolfo	"Quando le sere al placido"
	Macbeth	Macduff	"Ah, la paterno mano"
	I masnadieri	Carlo	"O mio castel paterno"
	Rigoletto	Duke of Mantua	* "La donna è mobile" "Parmi veder le lagrime" * "Questa o quella"
	La traviata	Alfredo	"De miei bollenti spiriti"
	Il trovatore	Manrico	"Di quella pira"
	I vespri siciliani	Arrigo	"Giorno di pianto"
Wagner	*Der fleigende Holländer*	Erik	"Willst jenes Tag"
	Lohengrin	Lohengrin	"Atmest du nicht" "Höchstest Vertraun" * "In fernen Land" "Mein leiber Schwann"

Composer	Opera	Role	Aria
Wagner, cont.	*Das Rheingold*	Loge	"Immr ist undank Loge Lohn!"
	Die Walküre	Siegmund	* "Winterstürme"
Weber	*Euryanthe*	Adolar	"Wehen mir Lüfte Ruh'"
	Der Freischütz	Max	* "Durch die Wälder"
	Oberon	Hüon	"Vater! Hör mich" "Von Jugend auf"
Wolf-Ferrari	*Sly*	Sly	"Un orso musoliera"

Dramatic Tenor (*Heldentenor*)

Composer	Opera	Role	Aria
Beethoven	*Fidelio*	Floristan	"In des Lebens Frühlingstagen"
Berlioz	*Les Troyens*	Aeneas	"Inutiles regrets"
Britten	*Peter Grimes*	Peter Grimes	"In dreams I've built myself" "Picture what that day"
	The Rape of Lucretia	Tarquinius	"Tarquinius does not wait"
Halévy	*La juive*	Éléazar	"Rachel quand du Seigneur"
Korngold	*Die tote Stadt*	Paul	"Verstumme"
Massenet	*Werther*	Werther	"J'aurai sur ma poitrine"
Meyerbeer	*Die Hugenotten*	Raoul	"Plus blache"
Saint-Saëns	*Samson et Dalila*	Samson	"Arrêtez, o mes frères"
R. Strauss	*Ariadne auf Naxos*	Baccus	"Circe, Circe"
	Salome	Herodes	"Ah! Du willst nicht"
Verdi	*Aida*	Radamés	* "Celeste Aida"
	I due Foscari	Jacopo	"No maledirmi, o probe"
	Ernani	Ernani	"Come ruggiada al cespite"
	Otello	Otello	"Ora per sempre addio"
	Simon Boccanegra	Gabriele	"Sento avvampar"
	Il trovatore	Manrico	"Di quella pira"

Composer	Opera	Role	Aria
Wagner	*Götterdämmerung*	Siegfried	"Brünnhilde, heilige Braut"
	Die Meistersinger	Walther	"Am stillen Herd"
			"Morgenlich leuchtend"
	Parsifal	Parsifal	"Nur eine Waffe taugt"
	Das Rheingold	Loge	"Immer ist Undank Loge Lohn"
	Rienzi	Rienzi	"Ich liebe glühend"
	Siegfried	Siegfried	"Nothung! Neidliches Schwert"
	Tannhäuser	Tannhäuser	"Dir töne Lob!"
	Tristan und Isolde	Tristan	"Wie sie selig, hehr und milde"
	Die Walküre	Siegmund	* "Winterstürme"

Character Tenor (*Charaktertenor*)

Composer	Opera	Role	Aria
Gershwin	*Porgy and Bess*	Sporting Life	"It ain't necessarily so"
Humperdinck	*Hänsel und Gretel*	Hexe	"Hurr hopp hopp hopp"
Mozart	*La finta giardiniera*	Don Anchise	"Dentro il mio petto"
R. Strauss	*Salome*	Herodes	"Ah! Du willst nicht"
Wagner	*Der fleigende Holländer*	Steuermann	"Mit Gewitter und Sturm"
	Das Rheingold	Loge	"Immer ist Undank Loge Lohn"

Lyric Baritone (*Lyricher Bariton*)

Composer	Opera	Role	Aria
Berlioz	*Benvenuto Cellini*	Fieramosca	"Qui pourrait me résister?"
Bizet	*Les pêcheurs de perles*	Zurga	"O Nadir, tendre ami"

Composer	Opera	Role	Aria
Britten	*Albert Herring*	Mr. Gedge	"Virtue, says Holy Writ"
	Billy Budd	Billy Budd	"And farewell to ye"
Debussy	*Pelléas et Mélisande*	Pelléas	"Ah! Je respire enfin!"
			"Oh! Qu'est-ce que c'est?"
Donizetti	*L'elisir d'amore*	Belcore	"Come Paride vezzoso"
	Don Pasquale	Dr. Malatesta	* "Bella siccome un angelo"
Gershwin	*Porgy and Bess*	Porgy	"Bess, you is my woman now"
Gounod	*Faust*	Valentin	* "Avant de quitter ces lieux"
Haydn	*Il mondo della luna*	Ernesto	"Qualque volta non fa male"
Korngold	*Die tote Stadt*	Fritz	* "Mein Sehnen, mein Wähnen"
Massanet	*Werther*	Albert	"Quelle prière"
Monteverdi	*L'Orfeo*	Orfeo	"Possente spirto"
			"Rosa del ciel"
			"Vi ritorni"
Mozart	*Così fan tutte*	Guglielmo	"Donne mie le fate a tanti"
	La finta giardiniera	Roberto (Nardo)	"Un marito, O Dio"
	La finta semplice	Don Cassandro	"Ella vuole"
	Die Zauberflöte	Papageno	* "Der Vogelfänger bin ich ja"
			* "Ein Mädchen oder Weibchen"
Rossini	*Il barbiere di Siviglia*	Figaro	* "Largo al factotum"
	La Cenerentola	Magnifico	"Mi sognai fra il fosco"

Composer	Opera	Role	Aria
R. Strauss	*Ariadne auf Naxos*	Harlekin	* "Lieben, Hassen, Hoffen, Zagen"

Cavalier Baritone (*Kavalierbariton*)

Composer	Opera	Role	Aria
Bellini	*I puritani*	Sir Richard Forth	"Bel sogno beato"
Berlioz	*Benvenuto Cellini*	Fieramosca	"Qui pourrait me résister?"
Bizet	*Carmen*	Escamillo	* "Votre toast"
	Les pêcheurs de perles	Zurga	"O Nadir, tendre ami"
Donizetti	*L'elisir d'amore*	Belcore	* "Come Paride vezzoso"
	Lucia di Lammermoor	Ashton	"Cruda, funesta smania"
Gounod	*Faust*	Valentin	"Avant de quitter ces lieux"
Lortzing	*Undine*	Kühleborn	"Es wohnt am Seegestade"
	Zar und Zimmermann	Zar	"Sonst spielt' ich mit Scepter"
Massenet	*Manon*	Lescaut	"Sei splendida e lucante"
			"O Rosalinde"
Mozart	*Così fan tutte*	Guglielmo	"Donne mie le fate a tanti"
	Don Giovanni	Don Giovanni	* "Deh vieni alla finestra"
			"Finch'han dal vino"
	Le nozze di Figaro	Count	"Vedro mentr'io sospiro"
Puccini	*Manon Lescaut*	Lescaut	"Sei splendida"
	Tosca	Scarpia	"Va, Tosca"
			"Ha più forte sapore"
Tchaikovsky	*Eugene Onegin*	Onegin	"Kogda bi zhizn domashnim"
Verdi	*Attila*	Ezio	"Dagl'immortali vertici"
	Un ballo in maschera	Renato	"Alla vita che t'arride"

Composer	Opera	Role	Aria
Verdi, *cont.*	*Don Carlos*	Posa	* "Per me giunto"
	Ernani	Don Carlos	"Lo vedremo, veglio audace"
	Falstaff	Ford	"È sogno? O realtà"
	La forza del destino	Don Carlos	"Urna fatale"
	I masnadieri	Francesco	"Pareami che sorto"
	La traviata	Germont	* "Di provenza il mar"
	Il trovatore	Count di Luna	"Il balen del suo sorriso"
	I vespri siciliani	Guido de Montfort	"Il braccio alla dovizie"
Wagner	*Tannhäuser*	Wolfram	* "O du mein holder Abendstern"

Dramatic Baritone (*Heldenbariton*)

Composer	Opera	Role	Aria
Beethoven	*Fidelio*	Don Pizarro	"Ha! Welch ein Augenblick"
Bellini	*I puritani*	Sir Richard Forth	"Bel sogno beato"
Berlioz	*La damnation de Faust*	Méphistophélès	"Voici des roses" "Devant la maison"
Borodin	*Fürst Igor*	Igor	"Ni sna ni otdyicha"
Charpentier	*Louise*	Vater	"Les pauvres gens"
Cilea	*Adriana Lecouvreur*	Michonnet	"Ecco il monologo"
Gershwin	*Porgy and Bess*	Porgy	"Bess, you is my woman now"
Giordano	*Andrea Chénier*	Gérard	* "Nemico della patria?"
Gounod	*Faust*	Méphistophélès	"Le veau d'or"
Hindemith	*Mathis der Maler*	Mathis	"Auf denn zum letzten Stück"
Leoncavallo	*Pagliacci*	Tonio	"Si può?"

Composer	Opera	Role	Aria
Mascagni	*Cavalleria rusticana*	Alfio	"Il cavallo scalpita"
Mozart	*Don Giovanni*	Don Giovanni	* "Deh vieni alla finestra"
			"Finch'han dal vino"
Mussorgsky	*Boris Godunov*	Boris	"Skorvit dusha!"
			"Uf, tja zhelo"
			"Prashchai moy sin"
Offenbach	*Les contes d'Hoffmann*	Coppelius	"J'ai des yeux"
		Dapertutto	"Scintille, diamante"
		Lindorf	"Dans les rôles d'amoureux"
Ponchielli	*La Gioconda*	Barnaba	"Ah, pescator"
Puccini	*La fanciulla del West*	Jack Rance	"Minnie, dalla mia casa"
	Gianni Schicchi	Gianni Schicchi	"Si corre del notaio"
	Il tabarro	Michele	"Perchè non m'ami più?"
	Tosca	Scarpia	* "Va, Tosca"
			"Ha più forte sapore"
Rossini	*Guillaume Tell*	Tell	* "Sois immobile"
Saint-Saëns	*Samson et Dalila*	Oberpriester	"Maudite à jamais soit la race"
R. Strauss	*Die Frau ohne Schatten*	Barak	"Aus einem jungen Mund"
Stravinsky	*The Rake's Progress*	Nick Shadow	"In youth the panting slave"
Tchaikovsky	*Pique Dame*	Tomsky	"Odnazhdy vy Versale"
Verdi	*Attila*	Enzio	"Dagl'immortali vertici"
	Don Carlos	Posa	"Per me giunto"

Composer	Opera	Role	Aria
Verdi, cont.	*I due Foscari*	Francesco Foscari	"O vecchio cor che batte"
	Ernani	Don Carlos	"Lo vedremo, veglio audace"
	Falstaff	Falstaff	* "L'onore! Ladri!"
	La forza del destino	Don Carlos	"Urna fatale"
	Luisa Miller	Miller	"Sacra la scelta"
	Macbeth	Macbeth	"Pietà, rispetto, onore"
	Nabucco	Nebuchadnezzar	"Chi mi toglie il region scettro?"
	Otello	Iago	"Credo in un Dio"
	Rigoletto	Rigoletto	"Pari siamo"
			* "Cortigiani, vil razza"
	La traviata	Germont	* "Di provenza il mar"
	Il trovatore	Count di Luna	"Il balen del suo sorriso"
	I vespri siciliani	Guido de Montfort	"In braccio alle dovizie"
Wagner	*Der fleigende Holländer*	Holländer	"Die Frist ist um"
	Götterdämmerung	Gunther	"Brünnhild' die hehrste Frau"
	Lohengrin	Telramund	"Erhebe dich"
	Die Meistersinger	Sachs	"Wahn, Wahn! Überall Wahn!"
	Parsifal	Amfortas	"Nein! Lasst ihn unenthüllt"
			"Mein Vater"
	Siegfried	Wanderer	"Du bist nicht"
	Tristan und Isolde	Kurwenal	"Das sage sie"
	Die Walküre	Wotan	"Leb' wohl"

Composer	Opera	Role	Aria
Character Baritone (*Charakterbariton*)			
Beethoven	*Fidelio*	Don Pizarro	"Welch ein Augenblick"
Berlioz	*Le damnation de Faust*	Méphistophélès	"Devant la maison"
			"Voice des roses"
Bizet	*Carmen*	Escamillo	* "Votre toast"
Borodin	*Fürst Igor*	Igor	"Ni sna ni otdyicha"
Cilea	*Adriana Lecouvreur*	Michonnet	"Ecco il monologo"
Donizetti	*Don Pasquale*	Don Pasquale	"Ah, un foco insolito"
Gershwin	*Porgy and Bess*	Crown	"A red-headed woman"
Mozart	*Le nozze di Figaro*	Figaro	* "Se vuol ballare"
			"Non più andrai"
Puccini	*La fanciulla del West*	Jack Rance	"Minnie, dalla mia casa"
	Gianni Schicchi	Gianni Schicchi	"Si corre del notaio"
	Il tabarro	Michele	"Perchè non m'ami più?"
	Tosca	Scarpia	* "Va, Tosca"
			"Ha più forte sapore"
Stravinsky	*The Rake's Progress*	Nick Shadow	"In youth the panting slave"
Verdi	*Rigoletto*	Rigoletto	"Pari siamo"
			* "Cortigiani, vil razza"
Wagner	*Das Rheingold*	Alberich	"Bin ich nun frei?"
Bass Buffo (*Spielbass*)			
Berlioz	*Béatrice et Bénédict*	Somarone	"Le vin de Syracuse"

Composer	Opera	Role	Aria
Donizetti	*Don Pasquale*	Don Pasquale	"Ah, un foco insolito"
	L'elisir d'amore	Dulcamara	"Udite, udite, o rustici"
Mozart	*Bastien und Bastienne*	Colas	"Befraget mich, ein zartes Kind"
	Così fan tutte	Don Alfonso	"Vorrei dir"
			"Tutti accusan le donne"
	Don Giovanni	Leporello	* "Madamina, il catalogo è questo"
	La finta semplice	Simone	"Troppa briga a prender moglie"
	Le nozze di Figaro	Figaro	* "Se vuol ballare"
			"Non più andrai"
Rossini	*Il barbiere di Siviglia*	Doctor Bartolo	"Manco un foglio"
			"Un dottor della mia sorte"
	La Cenerentola	Don Magnifico	"Sia qualunque delle figlie"
	L'italiana in Algeri	Mustafa	"Gia d'insolito ardore"
Verdi	*La forza del destino*	Melitone	"Toh, toh! Poffare il mondo!"
	Luisa Miller	Miller	"Sacra la scelta"

Heavy Bass Buffo (*Schwerer Spielbass/Bassbuffo*)

Composer	Opera	Role	Aria
Cornelius	*Der Barbier*	Abul Hassan	"Mein Sohn"
Flotow	*Martha*	Plunkett	"Lasst mich euch fragen"
Gounod	*Faust*	Méphistophélès	* "Le veau d'or"
Mozart	*Die Entführung*	Osmin	* "O, wie will ich triumphieren"

Composer	Opera	Role	Aria
Mozart, cont.			"Wer ein Liebchen hat gefunden"
Nicolai	Die lustigen Weiber	Falstaff	"Als Büblein klein"
Puccini	La bohème	Colline	* "Vecchia zimarra"
	Gianni Schicchi	Gianni Schicchi	"Si corre del notaio"
Rossini	Il barbiere di Siviglia	Basilio	* "La Calunnia"
Wagner	Der fleigende Holländer	Daland	"Mögst du mein Kind"
	Die Meistersinger	Beckmesser	"Den Tag she' ich erscheinen"
Weber	Der Freischütz	Caspar	"Hier im ird'schen Jammerthal" "Schweig', schweig'!"

Character Bass/Bass Baritone (*Charakterbass/Bass Bariton*)

Composer	Opera	Role	Aria
Boito	Mephisto	Mephisto	"Ave, Signor"
Britten	A Midsummer Night's Dream	Bottom	"When my cue comes"
Donizetti	Don Pasquale	Don Pasquale	"Ah, un foco insolito"
Mozart	Così fan tutte	Don Alfonso	"Vorrei dir" "Tutti accusan le donne"
	Don Giovanni	Masetto	"Ho capito, signor, si"
	Le nozze di Figaro	Figaro	* "Se vuol ballare" "Non più andrai"
Rossini	La Cenerentola	Alidoro	"Vasto teatro è il mondo"
Verdi	Ernani	de Silva	"Infelice! E tuo credevi"
	Luisa Miller	Walter	"Il mio sangue, la vita darei"
	Il trovatore	Ferrando	"Di due figli vivea"
Wagner	Die Meistersinger	Beckmesser	"Den Tag she' ich erscheinen"

Composer	Opera	Role	Aria
Wagner, cont.		Konrad Nachtigal	"Ein jedes Meistergesanges Bar"
	Das Rheingold	Alberich	"Hieher! Dorthin! Hehe, hoho!"

Serious Bass (*Seriöser Bass/Swartzer Bass*)

Composer	Opera	Role	Aria
Beethoven	*Fidelio*	Rocco	"Hat Mann nicht auch Gold"
Bellini	*I puritani*	Sir George	"Cinta di fiori"
Boito	*Mephisto*	Mephisto	"Ave, Signor"
Britten	*Billy Budd*	Claggart	"O beauty"
Donizetti	*Lucia di Lammermoor*	Raimondo	"Ah, cedi, cedi!" "Al ben dei tuoi qual vittima" "Dalle stanze, ove Lucia"
Gounod	*Faust*	Méphistophélès	* "Le veau d'or"
Handel	*Agrippina*	Claudio	"Vieni, o cara"
	Ariodante	King of Scotland	"Al sen ti stringo"
	Orlando	Zoroastro	"Lascia amor" "Tra caligni profondo"
Meyerbeer	*Die Hugenotten*	Marcel	"Pour les couvents c'est ici"
Mozart	*La clemenza di Tito*	Publius	"Tardi s'avvede"
	Die Entführung	Osmin	* "O, wie will ich triumphieren" "Wer ein Liebchen hat gefunden"
	Le nozze di Figaro	Bartolo	* "La vendetta"
	Die Zauberflöte	Sarastro	"O Isis und Osiris" "In deisen heil'gen Hallen"
Mussorgsky	*Boris Godunov*	Pimen	"Smirennii inok"
Ponchielli	*La Gioconda*	Alvise Badoero	"Si, morir ella de'"
Puccini	*La bohème*	Colline	* "Vecchia zimarra"
Rossini	*La Cenerentola*	Alidoro	"Vasto teatro è il mondo"

Composer	Opera	Role	Aria
Tchaikovsky	*Eugene Onegin*	Prince Gremin	"Lyubvi fse vozrasti pokorni"
Thomas	*Mignon*	Lothario	"De son coeur j'ai calmé"
Verdi	*Attila*	Attila	"Mentre gonfiarsi l'anima"
	Don Carlos	Philip	* "Dormirò sol"
	Ernani	de Silva	"Infelice! E tuo credevi"
	Luisa Miller	Walter	"Il mio sangue, la vita darei"
	Macbeth	Banco	"Come dal ciel precipita"
	I masnadieri	Maximilian	"Un ignoto tre lune"
	Nabucco	Zacharias	"Come notte al sol fulgente"
	Simon Boccanegra	Fiesco	"Il lacerato spirito"
	Il trovatore	Ferrando	"Di due figli vivea"
	I vespri siciliani	Giovanni	"O tu, Palermo" "Nell'ombra et nel silenzio"
Wagner	*Lohengrin*	König Heinrich	"Mein Herr und Gott"
	Die Meistersinger	Pogner	"Nun hört, und versteht"
Weber	*Der Freischütz*	Caspar	"Hier im ird'schen Jammerthal" "Schweig', schweig'!"

Glossary

German	English
Abendvertrag	evening contract
Agent	agent
Agentur	agency
Alt	alto
Altersruhesgeld	retirement money
anbieten	to offer
Änderungen	changes
Anfänger/Anfängerin	beginner
Anfängervertrag	beginner contract
Anhörung	contract negotiation
Anlage	enclosure
Anmeldung	announce; notify
Ansage	announcement
Apotheke	pharmacy
Arbeitnehmer	work-taker; worker
Arbeitsamt	work-office
Arbeitserlaubnis	work permission
Arbeitslos	out of work
Arbeitsuchend	looking for work
Arzt	doctor
Arztzettel	medical prescription
Atem	air; breath
Aufenthalterlaubnis	permission to stay (in the country)
Aufführung (Auff.)	performance, representation

German	English
Auffüren	present, perform
Aufgabe	problem, proposition, lesson, exercise, duty
Auftraggeber	employer
Auftragschein	notice of house audition (from agent)
Ausdauer	length (how long it lasts)
ausfühlen	to fill out
Ausländeramt	Foreigner Office
Bäckerei	bakery
Ballett	ballet
Bariton	baritone
Begleiter	accompanist
beiliegend	enclosed
Beitrag	contribution, share, premium
Beitragsnachweis	premium notice
Beleuchtung	lighting technicians
Beleuchtungsprobe	lighting rehearsal
bemühen	to make an effort
besetzen	to cast (a role)
Besetzung	cast (member)
besondere Vereinbarungen	special arrangements
Bestätigung	sworn certificate
Betriebsbüro	work office
Botschaft	embassy
Buffo	comic
Bühne	stage
Bühnenangehöriger	members of the stage professions
Bühnenbildner	set designers
Bühneneingang	stage door
Bühnenprobe	stage rehearsal
Charakterbariton	character baritone
Charakterbass	character bass
Charaktersoprano	character soprano
Charaktertenor	character tenor
Chor	chorus
Chor-Solo Vertrag	chorus-solo contract
Chorvertrag	chorus contract
Dekorationsprobe	set rehearsal
Dienstkarten	performer tickets; complimentary tickets
Dirigenten	conductors
Dramatischer Mezzo-sopran	dramatic mezzo-soprano
Dramatischer Tenor	dramatic tenor

German	English
Dramatischesopran	dramatic soprano
Dramaturg	music historian (musicologist)
Dramaturgie	dramatic theory or technique
Drehbühne	revolving stage
dritte Besetzung	third cast
Drogerie	drug store; pharmacy
D-Zug	local train
EC	Euro-City train
Einkommen	income
Einkommenerklärung	tax form; explanation of income
Einkommensteuer	income tax
einspringen	to "jump in" (assume) a role
Elektroakustik	audio engineers
empfehlen	to recommend; introduce
Empfehlung	recommendation; introduction
Empfehlungskarte	business card
engagieren	to be hired
Engagiert	engaged; hired
Ensembleprobe	ensemble rehearsal
Entgelt	pay received for working
Erdegeschoss	first floor (ground level)
erhalten	to receive
Erklärung	explanation
erste Besetzung	first cast
erste Partien	leading roles
Fach	specialty, category
Fachvertrag	contract with specified *Fach*
Festvertrag	ensemble contract
Finanzamt	financial office; tax office
Freiwillig	voluntary
Führerschein	driver's license
Gage	salary
Garderobe	dressing room
Gastvertrag	guest contract
Gehalt	salary
Gehaltsabrechnung	statement of salary
Generalkonsul	consul general
Generalmusikdirektor (*GMD*)	general music director
Generalprobe	final dress rehearsal
Gliederung	form (musical)
grosse Bühne	large stage

German	English
grosser Chorpartie (gr. Chp.)	a lengthened chorus solo section
grosser Partie (gr. P.)	lead solo role
Grundbeitrag	monthly charge
Grundsätze	rules; principles
Handlung	basic plot
Hauptmieter	primary renter
Hauptprobe	main rehearsal; preliminary dress rehearsal
Haus	house
Hausordnung	apartment house rules
Heldentenor	heavy dramatic tenor; heroic tenor
Hinweis	indication; hint
Hoch	high
Honorar	payment
Houseagentur	house agent
im Anlage	enclosed
im Vertrag	in the contract
Intendant	general manager; artistic director
Jahresvertrag	year contract
Jugendlicher Bariton	German dramatic baritone
Jungendlicher	youthlike
Kaltmiete	basic cost of an apartment; cold rent
Kantina	café
Kapellmeister	chorus conductor
Karte	map
Kaution	rental deposit
Kinderchor	children's chorus
Klangfarbe	tone color of the voice
Klangfülle	sonority
Klanglehre	acoustics
kleine Chorpartie (kl. Chp.)	small chorus role
kleine Partie (kl. P.)	small role
Konsul	consul
Konsulate	consulate
Kosten	costs
Kostenersatz	extra charge
Kostümabteilung	costume area
Kostümbildner	costume designers
Krankenkasse	health pay office
Krankenversicherung	health insurance
Kritiken	reviews
kündigen	to give notice

German	English
Kündigung	dismissal
Kündigungsfrist	final date for dismissal
Kündigungstermin	deadline for dismissal
Künstler/Künstlerin	male artist; female artist
Künstlerischen Mitlieder	artistic personnel
Künstlerisches Betriebsbüro	artistic management office
Lage	range
Landestheater	land (area) theater
Lichtprobe	lighting rehearsal
Lohnsteuerjahresausgleich	yearly tax statement
Lohnsteuerkarte	W2 form
Lungen	lungs
Lyrischer Bariton	lyric baritone
Lyrischer Koloratur	lyric coloratura
Lyrischer Sopran	lyric soprano
Lyrischer Tenor	lyric tenor
Maske	makeup/wigs
medium Chorpartie (m. Chp.)	medium length chorus part
medium Partie (m. P.)	medium length solo part
Mieten	to rent
Mieter	renter
Mietpreis	rental price
Mietvertrag	rental contract
Mitarbeiter	office workers
Möbliert	furnished
Monatsmiete	monthly rent
Monatsvertrag	monthly contract
Müll	refuse; garbage
Münzen	small change
Musikalische Oberleitung	musical direction
Musiker	musicians
nächsten	next
Nationaltheater	National Theater
Nebenkosten	other charges
Nicht möblier	unfurnished
Nichtverlängerung	notice of dismissal; not extended
Normalvertrag	normal contract
Nummerausweis	number identification
offizielle Urlaub	official vacation
Opernhaus	opera house
Orchester	orchestra

German	English
Orchester Stückprobe	orchestra rehearsal; "piece" rehearsal
Ort	city, place
Partie	role
Partien nach individualität	roles by agreement
Pflichtversicherte	required insurance
Photos	photos
Pianist	pianist, accompanist
Probe	rehearsal
Probejahr	probationary year
Probeplan	rehearsal schedule
Probezeit	time of probation
Referenden des Intendant	representative of the *Intendant*
Regisseur	stage director
Repertoire	list of roles performed, studied
Repititor	accompanist
Requisite	props
Residenzpflicten	residence obligations
Résumé/Resümee	summary; artist bio and repertoire
Rezept	medical prescription
Ruhezonen	quiet areas
Sänger	singer (male)
Sängerin	singer (female)
S-Bahn	commuter train
Schadenersatz	damage fee; deposit
Schauplätze	setting
Schauspielhaus	drama house, theater
Schleim	mucus
Schleimhaut	mucus membranes
Schminke	makeup department
Schreiben	letter
Secretäriat	secretaries
Seriöser Bass	serious (low) bass
Shoemacher	shoemaker
Sicherung	insurance
Sitzprobe	first full ensemble read-through (memorized) with orchestra
Solo-Chor Vertrag	solo-chorus contract
Soloisten	soloists
Soloprobe	solo rehearsal
Sopran	soprano
Soubrette	light soprano voice

German	English
Souffleurkasten	prompter's box
Souffleusen	prompters
Spiel	acting
Spielbass	acting bass
Spieldauer	performance length (in time)
Spielplan	schedule
Spieltenor	acting tenor
Spielzeit	season
Staatsoper	national opera
Staatstheater	state theater
Stadt Centrum	city center
Stadtplan	city plan
Stadttheater	city theater
Stadtverwaltung	city management office; local authorities
Stellprobe	blocking rehearsal
Steuer	taxes
Steuerberator	tax specialist
Steuerkarte	tax card
Steuerkarten	tax tickets; small tax surcharge on complimentary tickets
Steuernummer	tax identification number
Stimmbänder	vocal folds
Stock	floor
Strafzettel	penalty notice
Stückprobe	"piece" rehearsal
Stückvertrag	"piece" contract; single role contract
Stumme Rolle	nonspeaking role, mute role
Suchen	to look for
Tänzer	dancer (male)
Tänzerin	dancer (female)
Technische Leitumg	technical direction
Technische Probe	technical rehearsal
Teilvertrag	contract for a specific period of time
Tenor	tenor
Theaterphotographie	theater photographer
Tüte	plastic shopping bags; paper bag
Übernehm	to take over, transfer
Umfang (tessitura)	range
Unkündbar	tenured
Untermietvertrag	rental contract (official)
unterschreiben	to sign

German	English
Unterschrift	signature
Urlaub	vacation
Vakanzen	vacancies
Verabredung	appointment; agreement
Vereinbarung	agreement
Verlag	contract
Verlängerung	extension
Vermieter	landlord
Vermittlung	agency; office
Verpflichtung	responsibilities
Versicherte	insured person
Versicherung	insurance
Versicherungsnachweis	statement of insurance contributions
Versicherungsnummer	insurance number; account number
versorgen	to provide for; supply; take care of
Versorgungsanspruch	request for assistance
Versorgungsleistung	provisions
Verständigungsprobe	explanatory rehearsal
Verständnis	understanding
Vertrag	contract
Vertrag verlängern	to extend a contract
Verwaltung	house administration
Verwaltungsdirektor	house administrator
Vorsingen	audition
Vorsingentermin	audition date
Vorspiel	prelude, overture, curtain-raiser
wahrnehmen	to avail yourself of; make the most of
Warmmiete	basic cost plus extras
Weiterversicherung	continuation of insurance
Werkstätten	set construction area
Wiederaufnahme	first performance of the opera in its second season
Zahlstelle	payment office
Zeit	time, epoch, period, age, era, season, space of time
Zimmervermittlung	room rentals
zweite Besetzung	second cast
Zwischenfach	between categories
Zwischenfachstimme	between categories voice

Bibliography

BOOKS

Betteridge, Harold, ed. *The New Cassell's German Dictionary*. New York: Funk & Wagnalls, 1965.

Boytim, Joan. *The Private Voice Studio Handbook*. Milwaukee, Wis.: Hal Leonard, 2003.

Brook, Stephen. *Vienna*, Eyewitness Travel Guide. New York: DK Publishing, 2004.

Brown, William Earl. *Vocal Wisdom: Maxims of Giovanni Battista Lamperti*. New York: Taplinger Publishing, 1957.

Deutsches Bühnen Jahrbuch. Hamburg: Genossenschaft Deutscher Bühnen-Angehöriger im Verlag der Bühnenschriften-Vertriebs-Gesellschaft mbH, 2006.

Frisell, Anthony. *The Baritone Voice*. Boston: Crescendo Publishing, 1972.

Garcia, Manuel. *Hints on Singing*. Translated by Beata Garcia. New York: Ascherberg & Co., 1894.

Glass, Beaumont. *Lotte Lehmann: A Life in Opera and Song*. Santa Barbara, Calif.: Capra Press, 1988.

Hines, Jerome. *Great Singers on Great Voices*. New York: Limelight Editions, 1988.

Hessler, Ulrike, ed. *Bayerische Staatsoper Jahresvorschau*, 2007–2008. Munich, Germany: Max-Joseph-Platz 2.

Kloiber, Rudolf, Wulf Konold, and Robert Maschka. *Handbuch der Oper*. Kassel, Germany: Bärenreiter-Verlag, 2006.

Kobbé, Gustav. *The Definitive Kobbé's Opera Book*. Edited, revised, and updated by the Earl of Harewood (George Henry Hubert Lascelles). New York: G. P. Putnam's Sons, 1987.

Lehmann, Lilli. *How to Sing*. Translated by Richard Aldrich; revised edition translated by Clara Willenbücher. New York: Macmillan, 1929.

Mawson, C. O. Sylvester. *Dictionary of Foreign Terms.* Updated and revised by Charles Berlitz. New York: Thomas Y. Crowell, 1975.

McGinnis, Pearl Yeadon. *The Solo Vocal Music of American Composer John La Montaine: Compositions for Voice on Piano.* Lewiston, N.Y.: Edwin Mellen Press, 2004.

Menotti, Gian Carlo. *Amahl and the Night Visitors.* Milwaukee, Wis.: G. Schirmer, 1997.

Miller, Richard. *Training Soprano Voices.* New York: Oxford University Press, 2000.

Mordden, Ethan. *Opera Anecdotes.* New York: Oxford University Press, 1985.

Vennard, William. *Singing: The Mechanism and the Technic.* New York: Carl Fischer, 1967.

WEBSITES

www.germany.info/Vertretung/usa/en/Startseite.html, "German Missions in the United States," is a German-government site with information about visas, passports, legal and consular services, and more.

www.usembassy.gov/ is the U.S. State Department site with links to information about foreign travel, including passports, visas, taxes, security, and more.

Index

face, focusing attention on, 99–101
Fachvertrag (category contracts), 117–
19, 124–25, 127–28
facilities for opera, 62, 63–65
Fagan, Arthur, 83
fans of opera, 151
Fashing (carnival season), 174
fees, 106
Festvertrag, 117–19, 124–25
fifteen-year barrier, 161–62
Figaro in *Il barbiere di Siviglia*, 37, 38
Figaro in *Le nozze di Figaro*, 41
final rehearsals (*Hauptproben*), 144
financial support of opera houses, 63,
65–68
Fiordiligi in *Così fan tutte*, 21, 22
first associate conductor (*Erste
Kapellmeister*), 82
first cast (*erste Besetzung*), 121
first chair violinist, 85
first orchestra rehearsal (*Sitzprobe*), 143
flexibility, enhancing, 54
following up with agents, 105
foreign earned income exclusions, 134
France, driving in, 169
French language fluency, 164
frequency of performances, 9, 54–55,
94
full-time work, opera singer as, 137–38
funding of opera houses, 63
fun with audition arias, 92
furnished apartments, 167

Gaea in *Daphne*, 30
Garcia, Manuel, 48, 50
Gastvertrag (guest contract), 110–11,
119, 120, 158–59
general music director
(*Generalmusikdirektor*) (GMD),
81–82, 120
Generalprobe (dress rehearsal), 139, 145
German black bass (*Schwarzer Bass*),
43–44, 273–76
German language fluency, 103, 108–9,
164
Germany: Federal Employment Office,
134–35; opera houses, 186; salaries,

123; transportation, 169, 170; ZBF,
105, 177–78
Gianni Schicchi in *Gianni Schicchi*, 43
Giorgetta in *Il tabarro*, 23
Giuseppe in *La traviata*, 30, 31
Glockley, David, 94
GMD (*Generalmusikdirektor*), 81–82,
120
Great Singers on Great Singing (Hines),
54
Gretel in *Hänsel und Gretel*, 22
grosse Bühne (large stages), 64
grosse Partie (main role), 122–23
guest contracts: *Gastvertrag*, 110–11,
119, 120, 158–59; jumping in
(*einspringen*), 159–61; piece contract
(*Stückvertrag*), 119, 128, 130; time
(*Teilvertrag*), 110–11, 120, 128, 130

Handbuch der Oper (Kloiber), 17, 122
handshake audition, 158
Hänsel in *Hänsel und Gretel*, 27
Hauptproben (final rehearsals), 144
Haute-Contre (high countertenor), 32,
249, 285
health insurance, 132
Heldenbariton/Hoher Bass (baritone/
high bass), 39–40, 263–66, 296–98
Heldentenor (dramatic tenor), 35, 49,
123–24, 257–58, 292–93
hermit in *Der Freischütz*, 10, 123
Herodes in *Salome*, 36
Herodias in *Salome*, 28, 29
Hints on Singing (Garcia), 48
historian, music (*Dramaturg*), 72–73
Hochdramatischer Sopran (high
dramatic soprano), 25–26, 241,
281–82
Horne, Marilyn, 28
Hosen Partien (pants roles), 100
hotel monthly rentals, 166
Hotter, Hans, 113
house auditions, 98, 104–5, 106–10
house photographer
(*Theaterphotographie*), 87
housing, 165–68
How to Sing (Lehmann), 49, 51

About the Author
and the Editor

Following a career as an opera singer in Germany, **Pearl Yeadon McGinnis** earned her PhD in music at the University of Illinois (Champaign-Urbana) and went on to teach voice and direct the Opera Workshop program at Missouri State University (MSU) in Springfield, Missouri, from 1993 until her unexpected death in 2007. She founded and directed the prestigious Collectors Series opera scholarship program and the Missouri Chamber Players, who performed during four tours in Europe (1998–2004). MSU honors included multiple University Awards in research and teaching and College Awards in service. Dr. Yeadon, who performed and taught using her middle rather than last name, was nationally recognized as an educator and presented at many international conferences on service learning.

Dr. Yeadon's scholarly works include *The Solo Vocal Music of American Composer John La Montaine* (2004) and articles "Opera Out of the Box: Music as an Intervention for Rural Public Schools," *Academic Exchange Quarterly* (2003); "Teaching Music and Public Affairs," *SMSU Journal of Public Affairs* (1999); and "*La Traviata*, the End of a Dream," *Springfield Regional Opera Times* (spring 1997). She was a member of Actors' Equity and the *Bühnengenossenschaft* in Germany. Dr. Yeadon was also an accomplished poet, painter, photographer, and sculptor.

Her recordings and CDs include *Sixteenth Mass*, Haydn, PAR 1010; *Kyrie & Gloria*, Vivaldi, Crystal Records S 901; *Christmas Oratorio*, J. S. Bach, PAR 1009; *9 Lessons of Christmas*, La Montaine, Fredonia Discs FD 6; *Symphony No. 9 Beethoven*, Millikin Symphony Orchestra, MU 310; and *Christmas Is . . .* and *This Hallowed Season*, Fleet LLC Sound Works.

Dr. Yeadon had a daughter, Pamela Glasell, and two grandchildren, Matthew and Michelle.

A graduate of the University of Montana in drama and English, **Marith McGinnis Willis** has had a career combining teaching with performing and directing as she accompanied her husband, Army Colonel Dick Willis, on assignments to Germany, Japan, and Hawaii. Marith Willis's favorite roles were Maria in *The Sound of Music*, Eliza in *My Fair Lady*, and Dolly in *Hello, Dolly!* with the Yokota Players in Tokyo, Japan. She also directed and performed with the Aloha Players in Honolulu, Hawaii.

While teaching voice and working in early childhood education, Willis made commercials for Sony and Mitsubishi, conducted master classes in performance, and directed a high-school show choir. In the 1990s and early 2000s, she starred with her sister, opera singer Pearl Yeadon McGinnis, in a series of benefit concerts entitled *The Best of Broadway and Opera* and *The Magic of Music*, and together they recorded two Christmas CDs: *Christmas Is . . .* and *This Hallowed Season*.

In addition to singing, Willis's hobbies are writing music and fiction. She has just finished her first novel, *This Moment in Time*, based on her sister's experiences as an opera singer. She and her husband reside in Carlisle, Pennsylvania, and Bigfork, Montana, and have two sons, James and Joseph, who with wives Robin and Sandy have blessed the family with three grandchildren: Zachary, Austin, and Kate.